Feminist Theology and the Challenge of Difference

REFLECTION AND THEORY IN THE STUDY
OF RELIGION SERIES

SERIES EDITOR
James Wetzel, Villanova University

A Publication Series of The American Academy of Religion
and Oxford University Press

WORKING EMPTINESS
Toward a Third Reading of Emptiness
in Buddhism and Postmodern Thought
Newman Robert Glass

WITTGENSTEIN AND THE MYSTICAL
Philosophy as an Ascetic Practice
Frederick Sontag

AN ESSAY ON THEOLOGICAL METHOD
Third Edition
Gordon D. Kaufman

BETTER THAN WINE
Love, Poetry, and Prayer in the Thought
of Franz Rosenzweig
Yudit Kornberg Greenberg

HEALING DECONSTRUCTION
Postmodern Thought in Buddhism
and Christianity
Edited by David Loy

ROOTS OF RELATIONAL ETHICS
Responsibility in Origin and Maturity in
H. Richard Niebuhr
Melvin Keiser

HEGEL'S SPECULATIVE GOOD FRIDAY
The Death of God in Philosophical Perspective
Deland S. Anderson

NEWMAN AND GADAMER
Toward a Hermeneutics of Religious
Knowledge
Thomas K. Carr

GOD, PHILOSOPHY AND ACADEMIC
CULTURE
A Discussion between Scholars in the AAR
and APA
Edited by William J. Wainwright

LIVING WORDS
Studies in Dialogues about Religion
Terence J. Martin

LIKE AND UNLIKE GOD
Religious Imaginations in Modern
and Contemporary Fiction
John Neary

CONVERGING ON CULTURE
Theologians in Dialogue with Cultural Analysis
and Criticism
Edited by Delwin Brown, Sheila Greeve
Davaney, and Kathryn Tanner

BEYOND THE NECESSARY GOD
Trinitarian Faith and Philosophy in the
Thought of Eberhard Jüngel
Paul DeHart

CONVERGING ON CULTURE
Theologians in Dialogue with Cultural Analysis
and Criticism
Edited by Delwin Brown, Sheila Greeve
Davaney, and Kathryn Tanner

LESSING'S PHILOSOPHY OF RELIGION
AND THE GERMAN ENLIGHTENMENT
Toshimasa Yasukata

AMERICAN PRAGMATISM
A Religious Genealogy
M. Gail Hamner

OPTING FOR THE MARGINS
Postmodernity and Liberation in
Christian Theology
Edited by Joerg Rieger

MAKING MAGIC
Religion, Magic, and Science in the
Modern World
Randall Styers

THE METAPHYSICS OF DANTE'S
COMEDY
Christian Moevs

PILGRIMAGE OF LOVE
Moltmann on the Trinity and
Christian Life
Joy Ann McDougall

MORAL CREATIVITY
Paul Ricoeur and the Poetics of Moral Life
John Wall

MELANCHOLIC FREEDOM
Agency and the Spirit of Politics
David Kyuman Kim

AMERICAN ACADEMY OF RELIGION

Feminist Theology and the Challenge of Difference

MARGARET D. KAMITSUKA

UNIVERSITY PRESS

2007

OXFORD
UNIVERSITY PRESS

Oxford University Press, Inc., publishes works that further
Oxford University's objective of excellence
in research, scholarship, and education.

Oxford   New York
Auckland   Cape Town   Dar es Salaam   Hong Kong   Karachi
Kuala Lumpur   Madrid   Melbourne   Mexico City   Nairobi
New Delhi   Shanghai   Taipei   Toronto

With offices in
Argentina   Austria   Brazil   Chile   Czech Republic   France   Greece
Guatemala   Hungary   Italy   Japan   Poland   Portugal   Singapore
South Korea   Switzerland   Thailand   Turkey   Ukraine   Vietnam

Copyright © 2007 the American Academy of Religion

Published by Oxford University Press, Inc.
198 Madison Avenue, New York, New York 10016

www.oup.com

Library of Congress Cataloging-in-Publication Data
Kamitsuka, Margaret D.
Feminist theology and the challenge of difference / Margaret D.
Kamitsuka.
   p. cm.
Includes bibliographical references and index.
ISBN: 978-0-19-531162-4
1. Feminist theology.   I. Title.
BT83.55.K35 2007
230.082—dc22   2006028318

9 8 7 6 5 4 3 2 1
Printed in the United States of America
on acid-free paper

To the memory of my father,

Milenko Despot (1917–1998)

Acknowledgments

This project originally began in a much different form as a dissertation exploring the differences and convergences between several contemporary male theological voices and feminist theology. I am deeply grateful for my advisor at Yale, David Kelsey, who supported me when I proposed scuttling that project and starting anew on a dissertation with feminist theology as the focus. That dissertation eventually formed some of the basis for what is now *Feminist Theology and the Challenge of Difference*. I wish to acknowledge my other Yale professors, especially George Lindbeck, the late Hans Frei, and Peter Hawkins. Their teaching formed me as a theologian and gave me a model to which to aspire in the classroom and in my scholarship. I am grateful to the members of the Department of Religion and the Gender and Women's Studies Program at Oberlin College for their support of my scholarly endeavors, and to the members of the Workgroup on Constructive Christian Theology (a living testament to the power of collaborative theological work). My thanks go to my students at Oberlin College, and especially for the editorial help on this project from my former student Mara Brecht, who is well on her way to a promising scholarly career in religious studies. I wish to thank Professor James Wetzel, editor for the Reflection and Theory in the Study of Religion Series of the American Academy of Religion and Oxford University Press, for the professionalism and thoughtfulness he displayed in ushering my manuscript through the initial channels of academic publishing. The editorial staff at Oxford

University Press were very helpful in preparing the manuscript for publication. Chris Carter provided the original artwork gracing the cover.

Parts from several chapters appeared previously in somewhat different form in two journals: "Toward a Feminist Postmodern and Postcolonial Interpretation of Sin," *Journal of Religion* 84, no. 2 (April 2004); and "Reading the Raced and Sexed Body in Alice Walker's *The Color Purple*: Repatterning White Feminist and Womanist Hermeneutics," *Journal of Feminist Studies in Religion* 19, no. 2 (Fall 2003).

One is not born a feminist, one becomes one. Women friends are essential to that process. For this I thank in particular Yvonne Schibsted, my long-time friend and fellow writer, and Sally Peterson, whose untimely death in 2002 does not diminish the sustaining presence of her spirit in my life. My mother, Shirley Despot, and my sister, Katy Despot, are organic, practical feminists who subtly inspired much of what I wrote. My father, Milenko Despot, a Croatian immigrant, was neither scholarly nor feminist; yet, his subaltern discourse was probably the most influential of all in my postmodern and postcolonial turn. My deepest words of gratitude go to my husband, David Gen Kamitsuka, with whom all my intellectual, religious, and emotional experiences find their richest and most joyful place of nurture. Finally, I want to celebrate the blessing in my life of my two indefatigable five-year-old sons Mark Andrew and Paul Joseph Kamitsuka. They are not theologians, but their piercing questions about God keep reminding me why I am. They are not feminists—yet—but they have a fifteen-year-old imaginary sister who, I suspect, is.

Contents

1. An Introduction to the Challenge of Difference, 3

2. Critical Issues in Retrieving Women's Experience, 27

3. Reinterpreting Sex, Sin, and Desire, 63

4. Theorizing Power, 89

5. Negotiating with a Disciplinary Tradition, 115

6. Rethinking Solidarity, 137

   Notes, 159

   Select Bibliography, 201

   Index, 216

Feminist Theology and the Challenge of Difference

I

An Introduction to the Challenge of Difference

Feminist theology was born in struggle and continues to experience the pangs of birthing new spiritual images and discourses of resistance that empower women. The first wave of feminist scholarship in religion originated in women's attempts in the 1960s and 1970s to challenge sexism in religious and academic venues long dominated by men.[1] Because the battle against patriarchal attitudes and practices in the Christian tradition became an early defining factor, feminist theologians have been well acquainted with conflict.[2] Since the 1980s, another arena of contestation opened up—this time, closer to home, so to speak. The discipline began to experience its own internal fractures, with the result that one can no longer simply say "feminist theology" and mean a more or less unified discipline based on the assumption of a united sisterhood standing oppositionally to patriarchy. Christian feminist theology is increasingly recognized for what it has de facto been: a scholarly field dominated by white, middle-class, first-world, heterosexual women. Womanist, *mujerista*, lesbian, Asian American, two-thirds-world, and other self-named women's theologies are rapidly developing their own discourses, agendas, constituencies—and fractures as well. Thus, feminist theology, with relatively new institutional standing within the field of Christian theology, has become divided—and enriched, from my perspective—by difference. The extent to which this fracturing will be enriching depends ultimately not on the multicultural good intentions of those in dominant positions; rather, it depends on the extent to which feminist theologians make difference methodologically central to the way in which we approach our central subject (women). How can we speak of women in light of difference? More specifically, how can we speak of a gendered, sexually embodied female self who is a morally accountable agent and a creature of God, in ways that respect the irreducible diversity of women's experiences and that unmask persistent and deeply entrenched forms of privilege? It will be necessary for feminist theology to address the complex philosophical and theological components of this question, and new theoretical tools are required to do so.

In the course of this text, I will propose how feminist theology could make use of various sets of theoretical tools, in particular those borrowed from postmodern and postcolonial thought, in order to theorize difference in relation to female, embodied moral agents. Having embarked on this process of rethinking women's selfhood, we cannot simply return to feminist theological business as usual. We will see in subsequent chapters how this new theoretical perspective on women's selfhood helps expose troubling assumptions at work in the most venerable and deeply valued feminist theological themes such as the appeal to women's creation in the image of God; insistence on the oppressiveness of structural sins against women; rejection of the salvific significance of the maleness of Jesus; suspicion toward the masculinist, Christian creedal tradition; and the call for women's solidarity. The implications for feminist theology of attending to difference, thus, are not superficial but rather decisive, radical, and systemic. Attending to difference affects how feminist theologians engage each other's work, how we remain accountable to the needs and resistance activities of our various constituent communities, how we position ourselves in relation to the Christian tradition, and how we conduct ongoing self-critical reflection as we encounter new forms of otherness and new repressed voices.

The next two sections of this chapter launch us into the subject matter of difference by examining, first, one of the most historically central feminist methodological themes and one of the most hotly contested today—the appeal to women's experience—and, second, the status of feminist discussions about two markers of difference (and sites of privilege) that will be an ongoing focus of this project: race and sexuality.

I. The Appeal to Women's Experience as Source and Norm for Feminist Theology

Rosemary Ruether gives a classic articulation of the function of an appeal to experience for theological methodology, arguing that not just for feminist theology but for all theology "human experience is the starting point of the hermeneutical circle" since even the "objective sources of theology . . . scripture and tradition, are themselves collective human experience."[3] The feminist theological writings that adhere to this hermeneutical principle find their natural methodological home within liberal theology and its approach to correlating the Christian tradition with the experience of the modern subject. Feminist theological writings are set apart from largely male liberal theology in that they make *women's* experience (not that of the universal "man") the hermeneutical lens through which to interpret scripture, formulate doctrines, revise liturgical practices, and so on.

From its beginnings, feminist theology's appeal to women's experience as a source and norm has focused on oppression under patriarchy. While she was by no means the first to broadcast the notion of a global women's experience of sexism, Mary Daly was an early and powerfully formative voice enunciating the ubiquity of patriarchy and its insidious partnership with religion. *"Patriarchy is itself the prevailing religion of the entire planet,* and its essential message is necrophilia. All of the so-called religions legitimating patriarchy . . . from buddhism and hinduism to islam, judaism, christianity, to secular derivatives . . . are infrastructures of the edifice of patriarchy."[4] Daly appeals to women's global experience of sexism in order to combat this massively oppressive force. She states unequivocally that "[w]omen of all 'types,' having made the psychic breakthrough to recognition of *the basic sameness of our situation as women*, have been initiated into the struggle for liberation of our sex from its ancient bondage."[5] The notion of a collective women's experience of oppression, leading to revolutionary opposition to patriarchy, permeates the writings of first-wave women scholars in religion during the 1970s and into the early 1980s. These feminist writers (at this point, a largely homogeneous group of white, upper-middle-class women academics mostly in dialogue with the Christian tradition) made women's experience of patriarchal oppression a methodological norm for feminist religious thought.

Even in early white feminist appeals to women's experience, provisoes can be found regarding "variations in the consciousness of women, shaped by different cultural contexts and life experiences." However some kind of unifying oppression or consciousness is usually cited as underlying these variations. For example, Ruether speaks of a basic feminist awareness "which arises when women become critically aware of . . . falsifying and alienating experiences imposed upon them as women by a male-dominated culture."[6] Beginning in the 1980s, theological appeals to common women's experience began to come under fire. While virtually all feminist theologians would affirm Daly's claim that patriarchy is pervasive, there is serious disagreement about how women in different contexts and from different backgrounds experience patriarchy and other oppressive forces. For example, womanist theologian Delores Williams claims that white women experience a "patriarchally derived privileged oppression" in a white male-dominated culture; whereas black women suffer from "demonarchy," a word Williams coined meaning black women's experience of systemic race and gender oppression by white men and women.[7] Feminist theologians from marginalized communities have called into question the universalism of first-wave white feminist theology's appeal to a common women's experience of oppression; nevertheless, they also employ the language of women's experience, appealing specifically to African American, Hispanic, lesbian, Asian American, and two-thirds-world women's experience, to name a few. These feminists have a stake in defending the methodological appeal to women's experience—with experience redefined so as to focus on women in particular marginalized communities. Hence, white feminist theologians and feminist theologians in marginalized communities who methodologically appeal to women's experience in some form do so often based on two different (and potentially conflicting) agendas—each with different ways of generalizing women's experience and different attitudes about how to treat difference.

White feminist theologians currently no longer appeal overtly to a common women's experience, but they still tend to pursue an agenda of codifying women's diversity into symbols that assume some unified experiences and values. One example will suffice to demonstrate the persistence of this agenda. Elizabeth Johnson is exemplary in her attention to diversity in women's experiences when investigating "the ecumenical, interracial and international spectrum of women's theological voices" on the nature of God. She fully intends to be inclusively multicultural in her conclusion that "the Trinity as pure relationality...epitomizes the connectedness of all that exists in the universe.... [and] 'embodies those qualities of mutuality, reciprocity, cooperation, unity, peace in genuine diversity that are feminist ideals.'"[8] There is a universalist claim at work here that is, for Johnson, theologically unavoidable if she wants to posit God as the ultimate reality undergirding all that is. Nevertheless, just because something may be theologically necessary to claim does not mean that the way in which it is expressed is not loaded with problematic cultural assumptions and uninterrogated privilege. Susan Thisthlethwaite has analyzed white feminist theological claims in juxtaposition to womanist writings. She argues that "the selves of white women have been formed by connectivity. They have also been formed by the class prerogative of whiteness." Hence, white women must begin to see how the prerogative of whiteness is subtly at work in their appeals to universal connectivity and feminist ideals of mutuality and peace.[9] The appeal to women's experience by feminist theologians of color, on the other hand, usually serves an agenda of bringing into focus and affirming the differences among women's experiences, often emphasizing minority women's struggles related to race-based or neocolonialist injustices and the deep mistrust of and lack of connection to the images, metaphors, and ideals of white feminist theology.

By the late 1980s, concerns of what I would call a postmodern nature began to surface. A small number of white feminist theologians began to dispute, from a more postmodern perspective, the validity of an appeal to women's experience, whether universalized or particularized. This third group argues that notions of unitary selves and essential women's experience—even if diversely understood—have become so problematic as to have lost their purchase as authoritative sources or norms for theological claims and political programs.[10] These postmodern white feminist theologians echo certain critiques made by feminists of color that first-wave feminist notions of women's experience are universalizing; yet, there has been little common cause between postmodern feminist theology and the theologies of feminists of color on the issue of women's experience. Hence, the appeal to women's experience remains a live methodological issue, not least because it is a contentious one as well.[11] It seems that feminist theology can't live with this appeal (in light of the postmodern turn) but also can't live without it (at the risk of rendering marginalized women's lives invisible). For all her tendencies to universalize women's experience, Ruether's methodological point still stands: no theology can go forward that does not recognize its rootedness in experience.

Moreover, it would seem that the loss of the appeal to women's experience could mean a setback for feminist constructive theology in particular. One need only look at the long hard road first-wave feminists had to walk to break into this area of scholarship to see how experientially and methodologically vital the appeal to women's experience has been. Although many feminist theological writings date from the 1970s, feminist Christian systematic or doctrinal writings in particular took much longer to appear in any significant numbers. It is perhaps no coincidence that Ruether, who made an appeal to women's experience central, wrote the first book-length piece of feminist doctrinal theology, *Sexism and God-Talk*, in 1983. Ruether commented in her 1993 new introduction that as of the writing of that introduction, she knew of no other comparable text of feminist theology.[12] I believe there are two significant contributing factors to this reality. One factor has to do with the nature of theological education in the 1960s and 1970s (when first-wave feminist theologians were attending divinity schools and religious studies programs) and another has to do with the challenge feminist theologians faced in developing methodologies for accessing women's experiences as source and norm for constructive theological work in ways that would not replicate androcentric views of the experience of God for "man."

Regarding the first factor, Rebecca Chopp probably speaks for many other white feminist scholars in religion of this period when she writes:

> Entering St. Paul School of Theology in Kansas City, Missouri, in 1973, I was hardly a liberal feminist, having been unexposed both to women in ministry and to feminist literature! ... Through these years of education, I read avidly in feminist theology but wrote very little on the topic. In part, this was due to the influence of some of my women colleagues and teachers who warned me about what publishing in feminism would do to my career. But in part, it was due to my own need to first achieve a kind of theoretical and symbolic richness in feminism and other contemporary emancipatory theories. As my confidence grew, I started to write explicitly feminist theology.[13]

The curricula of most divinity and religious studies departments at the time were not oriented to feminist research projects; hence such studies were often conducted in ad hoc ways or at the margins of more traditional areas of curricular emphasis. Moreover, pedagogical methodologies in most schools followed traditional lecture/tutorial formats, whereas feminist pedagogy was exploring models of narrativity, metaphorical thinking, and collaborative dialogical learning.[14] Prior to the 1980s, one can barely imagine a student turning in a paper to a (male) professor in which she describes the process of theological reflection as akin to quilting: "Just as women quilters gathered in groups and shared their life experiences with each other so does a Christian feminist preacher start with the communal sharing and claiming of women's stories."[15] Theological education has changed, but the change took time— hence the lag in feminist constructive theological publication.

We can garner some additional insight into the question about the paucity of feminist theological works in the 1980s by looking at one of the few other texts of feminist theology during this period, Mary Grey's 1989 *Redeeming the Dream*. Grey elucidates what virtually every Christian feminist theologian knows to be true: because "the very categories of Christian theology have seemed to reinforce the inferiority of women," to reimagine symbols, doctrines, and rituals that might promote women's equality, empowerment, self-worth, and liberation, one needs to search out "'another voice,' another strand in human experience which may offer a critique of certain dominating values."[16] It became clear to feminist scholars of religion at the time that this necessary task would be an arduous and uncharted process, which has been variously called: "reclaiming lost experiences," "reclaiming the myth," "hearing silence," reconstructing "herstory," and so on.[17] Some of this process has entailed searches for women's suppressed voices in Christian scripture and deuterocanonical ancient texts and in women's spiritual autobiographies, diaries, and letters throughout history. Although exegetical methodology differs from theological methodology, feminist exegesis focusing on women's roles in the biblical text has been pivotal for feminist constructive theological reflection. One sees the fruit of feminist exegetical-theological partnership in texts like *Sisters in the Wilderness*, where feminist exegesis of the Hagar story in Genesis figures centrally in Williams's womanist proposals for reworking themes of liberation in the experience of African American women.[18] Some of the process has entailed foraging for symbols of women's spirituality in poetry, art, and literature—hence, the pervasiveness of theological use of women's literature in feminist theological and ethical writings (Doris Lessing, Zora Neale Hurston, Alice Walker, Louise Erdrich, Isabel Allende, and others).[19] Although Ruether's *Sexism and God-Talk* exemplified a then-revolutionary feminist methodology, it is written in a more or less traditional manner following common doctrinal themes (with the exception of her own creative midrash, "The Kenosis of the Father"[20]), and there is a notable absence of literary references. Even a cursory glance at feminist theological writings in the late 1980s and 1990s and up to today shows how the genre of feminist theological writing has changed. Currently, there is also an increased interest in ethnography as a starting point for feminist theological writing (a topic I will return to in chapter 2).

With some few exceptions, most first-wave feminist scholars were essentially operating under a self-imposed policing regarding constructive Christian doctrinal writing directly challenging the androcentric tradition. Theologically trained feminist scholars were not only reticent to do explicitly feminist Christian theology because of hiring and tenure considerations but they were still looking for resources for critical and imaginative perspectives to bring to traditional doctrinal loci. Having fortified themselves with narratives and ethnographies about women's experiences of suffering, survival, and hope (and having benefited from changes in the way theological education is being conducted), feminist scholars are now turning again to the task of reinterpreting the Christian tradition.

Looking back on this situation from a point in time after that first wave has deposited its shells on the beach, so to speak, a number of questions arise about the assumptions that first-wave religious feminists carried into their project of reclaiming women's voices—especially as these voices are heard in biblical and women's literature. Reading this literature from a feminist perspective has been pivotal for feminist theologians, but that does not mean that critical review of their methods and assumptions is not necessary. Ethnographic studies in religion have yielded rich data on women's material religious practices, but, again, feminist critique of assumptions and methodologies is vitally necessary at this point in time. Just as first-wave feminists paused in order to scrutinize the then largely androcentric theological and exegetical guild, so feminists today would do well to pause again—in light of issues of difference—for the purpose of self-critical evaluation of the methodological and theoretical assumptions that are directly shaping the search for and interpretation of women's experiences funding feminist theological writing.

Difference comes in many forms: sex, race, class, age, ethnicity, nationality, physical ableness, and so on. In my reading of feminist theological literature, two hot-button issues have emerged: race and sexuality. While these two issues do not have any intrinsic importance over the other items in the above list (and other issues not listed), the intensity of feminist rhetoric surrounding them makes them especially pertinent for analysis. Throughout this text I will examine how they are discussed and propose theories that will increase attentiveness to difference related to race and sexuality. Let me outline here what makes these two issues so complex and challenging for feminist theology.

II. Decentering Privileged Whiteness and Heterosexuality

"Race, See: Women of color"

In the previous pages I have at times used the term "feminist" and at other times, "white feminist." These are not interchangeable terms. A small group of white feminist theologians are calling for an intentional naming of ourselves as such.[21] Such self-naming is part of breaking a decades-long pattern of allowing "feminist" to act as an unmarked code for, among other things, white feminist theology. In other words, "white feminist theology" should join other self-named women-oriented theologies, such as those listed above, each of which will eventually be further qualified in order to be attentive to new manifestations of difference (e.g., lesbian womanist, white disabled, and so on). In light of this reality, it would be valuable to be able to recuperate "feminist theology" as an overtly neutral, noncoded term that can, at certain times, be used to refer to the diversity of these and other yet-to-be-named women's theological writings (with care always taken by hegemonic positionalities to self-name). Indeed, in the current scholarship, "feminist" continues to be intertwined in complex and sometimes contentious ways with many other designations for particular communities of women-oriented theologians (womanist and black feminist theologians, or *mujerista* and Latina feminist theologians).[22] Is my call for white feminist theological self-naming too easy? Is it just a semantic change with nothing of substance beneath? Unless white feminists are willing to delve into the issues surrounding white racial privilege, such self-naming will not only lack substance but will work to reinforce the privilege it is supposed to acknowledge and decenter.

The predominant way white feminist theology has dealt with race issues until very recently is to defer substantive discussions.[23] There is much appropriateness to white theologians standing back and listening to theologians of color present their analyses and accounts of racism; yet, deferring to another can function as avoidance. Eventually what is avoided becomes someone else's issue, as reflected in the subtitle of this section (an index entry in a recent feminist book[24]). The burden is put on people of color to explain racial differences and to help white people work through their racial prejudices and anxieties. Gloria Anzaldúa speaks of how this burden is internalized by women of color and how an unhealthy parasitic relationship is formed. "It is a great temptation for us to make white women comfortable.... Some of us get seduced into making a white woman an honorary woman-of-color—she wants it so badly....A reversed dependency of them upon us emerges."[25] White feminist theologians must do self-critical theorizing about race as well, and feminist theologians of color must resist the temptation to carry the burden of resolving the race anxiety of white feminists. However, if white feminist theologians do begin to comment on race issues, another potential danger crops up—the danger that whatever white theology turns its attention to will be absorbed into its institutionally dominant discourse, domesticated and neutralized. Neither avoidance nor domestication of race issues is satisfactory. In what follows, I will look briefly at three examples of how secular white feminists (Elizabeth Spelman, Nancie Caraway, Ruth Frankenburg) have struggled with race issues in order to demonstrate the difficulty white feminist theologians face in the necessary task of confronting the white race privilege that undergirds racism.

In the aftermath of the first hard-hitting charges of racism in early white feminist calls for "sisterhood," many white feminists fell into a pattern of recycling what Susan Friedman calls "feminist scripts about race." These include principally scripts of denial ("I'm a feminist, so how could I be a racist?") and scripts of guilt or confession ("I am a racist"; "Women of color are...more oppressed than me, better than me, and always right").[26] While there are times when these scripts are appropriate, if acted out over and over, they do tend to create a stage where white feminist race anxiety takes the spotlight instead of the actual realities of racism's destructive effects or the resistance practices of women of color. The scholarship of North American feminists of color on racism is extensive.[27] White feminist theorists attempting to take seriously the deconstruction of a feminist "sisterhood" as a basis for feminist theorizing and practice have been actively debating where to go from here in their own scholarship.

Elizabeth Spelman's *Inessential Woman* (1988) was a landmark work on feminism and difference, which tried to avoid the nonproductively repeating scripts of which Friedman speaks. Spelman did not inaugurate the discussion on racism in white feminist writings but she made two crucial points beyond the acknowledgement of the interlocking nature of gender, race, and class differences in women's experience. First, inclusion is no solution. The problem of differences between white women and women of color is not so much an issue of racial exclusion (which could be solved by merely including "others" in dominant white circles); rather, "the 'problem of difference' is really a problem of privilege." Simply including the voices of women of color in the predominantly white feminist conversation does not address privilege; it reinforces it, since "[t]he power to include implies the power to exclude."[28] Second, empathy is no solution. Spelman unmasks white women's attempts to hear and empathetically understand the experiences of women of color by trying imaginatively to enter their worlds. While not underestimating the power of the utopian imagination and compassion, Spelman worries that imaginative empathizing with women of color is a form of objectification. "When simply imagining" the woman of color, Spelman explains, "I can escape from the demands her reality puts on me and instead construct her in my mind in such a way that I can possess her." Again, privilege (as intellectual property ownership) is reinforced.[29] What could address privilege? Spelman suggests a pedagogical relationship: white women should "apprentice" themselves under women of color, since "making oneself an apprentice to someone is at odds with having political, social and economic power over them."[30] Her proposal is, fundamentally, that white feminists need to surrender their sense of entitlement to determine how dialogue and work on race matters will proceed.

Nancie Caraway objects to part of Spelman's analysis strenuously. Caraway agrees with Spelman that the notion of "generic woman" is "the 'Trojan horse of feminist ethnocentrism,'" which depends on an essentialized view of the other. Like Spelman, Caraway is a liberal white feminist interested in investigating differences between white feminists and feminists of color with the goal of reenvisioning a noncoercive multicultural feminism. She differs from Spelman in her insistence that progress will not be made toward multicultural alliances unless one interrogates the Trojan horse of ethnocentrism on *both* sides. After investigating various dimensions of how black feminist theory and practice challenge the multiple ways in which white women essentialize and try to dominate black women, Caraway turns to the problem of women of color creating "equally non-negotiable constructions of self" regarding white women.[31] Caraway recounts an episode of a white feminist being rendered "invisible" by feminists of color at a multicultural feminist conference. She finds it disturbing that a white woman can be prejudged simply by "her (lack of) color. She, with her undifferentiated 'whiteness,' is homogenized, trapped in images which define her in a certain way, align her with politics she doesn't support."[32] There may be a veiled autobiography here, since Caraway notes her own white southern working-class background and declares: "I dare anyone to shut me in the bloodless, airless tomb of 'privileged white woman.'"[33] Here, class is used to trump the charge of privileged whiteness. Caraway is adamant that the road to feminist multiculturalism is going to be a rocky one of resisting essentialisms and exclusions on both sides. For this reason, she objects to Spelman's one-sided "corrective postures...for white women." She criticizes Spelman's apprenticeship metaphor because no indication is given as to how "the apprenticeship might evolve into dialogue or debate between equals."[34]

Caraway's points are both refreshing and disturbing. I find Caraway's retrieval of the rich history of black feminist theory and activism refreshing because it calls into question the notion that oppression has reduced black women to mere silent victims. I am disturbed, however, by the lack of attention given to the differing effects of white versus black ethnocentrism (as she calls it). Caraway seems at times to be suggesting that the way in which black women might render white women invisible at a feminist conference is in some way analogous to the way in which women of color are rendered invisible in the city streets, restaurants, classrooms, and hospital corridors of America. In what comes close to a script of denial, she also suggests that professional white women's past experience of class discrimination undercuts their white privilege—a point I would contest. Nevertheless, despite the drawbacks and defensiveness of Caraway's text, she can be credited for turning the focus of white feminist writings toward analyses of how whiteness is socially constructed and, hence, something which has "functioned at a structural level (beyond individual intentionality)."[35]

Ruth Frankenberg further investigates the constructed nature of whiteness in her ethnographic study, *White Women, Race Matters: The Social Construction of Whiteness*. Frankenberg explains that from the perspective of white privilege, naming one's racial identity is what minorities are seen to do on the margins, taking as their reference point whiteness at the center, which itself (in the minds of whites) needs no reference point or name. Whiteness, to those at the center, is ..., well, just colorless. Frankenberg calls this function of whiteness the "unmarked marker of others' differences."[36] This makes whiteness functionally a normative relational category "defined by reference to those named cultures it has flung out to its perimeter." Frankenburg argues that for all its apparent lack of identifying markers, whiteness is not "'empty' cultural space."[37] It shapes identity in various ways and is complexly linked to other cultural markers such as class and gender. Frankenburg concludes that whiteness also confers privilege even when one views oneself in some contexts as a nonprivileged, marginalized person. Some of her interviewees denied that their whiteness is a privileged position, appealing to past experiences of marginalization or to the memory of their family's societal marginalization because of ethnicity or poverty (this echoes Caraway's stance). Frankenberg found, however, that those memories of marginalization usually outlasted the marginalization itself.[38] Only for a few groups of the white women she studied (such as Jews and lesbians) did marginalization on any pervasive, structural level continue to be an existential factor for them.[39]

This discussion of Spelman, Caraway, and Frankenburg in no way represents the totality of secular white feminist theorizing on race but it gives some insight into the range of issues relevant to white privilege. The lesson we can draw is that if whiteness remains unnamed and uninterrogated, it will most likely continue to function as an unmarked marker in relation to overtly named racial minorities. As a result, privilege and nonproductive white race anxiety will accrue. If, however, whiteness is seen for what it is—a diverse privilege-conferring culture—then it will be a more manageable factor in feminist interracial discussions.[40]

I am not suggesting that no meaningful attempts have been made thus far among feminist theologians of diverse races and sexual orientations to dialogue, learn of one another's differences, and interrogate white privilege. Notable among these attempts was that of the Mud Flower Collective, a group of women scholars in religion whose multicultural reflections were compiled some two decades ago in God's Fierce Whimsy.[41] Such interchange is important, but we must be careful about concluding that, because groups of women from diverse backgrounds have previously come together and shared with each other in this way, the bases for dialogue have been established. One example from the Mud Flower Collective's dialogues will make my point. Emerging from their reading of Alice Walker's The Color Purple, African American theologian Katie Cannon and white lesbian theologian Carter Heyward began a dialogue through letters titled "Can We Be Different but Not Alienated?" which continues to be reprinted.[42] In this exchange, Cannon and Heyward explore themes of racial difference and the possibility of finding commonalities among black and white women's experiences. In one especially frank and poignant moment, Cannon addresses Heyward's experience of being molested as a child by a black man—an experience Cannon also suffered. Cannon uses themes from *The Color Purple* (Celie, the protagonist, is also sexually abused) to share with Heyward how she is finding healing and to encourage Heyward in her path of recovery.

An uncritical reading of these letters might lead one to conclude that finding experiential commonalities of a significant sort (e.g., having suffered sexual abuse) can be the basis for conversation in which differences melt away. In particular, a "sentimental" reading of these two women's letters might attempt to dispel differences of race and to forge sisterhood through "the invocation of tears" on the part of the empathetic reader.[43] However, the discovery of this shared, very personal, and painful experience is also a discovery of deep racial differences (differences of class or sexuality are not really discussed). Heyward makes a frank confession of experiencing a disturbing distrust of black men.[44] Cannon empathizes with the ongoing trauma of living with a "place inside you that has not healed from violation" but expresses no similar aversion to black men as a whole—only to "those who remind me of the boy who molested me."[45] One sees immediately that Heyward's trauma is shaped by a dominant white racist cultural myth of the predatory black male, whereas Cannon's trauma is not. The two women cry the same salty tears as a result of their childhood violation, but the experience and its effects are different. A reader's sentimental appeal to shared suffering masks the differences between interracial versus black-on-black sexual molestation within a white racist society.[46]

This interracial conversation suggests that sharing differences is only the beginning of understanding what separates women and how privilege functions. "Difference" is itself a complex notion that needs to be theorized. Feminist theology has been slow to commit itself to this task; hence, the path to multicultural feminist dialogue will not be easy. It will require a rigorous analysis of how feminist theologians in dominant positions overlook difference and thereby inculcate privileged perspectives. Be that as it may, this project is not intended as an exercise in blame laying for racist, classist, heterosexist, or any other hegemonic attitudes and practices. On the whole, feminist theology takes a strong position condemning such things. The manifestations of privilege in feminist theological writings are usually more subtle and implicit— but, not for that reason, any less problematic. Privilege might take the form of a well-meaning liberal call for dialogue itself, which is a pervasive ethos in white feminism. Too often, however, the scholarly attempt to reach out to and "include" the marginalized other in dialogue has the opposite effect. The invitation to the marginalized "other" to converse with the dominant "us" subtly yet indisputably underpins the privilege and hegemony of the position of the one with the power to include or exclude (as Spelman has aptly noted). One example cannot entirely represent this phenomenon, but it will help to illustrate my point in relation to how white racial privilege can function in an otherwise collegial interracial dialogue.

The example again comes from a published exchange between two feminist scholars in religion: Susan Secker, who is white, and Jeanette Rodríguez, who is Latina. Both these Seattle University professors read the papers each was planning to give at an upcoming feminist theological conference and then wrote about the experience of finding so many differences between them. Secker describes the difference between her and Rodríguez's points of view in this way: when she herself thinks about the term "experience," Secker "presume[s] the quest for generalizations about features of women's lives," whereas Rodríguez focuses on differences among women.[47] Nothing in Secker's worldview prevents her from imagining some basic features common to all women, despite her awareness of women's differences. Indeed, for Secker, seeking out theologically some universalizing features of women's experience reflects a vital truth about what constitutes all women's dignity before God. Rodríguez's position on difference is just the opposite: her worldview prevents her from attempting theologically to transcend differences. The reality of her current "'struggle of flesh . . . struggle of borders'" (as the daughter of Ecuadorian parents, theologically trained and residing in North America) impels her to emphasize interracial differences as well as differences among the experiences of Latina women of various nationalities, age groups, and educational levels.[48]

Secker is not unmoved by Rodríguez's comments on the differences between them. They have an impact on Secker who asks, naming her whiteness: "Have we white feminists unconsciously mistaken our own 'room' for the entire house?"[49] Secker begins to feel uncomfortable with a comment she remembers by a white male colleague in her department who told her that he believed that "[a]ttentiveness to the many ways in which humans are different inhibits theological reflection. . . . [C]laims by women, Asians, Hispanics, African-Americans, etc., about the uniqueness of their group 'experience' result in . . . cultural- or racial- or gender-based relativism . . . [that] renders impossible the theological task itself."[50] Secker is disturbed by her male colleague's patriarchal insistence on doing theology undistracted by differences.

In disagreement with that colleague, Secker takes a feminist stance affirming particularity and diversity. Moreover, she understands that taking such a stance will have "ramifications for feminist theological method." Secker has clearly had her consciousness raised about the reality of white racial bias among "we white feminists." This admission, however, does not constitute a rigorous enough analysis of the nature of white race privilege. Hence, there is a not-unexpected lapse back into unnamed whiteness at the end of her article when Secker writes: "I remember, ironically, how often some [white?] women colleagues and I have chuckled at Adrienne Rich's description of 'objectivity.'... Yet, we [white feminists?] seem oblivious to the stark similarity of our own presumptions about...objective womanness."[51]

Naming oneself as white cannot be a momentary epiphanic mea culpa followed by a return to "our" (unmarked white) business as usual. Why is it so easy to forget whiteness and inadvertently start talking about "some women colleagues and I..."? Secker, as a feminist, certainly does not lapse unintentionally into language about her generic "humanness" (as her male colleague does). The problem I have identified can be subtle and does not indicate a complete lack of multicultural sensitivity to racial difference. Rodríguez, for example, describes Secker as having been "changed because of her encounter with another"; hence, a fruitful dialogue took place.[52]

My point in this illustration is that white racial privilege is devilishly hard to decenter and not doing so has a direct impact on the possibilities for interracial, intercultural dialogue among feminist theologians. Indeed, the very assumption (especially on the part of white feminist theologians) that we are at a point where dialogue of any depth can take place must itself be carefully interrogated. Dialogue, which seems by definition to be a good and enriching thing, can also be disempowering in certain contexts and for certain groups. Stephanie Mitchem surveys the arduous road that womanist theologians have had to climb to carve out their own theological voice in the context of dominant white theology. Given womanist needs to devote time for retrieving resources, images, histories, and ethnographies from within the African American community, Mitchem asks pragmatically and pastorally, "Should womanists limit dialogue with white feminists?"[53] Moreover, when the subject matter for dialogue is about theory, additional complications arise. A too facile appeal to the use of critical theories might ignore the warning voiced by Barbara Christian: "'My fear is when theory is not rooted in practice, it becomes prescriptive, exclusivist, elitist.'" Moreover, Mitchem, adds, "there will be differences between black and white feminist scholars in the uses, extensions, and applications of...[theory] constructions." Mitchem contends, and I agree, that we are only "at the beginning" of finding "a common vocabulary, address[ing] differences, and reconcil[ing] fissures between womanists and white feminists."[54] She issues a warning about turning to theories that are not widely used or are differently used by womanist theologians who are immersed in other theory constructions. Emilie Townes gives poetic voice to womanist reticence regarding dialogue about theory:

> if we rush in too quickly
> > without tools of correct analysis
> > and sisterly solidarity
> the voice we will hear is our own echo
> > a distortion of the original
> > but dolby in sound....
> I do want you to hear my story
> > take it in
> > consider how you have been a part of it
> > > or not[55]

Dialogue among communities of feminist scholars of different races and ethnicities is a road fraught with potholes that must be negotiated with care. Such dialogue must be prefaced by rigorous self-critique on the part of well-intentioned white feminists who may erroneously think that calls for more inclusivity in feminist theology constitutes a decentering of white privilege.

"What is 'Sex' Anyway?"

As with racial privilege, heterosexual privilege is difficult to decenter. In part, this is because theologians generally tiptoe delicately around or avoid completely issues of sexuality and are unwilling or unable to take on questions such as Judith Butler's quoted in the subtitle to this section.[56] Underlying much of this theological reticence is an implicit suspicion toward the body, especially the female body and the nonheteronormative body. Anti-body attitudes that have influenced Christian thought have roots in late antiquity with the prevalence of Hellenistic body-soul dualisms. Greco-Roman men (of a certain social class and citizenship status) were associated with the mind and women were associated with materiality. Despite the acceptance of male homosexual activity in ancient Roman culture, elite male citizens were encouraged to pursue bodily discipline and even a kind of asceticism. Emerging from this context, patristic theology viewed material, sexual bodies negatively, despite attempts to oppose Marcionism and Manichaeanism. Celibacy and virginity were valued above even chaste marriage.[57] In medieval writings, women were depicted as particularly susceptible to the devil's deception, due to their supposedly deficient rationality and excessive physical "humors," and hence their claims about embodied mystical experiences were closely monitored by church authorities.[58] Women were the misbegotten daughters of Eve (on whom primary culpability for the Fall rested). The female body was seen as defectively conceived, inferior, fleshly, and dangerous.

First-wave (mostly white) feminist scholars have vociferously criticized the church's long-standing misogynous associations between the female body and evil.[59] Later, feminist "body" theologies emerged with constructive theological attempts to counteract androcentrism and misogyny in the tradition by making women's embodiment methodologically central.[60] Body theologies coincided and in some cases overlapped with the emergence of the first lesbian (and gay) theologies, and paved the way for more recent queer theological writings addressing other marginalized sex and/or gender identities.[61] The very notion of gynocentric feminism seems to necessitate inclusion of some discussion of embodiment, sexuality, and sex, which feminist theologians are increasingly integrating into theological writings. Understanding the very being of God is, for some feminists, contingent on not only accepting that "sexuality lies at the heart of all creation" but making that reality integral to theological epistemology: "sexuality is a clue that our existence is grounded in a being for whom To-Be is To-Be-For."[62] However, despite the prevalence of references to bodies and sexuality, feminist theologians are often very reticent in their embrace of, shall we say, bodies embracing—especially bodies outside of heteronormative categories.

The bulk of feminist theologies addressing sex and sexuality have been by white women. An important exception is Kelly Brown Douglas's *Sexuality and the Black Church*, which lays bare how white feminist discussions of sex and sexuality elide the African American experience.[63] Douglas's views, by her own account, have had some shock value in African American circles because of the way she shines a strong self-critical light close to home, asking, why is "womanist theology—a theology recognized by some as providing one of the most holistic visions of human life and freedom—so silent on sexuality" generally and so slow to "confront the potentially divisive issue of homosexuality" and HIV/AIDS particularly?[64] Most white heterosexual feminist theologians have not made it a priority to engage in self-critique regarding heterosexual (and racial) privilege within white feminism.

I am not saying that feminist theologians have been remiss in addressing heterosexism in complex ways. Two examples illuminate both how far we have come as well as how much work lies ahead for dialogue to continue fruitfully on the subject of sexuality. In a 1986 roundtable discussion in the *Journal of Feminist Studies in Religion*, Carter Heyward and Mary Hunt threw down the gauntlet, so to speak, to their feminist theological colleagues, challenging them to three tasks: (1) to "pay critical attention to their heterosexual privilege"; (2) to recognize the solidarity between heterosexual women and lesbians because the oppression lesbians have suffered "publicly—often in the name of God—represents dramatically what is done daily to all women"; and (3) to struggle with lesbians to find ways "to affirm women's bodies and sexualities" without "becoming...objects of male fantasy."[65] Bernadette Brooten, Evelyn Torton Beck, and Clare Fisher all spoke to how these concerns could and should be further explored in New Testament studies, Jewish studies, and the classroom. Based on these three responses, the dialogue seemed to be lacking in any points of tension. A fourth respondent, Delores Williams, however, interjected a different set of concerns. Stating her positionality "as a black, heterosexual woman," she challenged several of Heyward's and Hunt's claims. While she insisted on the necessity of attentiveness to lesbian experience, she questioned whether "black heterosexual women in white America have any kind of 'heterosexual privilege' above the privilege of white lesbian women" (such as Heyward and Hunt who self-identify as white in their segment of the piece).[66] To my knowledge, Williams's point has not been addressed substantively in subsequent white lesbian feminist theological writings.

What this conversation demonstrates is how discussions that are ostensibly about heterosexism can turn out also to be about other markers of power and privilege—in this case, white racial privilege. It goes without saying that this issue may never be satisfactorily addressed if this were to remain solely a two-way dialogue between white lesbians and black heterosexual women. As lesbian womanist theologian Renée Hill has argued: "I have stopped trying to acquiesce to the demands that I choose between my race, my gender and my sexual orientation as a starting or ending point for protest against personal or communal experience."[67] This early example of a foray into a relatively new area for feminist theology reveals how vital issues emerge not only in the presence of supportive agreement but also as the result of dialogical conflict related to differences in women's experiences.

My second example of feminist dialogue on sexuality comes from a recent issue of *Feminist Theology*, devoted to Marcella Althaus-Reid's provocative *Indecent Theology* written from a Latin American (urban Argentinean) liberationist, queer theological perspective.[68] Althaus-Reid's book unveils the repressiveness of the sexual ideology of traditional theology (Roman Catholic theology generally and Latin American liberation theology specifically) through a focus on women's sexuality—especially poor, urban Roman Catholic women in her native Argentina. She envisions and models a methodology and discourse that exposes the sexually, politically, and economically repressive nature of dominant religious dogma (e.g., about the Virgin Mary) and envisions liberating aspects of sexually, politically, and economically transgressive grassroots Latin American religiosity (e.g., veneration of the cross-dressing Jesus, known as *Santa Librada*).

There were many appreciative comments in this print forum to Althaus-Reid's work.[69] However, for my purposes of examining how difference and privilege play out in feminist theological dialogue, I want to focus on two critical points that were raised. Hong Kong–born feminist theologian Kwok Pui-lan applauded Althaus-Reid's claim that postcolonial theory needs queering, but she was troubled by the superficiality of Althaus-Reid's interaction with other streams of Latin American and other two-thirds-world feminist theologies, much of which is often conservatively "decent—meaning it supports the sexual codification of society and heterosexual norms."[70] The unspoken question here is: Can a new feminist theological method go forward productively when it does not deeply engage the voices of other non-first-world feminist theologies reflecting traditional theological perspectives and non-erotic-oriented forms of liberation? Emilie Townes questioned whether Althaus-Reid's discussion of the sexuality of poor urban Argentinean female lemon vendors was voyeuristic and hence objectifying (reminiscent of the objectifying exploitation of "the Hottentot Venus...the black African woman who was put on public display" in scientific exhibitions in nineteenth-century Europe).[71]

In response to Kwok's challenge, Althaus-Reid admitted unapologetically that her "queer and continental" philosophical approach is "foreign" to more conservative Latin American feminist theologians; yet, Kwok's points caused her to think more about how she herself relates to the "foreignness of [dominant Christian] theology" which she is trying to make indecent.[72] She also defended her discussion of the sexuality of the lemon vendors against Townes's claims of colonialist objectification, because Althaus-Reid places herself as an insider among these urban *Porteña* women.[73] I think she would admit, however, that as an academic theologian, she is in many ways other to those lemon vendors. Hence, when she speaks of them and herself as "we *Porteñas*," she should have in the forefront of her mind her own critique of how colonial theologians used to say "[w]e with confidence," as if "we" were "a homogeneous, unified group of people with similar experiences and desires."[74] What this conversation about Althaus-Reid's book demonstrates is how discussions that are ostensibly about the liberation of queer erotics can turn out to be also about the restrictiveness of the expectation that one's sexuality should be liberated in an erotically oriented way and about the risk of voyeurism in any claim about "we" women and our bodily pleasures.

There are two lessons I take away from exchanges on sexuality such as these. First, in order to interrogate heterosexual privilege, sex and sexuality need to come more front and center in feminist theological writings. But having said that, theorizing is necessary in order to understand the nature of differences among gendered and sexed bodies in ways that do not merely replicate patriarchal, heterosexist, racist or colonialist modes of thought on the subject. Second, even feminist or queer discussions about sex can also manifest problems of privilege, be entangled in ambiguities of the erotic, and waver on the sometimes fine line between a sexually empowering versus an objectifying academic gaze. Feminist theology will need to find ways to theorize sex, bodies, desires, and power in ways that fully face these complex issues.

III. A Road Map

I have organized this book in such a way that the argument builds incrementally in terms of the theoretical complexities of the challenge of difference as it plays out in the methodological, hermeneutical, and doctrinal aspects of feminist theology. In this summary of subsequent chapters, I will introduce a number of technical terms that will receive fuller explanation later. I turn in chapter 2 to the ostensibly most concrete and accessible issue: women's experiences as portrayed in literature, biblical narrative, and ethnographic writing. Such accounts have always been the mainstay of feminist theology, which is committed to remaining accountable in some way to women's suffering and hopes. That commitment is commendable, but it is incumbent upon feminist theologians to revisit their methodological practices in light of the considerations about difference and privilege discussed above. This chapter analyzes some problematic assumptions at work in the way feminist theologians retrieve women's experience textually and ethnographically. Using as my literary test case Alice Walker's *The Color Purple*, I examine how white feminists elide race in their color-blind appropriations of the spiritual themes in Walker's story. A troubling pattern found in white feminist and womanist readings of this novel is ignoring or downplaying the characters' sexualities, especially sexualities outside the dominant heterosexual paradigm. These reading practices reflect an implicit assumption that spirituality can be abstracted from embodied and cultural experience. We can also detect a general ambivalence around issues of sexuality and how to speak of sexed identity. I turn to the Genesis narrative of Sarah and Hagar in order to analyze the range of ways feminists interpret these two female characters as tropes for modern women's experience. At one extreme are approaches that eclipse women's agency by interpreting Sarah and Hagar in terms of a narrow victim/victimizer binary. At the other extreme are approaches that eclipse women's oppression through overly utopian representations of Hagar and Sarah's sisterhood. The readings at either extreme are marked by various problematic assumptions of the nature of oppressive power, women's agency, or women's resistance practices. The work of *mujerista* theologian Ada María Isasi-Díaz will be the focus of my comments on feminist ethnographic approaches to retrieving women's experience. I defend Isasi-Díaz's ethnographic feminist theology (which I read in light of black feminist "standpoint" theory) against one critic who claims that Isasi-Díaz inserts her own agenda too much into the ethnographic process. This discussion leads us into the center of current debates in cultural anthropology regarding objectivity, reflexivity, and the very possibility of doing advocacy feminist ethnography at all.

At the conclusion of chapter 2, the reader will find that she has been brought face to face not just with the challenge of retrieving women's diverse experiences of suffering, survival, and resistance (textually and ethnographically portrayed), but she has also been confronted with a number of complex questions. How should we think about selfhood—especially sexed selfhood and sexual desire—in light of our dominant heteronormative culture? How should feminist theologians theorize agency, oppression, ethical accountability, and resistance? Chapters 3 and 4 provide sustained arguments for the kind of theorizing I believe is necessary to begin to address adequately the challenging and sometimes controversial philosophical issues woven throughout these questions. These chapters also launch us into discussions of the theological—specifically, doctrinal—implications of employing new theoretical perspectives.

Chapter 3 approaches questions of selfhood and moral agency in light of embodiment—specifically, sexed and sexual bodies. This subject matter emerges in various loci of feminist theological writings. I will focus on feminist writings on sin and women's creation in the image of God in order to analyze critically the prevalent problematic assumption about a natural male-female sex binarism. In the field of gender studies, the work of white feminist scholar Judith Butler has been pivotal in discussion about maleness and femaleness. Butler's poststructuralist approach to "performative" gendered and sexed identity, I argue, provides feminist theology with an effective way to theorize the embodied self who sins and is created in God's image—without falling into a male-female binarism that arguably sustains heterosexist modes of thinking. After presenting how sexed selfhood can be formulated in a poststructuralist way, I offer a constructive feminist proposal on sin and creation in the image of God. If selfhood is viewed poststructurally and performatively, sin would be the self engaging in "discursive" relations in ways that distort godly performativity. The image of God, correlatively, would be the graced possibility for godliness in every discursive identity performance, including gender, sex and sexual desire. This reformulation of sin and the *imago dei* not only avoids assumptions about a natural sex binarism but helps sustain a commitment to difference because it highlights the multiple and diverse intersections of cultural discourses that constitute the subject. I conclude by addressing two positions that would challenge my poststructuralist approach to women's spiritual performativity: Elizabeth Johnson's position on the necessity of theologically presupposing an ontological basis for women's connection to God; and Grace Jantzen's position on the necessity of positing a feminist semiotic and symbolic realm outside of "phallocratic" discursive systems, within which women's desire for the divine can flourish. My poststructuralist counterproposal to their positions presents desire not as a prethematic given or a semiotic horizon but as discursively constructed in specific contexts and always in relations of power. A Christian poststructuralist feminist approach to desire for the divine would entail negotiating with the dominant masculinist "disciplinary" (Michel Foucault's term) discourse of the Christian tradition. This seems counterintuitive from most feminist perspectives today. In order to envision the possibility of productive feminist negotiations with the oppressive symbols of the Christian tradition, we need to theorize the nature of power adequately.

In chapter 4, I begin with the basic question regarding the nature of dominating power by looking at how it is often dualistically portrayed in feminist discussions of structural oppression (theologically referred to as social sin) and in feminist theological critiques of oppressive cultural formations, such as Christian symbols. Feminist theologians want to depict women as empowered agents who can resist societal structures, such as racism and sexism. The tendency has been to associate women's agency with good power over against the bad power of that which is oppressing them, which inscribes potentially restrictive essentialisms about women as victims in relation to power viewed too monolithically. I will propose balancing postcolonial theories about strategically positing a "subaltern" standpoint in relation to oppression (Gayatri Chakravorty Spivak) with poststructuralist theories about the construction of subjects, even those with insurrectional agency, in relation to disciplinary "power/knowledge" (Michel Foucault). I will apply the latter poststructuralist theory as part of a critical theological analysis of the cross (with its implications about enforced surrogacy and the glorification of sacrificial violence) and Jesus as the Christ (whose sex makes women dependent on a male savior who mirrors a male God). In this chapter and the next, I make the case for how a poststructuralist feminism that is attentive to difference can go forward productively in negotiation with the (patriarchal, heteronormative, etc.) Christian tradition.

Chapter 5 tests this theoretical possibility of negotiating with the tradition in two areas that pose seemingly insuperable obstacles for a diversity of feminist thinkers: the masculinist, heteronormative, christocentric, or imperialist Christian creeds and New Testament texts. First, I argue that a "postliberal" rule theory approach to doctrine allows us to see how contemporary feminist theologies that are ostensibly disconnected from the creedal tradition (and possibly even at odds with each other) are regulatively instantiating a stream of that tradition in diverse ways. Having established a formal rule theory connection to a common creedal tradition, we can see that productive negotiations with the tradition's heavily disciplinary aspects are possible and even well underway. Second, I face the challenge of what to do with those New Testament texts that seem to undermine liberal Christian feminist claims that the core of Jesus' message is woman-friendly, liberatory, and attentive to the marginalized. These liberal feminist canon-within-the-canon approaches are ill equipped to address New Testament passages that harbor imperialist, exclusivist, masculinist, and heteronormative messages, such as Jesus' encounter with the Samaritan woman in John 4.[75] Employing deconstructive, postcolonial, and queer hermeneutical tools, I try to meet head-on the text's biases and tease out meanings that subvert the dominant tradition's celebration of this story as an account of the successful conversion of a woman with dubious morals, misguided messianic notions, and illicit desires. I offer this reading as an example of one way in which diverse feminist scholars might resist disciplinary biblical texts, even while (perhaps surprisingly) finding themselves still desiring to continue to read such texts at all.

Chapter 6 concludes with one of the most contested (and rightly so to my mind) issues in feminist theology today: solidarity. Given the difficulties feminist theology has experienced in trying to attend to difference and root out privilege, should feminists today invoke the notion of women's solidarity? I examine three important contemporary approaches to this issue articulated by white feminists Sharon Welch and Sheila Greeve Davaney and womanist M. Shawn Copeland. In critical conversation each one's views, I discuss some conditions under which feminists might continue rethinking the notion of solidarity. I also propose a metaphor (borrowed somewhat eclectically from the field of dance improvisation theory) that can help us look anew (though still very skeptically) at solidarity in light of inescapable and determinative differences in women's experience.

The objective of this book is thus threefold. I wish to make the case for why ongoing and in-depth attentiveness to difference in feminist theology today is needed in order to avoid hegemonic impositions of privilege, especially white racial privilege and heterosexual privilege. This is a necessity even in the presence of multicultural good intentions, productive dialogue across differences, and genuine collegiality among feminist theologians of various backgrounds. The challenge of meeting this first objective requires a second one: employing new theoretical perspectives on embodied selfhood, moral agency, and social and institutional power which maximize the ways in which we can complicate our understanding of identity construction and resistance to oppression. I endeavor to make creative use of poststructuralism principally, but also postcolonial, queer and other theoretical resources. Theorizing selfhood, agency and power in light of these resources has ramifications throughout feminist theological practice: methodology, hermeneutics and doctrine. Hence, the third objective of this book is to make proposals in all three of these areas that hopefully contribute productively to feminist theological debate on methodological issues (such as the appeal to women's experience or to the erotic), hermeneutical issues (such as interpreting biblical texts that are morally ambiguous or outright patriarchal, imperialist, etc.), and doctrinal issues (such as sin and christology).

This text does not propose a criterion of feminist political correctness vis-à-vis difference; rather, it explores how certain theoretical tools might be deployed to face the challenge of difference for constructive theological purposes. Theory is by no means the complete solution to the fractures running deep throughout feminist theology; indeed, even the assumption that those fractures could or should be healed risks foreclosing important critiques from newly emergent marginal sectors. Nevertheless, new theoretical resources seem indispensable for rigorous analysis of the complex and often divisive issues that must be addressed in feminist theology today, and they seem indispensable for carving out new avenues for engagement with a religious tradition that feminists see as both alienating and sustaining, repressive and empowering. Without the means for thinking afresh about the challenge of difference, feminist theology will, in the years to come, fight an increasingly uphill battle to reach whatever new goals it sets for itself in the name of women's survival, spiritual well-being, agency, and hope.

2

Critical Issues in Retrieving Women's Experience

I have called for complicating the notion of women's experience and decentering privileges of whiteness and heterosexuality in feminist theology. I am confident that all feminist theologians marked by those privileges would agree, but cultivating awareness of how those (and other) privileges are actually subtly at work in theological writings is difficult. In the search for images, metaphors, narratives, and practices that could counteract dominant discourses and mechanisms of patriarchy, racism, heterosexism, and so on, feminist scholars from the first wave to the present have turned to women's literature, women's stories in the Bible, and women's everyday lives as sources for their constructive and critical writings. Because retrieving women's experience is such a pivotal task for feminist theology, a critical examination of how this task is being carried out is crucial. This chapter focuses critical attention on two important methodological approaches. In parts one and two, I examine feminist textual approaches to retrieving women's experience, using as my literary example Alice Walker's *The Color Purple* and as my biblical example the narrative of Sarah and Hagar in Genesis 16 and 21. In relation to Walker's text, I will bring specific attention to bear on how some white feminist and womanist theological reading practices either promote or inhibit awareness of differences of race and sexuality in women's experiences portrayed literarily. I examine eight scholars' interpretations of the Hagar-Sarah accounts, mapping their views of women's agency along a continuum between two extreme poles—the pole of oppressive victimization, suggesting virtually no agency, and the pole of utopian sisterhood, suggesting almost unlimited agency. Part three examines how ethnography is used for the purpose of feminist theological reflection on women's experience. Whereas first-wave (mostly white) feminist theologians tended to turn to textual and historical sources to uncover suppressed women's voices, currently some feminist scholars (including many women of color) are using ethnographic methods in order to find source material for theological reflection and to give voice to women in marginalized communities with whom they identify. In this section, I will address conflicts that have emerged regarding whether one can retrieve "real" women's experiences unmediated by the feminist theologian's own agendas.

This chapter looks at the writings of a representative group of feminist scholars on these three topics in order to build the case that these problematic patterns and conflicts can be attributed not to some lack of multicultural good intentions but to the kinds of assumptions that these scholars carry into the task of retrieving women's experience—assumptions about the nature of embodied selfhood, moral agency, oppressive power, resistance, and how to represent the voice of the marginalized "other." By identifying those assumptions, we can move productively forward, in future chapters, with the work of theorizing afresh about them. Hence this chapter's analysis paves the way for the subsequent chapters' constructive philosophical and theological proposals on these issues.

I. Obscuring Difference in Feminist Theological Interpretations of *The Color Purple*

As I noted in chapter 1, since the publication of such groundbreaking texts as Carol Christ's *Diving Deep and Surfacing* and Katie Cannon's *Black Womanist Ethics*, white feminist and womanist scholars in religion have promoted the notion that vital theological and ethical writing must remain connected to the subtleties of human experience as a source and norm.[1] Literature has often been an important means to this end. Theological uses of a diverse canon of literary works have captured the imagination of a broad spectrum of women. The scholars' intentions and literary sources may be multicultural, but some troubling reading practices are also evident. Alice Walker's *The Color Purple*— still one of the most often quoted pieces of literature in feminist theological writings[2]—is a novel well suited for bringing critical attention to some ways in which differences of race and/or sexuality are overlooked in white feminist and womanist reading practices. Specifically, some white feminist theologians engage in what I would call color-blind appropriations of the spiritual themes in Walker's text. Furthermore, some white feminist and womanist theological readings of *The Color Purple* largely ignore or downplay the protagonist Celie's lesbianism and the way that her discovery of her own sexuality is part and parcel of her discovery of a divine, loving Spirit in the world.[3] In effect, these readings render the black lesbian body invisible. These problems occur even when every good intention is exerted to be open to racial and sexual otherness. Intentions, however, are not my focus here. I am interested in identifying problematic methods and assumptions in a way that moves us forward in the feminist theological task, not in blame laying from some position of moral superiority.[4] I will illustrate that these reading practices reflect two implicit assumptions. There is the assumption that one can speak of spirituality disconnected from racial and sexual embodiment and particular context. A more complicated assumption is that sexuality or sexed identity is natural, an assumption which risks constituting a hegemonic assertion of what Butler calls "naturalized heterosexuality" (a point to be discussed at length in chapter 3).[5]

"Seeing" Color in The Color Purple

In some ways, Alice Walker's *The Color Purple* almost invites color-blind readings from a white readership. Because of the personal, introspective, timeless tone created in Celie's letters to God, white readers are tempted to forget that Celie's story begins in the pre–World War II, rural, segregated South. Because of the novel's focus on the abuse of women within black families,[6] white readers are tempted to forget that this is also a story of white racism. But, just as readers of *The Diary of Anne Frank* should not forget that Anne was Jewish, with all that being Jewish connoted under Hitler's rule, white readers of *The Color Purple* should not forget that Celie is a poor, semiliterate black woman, with all that connotes in the United States. Celie's reimaging of God in *The Color Purple*—the focus of most white feminist theological readings—can be understood only as it intersects with, among other things, racial discrimination.

The novel opens with the voice of Celie's sexually abusive stepfather threatening the fourteen-year-old Celie—"*You better not never tell nobody but God*"—thus implicating God in the conspiracy of silence surrounding the sexual abuse of which Celie is a victim. Before she is twenty years old, Celie has been impregnated twice by rape, has been forced to give up her babies for adoption, and has been married off to a much older and abusive man. All the while, she prays and writes letters to a silent God: "Dear God...Maybe you can give me a sign letting me know what is happening to me."[7] Her suffering and the silence of God galvanize an image of God in Celie's mind that is dislodged only after Celie meets Shug Avery, her husband's mistress. Shug befriends Celie and eventually becomes her lover, giving Celie some of the affection and nurture she had neither as a child nor as an adult. While encouraging Celie to stand up to her husband and to enjoy her own sexuality, Shug also teaches her a new spirituality—a belief in a divine Spirit that imbues all creation. The spirituality Celie embraces has concrete interpersonal ramifications for Celie's family and friends. The story culminates in a reconciliation between Celie and her husband, Albert (previously identified only as "Mr. ———" by Celie), who himself undergoes a kind of conversion that allows him to see Celie as a person to whom he must make amends. The closing scene, in which Celie is reunited with her children and her long-lost sister, is an idyllic vision of a black woman who has battled for personal survival and, having achieved it, reaps reconciliation and peace for her extended family as well.

I do not think Celie's rejection (under Shug's tutelage) of the belief that God is "big and old and tall and graybearded and white" (*CP*, 201) can be divorced from her firsthand experience of oppression by white people. Walker does not engage in diatribes against racism and white privilege, but the theme is powerfully communicated narratively in one episode in particular, when Celie's stepdaughter-in-law, Sofia, a formidable-looking woman who does not suffer fools of any color, drives into town with her children. The narrative about Sofia continues in Celie's voice:

> Clam out on the street looking like somebody. Just then the [white] mayor and his wife come by.
>
> All these children, say the mayor's wife, digging in her pocketbook. Cute as little buttons though, she say. She stop, put her hand on one of the children head. Say, and such strong white teef.
>
> Sofia...don't say nothing.... Miss Millie finger the children some more, finally look at Sofia.... She eye Sofia wristwatch. She say to Sofia, All your children so clean, she say, would you like to work for me, be my maid?
>
> Sofia say, Hell no. (*CP*, 90)[8]

The mayor intervenes, tempers flare, and a physical altercation ensues. The inevitable happens: Sofia is beaten to within an inch of her life and imprisoned. I suggest that the meaning of Celie's rejection of a white (male) God is defined by this scene, in which Sofia dares to challenge—directly and physically—white (patriarchal) privilege and is cruelly punished for her defiant act.

White feminist theological interest in this story is a positive move; however, as Susan Brooks Thistlethwaite warns in *Sex, Race, and God*, white feminist theologians such as herself should not "use the fiction of black women as a source in the same way [we]...have been able to use the fiction of white women...for white feminist theology."[9] Not only have white feminists often overlooked the racial component of the texts of African American women writers, but also the way they have read these texts reinforces their tendencies to universalize women's experience under white racial and cultural codes of women's authentic spirituality. Thistlethwaite notes that white feminist theologians are drawn, in particular, to the reimaging of God in a conversation between Shug and Celie where Shug explains, "My first step from [God as] the old white man was trees. Then air. Then birds. Then other people" (*CP*, 203). However, as Thistlethwaite rightly observes: "[N]o white feminist who has quoted this passage from *The Color Purple* has ever remarked on the rejection of the whiteness of God."[10] White feminists need to recognize that their interpretive lenses are different from those of womanists. White feminists deceive themselves if they believe that the ways they have interpreted texts like *The Color Purple*—a novel quoted, Thistlethwaite notes sardonically, by "virtually every white feminist" she knows—are not implicit assertions of their "class prerogative of whiteness."[11] Thistlethwaite's text, published in 1989, set us on a needful course of thinking regarding race and color-blind white feminist uses of African American literature. Nevertheless, color-blind uses of *The Color Purple* can still be found in many white feminist theological writings, hence the need to revisit this issue in an effort to identify how such reading practices can be repatterned.

Daphne Hampson uses *The Color Purple* as part of her attempt to reconceptualize God from a post-Christian feminist perspective in her *Theology and Feminism*.[12] Her theological project is aimed at "a non-anthropomorphic understanding of God, in which God is not conceived of as a discrete entity of which a personal pronoun [whether He or She] could be used."[13] Hampson credits Walker with exemplifying the type of feminist theological imagination free from the strictures of the anthropomorphic, androcentric Christian paradigm. She quotes at length from the section of Walker's novel in which Celie and Shug discuss the nature of God: "I believe God is everything, say Shug. Everything that is or ever was or ever will be. And when you can feel that, and be happy to feel that, you've found It" (*CP*, 202–203). Given that Shug tells Celie that "[a]ny God I ever felt in church I brought in with me" (*CP*, 200–201), Hampson concludes that Walker's text teaches us that being religious means getting rid of a church-linked God and relating to a divine Spirit who is everywhere and inside everyone.[14]

Although Hampson is on target in identifying the nonanthropomorphic orientation of Shug's spirituality, I would argue that Hampson reads that spirituality through a too exclusively white feminist interpretive grid and thus misses the meaning that Shug's words might carry for many African American women readers. As Thistlethwaite might point out: On the one hand, Hampson's interpretation of Shug's spirituality highlights typically white feminist religious sensibilities (e.g., themes of connectedness with nature and distancing from God the Father).[15] A hermeneutic informed by womanism, on the other hand, might highlight the African American aspects of Shug's spirituality. For example, when Shug says, "[O]ne day when I was sitting quiet and feeling like a motherless child...it come to me: that feeling of being a part of everything" (CP, 203), womanist-informed readers might point out the African American Christian subtext for Shug's words. Shug is referring to "what 'everybody knows' in the black church, that 'God is a mother to the motherless and a father to the fatherless'"—biblically derived images found in many black church sermons and hymns.[16] In other words, Shug's nonanthropomorphic experience of spiritual oneness with nature through love for "the color purple in a field" (CP, 203) can be read as mediated via her particular experiences as an African American woman.[17] Furthermore, her spirituality, though not traditionally Christian, is articulated at times via imagery from the black church. Hence, although Walker distinguishes Shug's spirituality from the institutional black church, she nevertheless portrays that spirituality as retaining important links to the emancipatory struggles of the African American Christian community by sharing its imagery.

When Hampson describes the spirituality of Celie and Shug, she affirms the post-Christian aspects of their spirituality but makes no reference to how the two women are linked to the black community. The unavoidable, if unintentional, effect is that womanist spiritual exploration is appropriated into a white feminist paradigm, and a rift is created between the spirituality of Celie and Shug on the one hand and more traditional black Christian spirituality on the other. A reader informed by womanism, however, might emphasize that Celie's noninstitutional spiritual journey and the religious commitment of her missionary sister, Nettie, are never put into conflict. In the narrative world of Walker's story, these two spiritualities coexist peacefully, joined by the love and solidarity between the two long-separated African American sisters whose lives have taken such divergent paths.[18] From this perspective, the racial differences between Hampson and Shug are at least as significant as the theological differences between Shug and Nettie. I have no doubt that Hampson quotes from Walker's novel to convey an appreciation of nature-oriented spirituality and to credit Walker for showing her a post-Christian way toward God. However, by rendering race an extraneous detail of Shug's spirituality, Hampson's reading elides the racial differences between womanist post-Christian and white feminist post-Christian spiritualities. Furthermore, the solidarity between Christian and post-Christian black women in Walker's text is hidden from sight in Hampson's account.

In Hampson's reading, we see how white feminist theology can impose a universalizing, color-blind grid on Walker's text, which reflects the assumption that spirituality can be abstracted from the embodied and cultural context from which it emerges. This white feminist tendency seems to confirm the need for a hermeneutic richly grounded in the social, historical, and political realities affecting African American women's experience in order to contest color-blind reading practices. Delores Williams's and Emilie Townes's readings of *The Color Purple*, which model some aspects of this kind of hermeneutical approach, stand in contrast to Hampson's.

Williams and Townes are interested in promoting African American women's moral and spiritual identity as a basis for ethical and political engagement on the part of the black church.[19] Williams asserts that *The Color Purple* exemplifies a "catalyst and moral-agent model" of "black women's social and religious experience" whereby one strong black woman is instrumental in helping another move from abuse and bondage to "full moral agency" and "liberation."[20] Williams is saying not that this model functions only in an African American setting but that it reflects the reality of how and why Celie needs black women as catalysts in her life, because of the specific "racial oppression and cultural traditions shared with all black people." Shug helps Celie see a loving Spirit beyond the old-white-man God, and Celie learns (especially through Sofia) how her own personal survival is precarious unless it is part of a communal "black family liberation."[21] In other words, Celie's moral and spiritual liberation takes place in the context of racial marginalization. Williams emphasizes that a reading practice that pays attention to racial markers of difference also illumines white women's need to liberate themselves not just from patriarchal victimization but also from their own "participation with white men in the oppression of black women."[22] Townes paints a similar liberationist image: "As Celie's horizons expand, she moves from her restricted, individual world in which exploitation is daily common fare into a universe of Black folk moving into Spirit-filled tomorrows."[23] Townes lauds this new spirituality, which not only clearly indicts a white racist God but also transcends any particular image of God as male or female by presenting God as living Spirit. She heralds Walker's portrayal of Celie's spiritual journey as paving "the way for a new understanding of God for Black children, men and women...a pathway to a deepening spirituality and a liberating hope" that can renew the African American religious community.[24] Williams and Townes contest Hampson's color-blind reading by virtue of the way they "see" color in *The Color Purple.* Their emphasis on the (visible) markers of race-based oppression in Walker's novel reflects a political and ethical commitment to address black women's experience in a racist society.[25]

Racism, however, is not the only locus of oppression and identity formation in this novel—another significant one being sexuality. White feminist and womanist theologians tend to stumble in different ways when race, sexuality, and gender issues intersect—with the result, in the case of feminist uses of *The Color Purple,* that the sexuality of the black lesbian and bisexual body is elided.[26]

Reading the Black Lesbian and Bisexual Body

A troubling pattern shared by many white feminist and womanist theological readings of *The Color Purple* is overlooking or downplaying themes of lesbianism and bisexuality. In general, most theologians avoid discussing sexuality.[27] Suffice it to say that most Christians suffer from negative body attitudes that have infused the church for centuries, and that gays, lesbians, bisexuals, and persons with other marginal sexual and gender identities suffer in particular from legacies of heterosexism. Attitudes toward embodiment and sexuality have a manifestation in the African American church that is inextricably connected to the experience of slavery and ongoing white racism (as we will see Williams and Townes emphasize in this section). Feminist scholars have initiated much new thinking about the goodness of the body and embodied spirituality but have often been tentative about discussing sexual expressiveness between women. Even feminist theologians accustomed to discussions of women's bodies shy away from Walker's depictions of physical affection between Shug and Celie:

> I believe God is everything, say Shug. . . .
> It sort of like you know what, she say, grinning and rubbing high up
> on my thigh.
> *Shug!* I say.
> Oh, she say. God love all them feelings. (*CP,* 202–203)

Few theologians affirm Shug's sexually expressive spirituality. The feminist theological gaze is discretely averted from that thigh rub.[28]

For white feminists, abstracting the black female experience in a color-blind way often goes hand in hand with overlooking black female sexuality, since both problematic reading practices implicitly assume a disembodied spirituality. The effect, in the case of Walker's novel, is that the black lesbian and bisexual body is rendered invisible. With womanist theology we have a different but related situation. In some womanist theological readings of *The Color Purple*, the black body is pulled into focus as a site of racial oppression while lesbian and bisexual markers of difference are downplayed. Among white feminist and womanist theologians, one type of reading practice that renders the lesbian and bisexual body invisible is the practice of characterizing Celie and Shug's relationship as primarily friendship or sisterhood. This reading practice is often quite subtle. I highlight two examples to show how feminist theologians might helpfully repattern the ways we talk theologically about bodies, sexuality, and spirituality.

I use as my first example an article by white feminist theologian Mary Catherine Hilkert, who explores how feminist thinkers negotiate fidelity to a religious tradition in light of new contextual challenges. Hilkert turns to Walker's text because it exemplifies the notion that "God is to be discovered in human experience...in the depth of the human heart." This revelatory discovery of the divine within humankind happens especially, she argues, in the experience of women's friendships. Hilkert refers to *The Color Purple* as an illustration: "Human friendship, such as that between Celie and Shug, is often used as the key metaphor for the experience of divine-human relationship."[29] I agree with Hilkert's theological insight about the importance of the metaphor of friendship; however, appeals to friendship without qualification can mask important particularities. In this case, Celie and Shug's race is not mentioned, and lesbianism is only alluded to by Hilkert's citation of Mary Hunt's *Fierce Tenderness* in a footnote.[30] The problem here is twofold. First, the significance of Hunt's text is lost on all but feminist theological insiders who are aware of the lesbian perspective in Hunt's book. Second, the text by Hunt, who is a white lesbian, is left to do the work of marking the sexuality of Celie, a black woman. I believe Hilkert would agree with me that this is an opportunity for hermeneutical repatterning in white feminist reading practices in order to give more emphasis to the complex interworkings of racial and sexual identity and thus to increase appreciation of differences in women's experiences.[31]

A different but related dynamic is at work in an article by womanist scholar Cheryl Kirk-Duggan, who emphasizes the black sisterhood of Celie and Shug but de-emphasizes their lesbian relationship. Kirk-Duggan approaches Walker's novel by setting it within a larger context of "the violent abuse that characterizes the human condition," using as her theoretical framework René Girard's psychosocial philosophy of religion as an approach to the issue of violence and sacrificial death.[32] From his study of religious rites, Girard concludes that scapegoating and violence, which originate in mimetic desire, are central to (Western) religion and have pervaded all kinship, civil, and taboo structures in the West. The cycle of violence continues because the tendency to resolve desire through conflict is learned and passed on. Kirk-Duggan insightfully reads Celie's story as marked, in some respects, by the kind of primal scapegoating myth of which Girard speaks. For example, Celie, in an effort to protect her younger sister from their stepfather's sexual abuse, "offers herself to be raped instead. Thus Celie as victim of incest becomes her stepfather's scapegoat, taking on violence otherwise directed toward her sister Nettie and their ailing mother."[33]

Kirk-Duggan argues (against Girard) that Shug and Celie's relationship exemplifies desire *without* violent rivalry, thus noting the (sexual) desire between the two women. Nonetheless, Kirk-Duggan states that instead of "mimetic violence...intensify[ing] between them..., Celie and Shug become friends!"[34] This statement is appropriate insofar as it attempts to show how Walker's novel breaks the Girardian pattern. However, Kirk-Duggan goes further when she argues that "many readers conclude that *The Color Purple* is a story about lesbian love. Yet Walker's novel focuses more broadly on the bonds of love shared in sisterhood." Here Kirk-Duggan seems to prioritize sisterhood over lesbian love, and one sees this prioritizing subtly played out when she discusses how Celie and Shug's relationship developed out of the "natural bonding between women as sisters and as mother and daughter."[35] Lesbianism is not mentioned among these "natural" liaisons—even though Walker does everything she can in her narrative to portray Celie and Shug's lesbian love as a natural event in their community of heterosexual friends and family.[36] Here again we have an opportunity for hermeneutical repatterning in order to avoid any unintentional hierarchies of sexual and nonsexual forms of love among women and to avoid an uninterrogated assumption of natural sexuality. I believe Kirk-Duggan would agree at least with the value of avoiding hierarchies, given that elsewhere she takes an explicit stance affirming black women's various sexualities.[37] (The issue of naturalness is more complex; I can only flag it here, since it will receive in-depth discussion in the next chapter.)

An approach to Walker's text that demonstrates attentiveness to racial and sexual particularity and avoids hierarchies in women's sexuality can be found in Delores Williams's and Emilie Townes's writings. Williams's reading of *The Color Purple* combines attentiveness to racial and sexual particularity by virtue of the way she construes Celie's lesbianism as integral to the novel's message about her survival and transformation as a black woman. Because, as we have seen, Williams emphasizes the role of a strong black woman as a catalyst in the life of another oppressed black woman, Shug's relationship with Celie receives direct attention. Although Williams points out that sex is not the sum total of their relationship, she nevertheless presents Celie's spiritual journey as inextricably linked to her lesbian sexual self-discovery. Celie's development into "a self-confident lesbian woman" and "fully responsible moral agent" enables her to confront the sexism of the black men in her extended family—which in turn ultimately precipitates restitution and healing in those relationships. Williams draws from *The Color Purple* the theme that lesbian relationships can be "redemptive" and strengthening for the fabric of the black family.[38] Williams includes Celie, a lesbian, and Shug, a bisexual, in the list of people who communally nurture one another's children. At the end of the novel, Williams explains, "Celie refers to her children as 'our children,' meaning she, Nettie, Samuel, Shug, Mr. Albert, Sophia, and Harpo will provide care and nurture" for them.[39] Thus, Williams's reading exemplifies attentiveness to color in *The Color Purple* (i.e., to the racist exploitation of black women's bodies, the fragility of the black family, black women's moral agency, and Celie's rejection of a white God) as well as attentiveness to diversity in the sexual identities of African American women.

I attribute Williams's attentiveness to themes of sexuality in part to her commitment to a thoroughgoing historicist analysis of black women's bodies. Elsewhere, Williams investigates the complex history of the exploitation of African American women's bodies by white slave masters and by black men who, "since slavery, have tended to re-create their manhood to conform to the [patriarchal] model of manhood."[40] She points out that colonialist white attitudes have insidiously influenced black aesthetic values so that light skin and smooth hair are valued among many African Americans.[41] Townes also analyzes the way in which the "Black body has long been a site of contention."[42] Female and male black bodies have been seen as "grotesque" or sexually "deviant" in the Western mind from ancient days to the present.[43] Thus, to understand sexual attitudes and identities in the African American community, one needs to analyze the structural *"production* of images of Black bodies"—male and female—in a white racist and heterosexist society.[44]

The readings of *The Color Purple* given by Williams and Townes call into question any mistaken assumptions that literary portrayals of spirituality can be used effectively by feminist theologians (who want to be attentive to difference) apart from discussion of the characters' racial and sexual embodiment or broader cultural contexts. Historicist analyses of the black female body and stereotypes of it (and of the black male body as well) should also be a necessary component of feminist interpretations of texts like *The Color Purple* because they impel white readers to see identity markers of race and impel both white and black readers to recognize the complexity of socially constructed sexual stereotypes. My proposal in the following chapter for using poststructuralist tools for theorizing embodied, sexed selfhood and sexual desire supplements the type of historicist analyses offered by Williams and Townes. Poststructuralism, I will argue, not only analyzes selves in terms of their historical and "discursive" construction but also specifically addresses assumptions about natural desires or a natural sexed self. If it is important to display how negative sexual stereotypes are culturally constructed, should we not also speak of sexual desire and maleness and femaleness as constructed as well? (Historicist analyses alone can be ambiguous on this point.) How does seeing gender as well as sex as a cultural construct contribute to addressing privilege? In chapter 3, I propose theoretical resources that help us think about the issue of the construction of gender, sex, and sexual desire, especially as related to heterosexual privilege. Rigorous theorizing on these issues would seem to be a vital part of a strategy to avoid obscuring nonheteronormative sexuality when retrieving women's experience.

II. Hagar and Sarah: Women's Agency beyond Victimization and Utopia

The issue of the role of women in the Hebrew Bible has long intrigued women scholars generally, and Hagar has a long history specifically in the African American Christian community. Hagar came to the forefront of first-wave (white) feminist exegesis with the publication of Phyllis Trible's *Texts of Terror*.[45] Trible's text shocked its readership by eulogizing the abused women whose neglected stories of suffering are recounted in the Hebrew scriptures. Suddenly, instead of praising, for example, the female friendship of Ruth and Naomi, feminists scholars were confronted with conflict between Sarah and Hagar in Trible's chapter "Hagar: The Desolation of Rejection." Feminist exegetes and theologians have been trying to respond ever since. The Hagar-Sarah accounts have been the focus of sometimes conflicting interpretations by scholars from a wide spectrum of nationalities, religious backgrounds, races, theological orientations, and religious studies approaches.[46] White exegetes working on the Sarah-Hagar texts from a feminist perspective have endeavored to rescue this story from the obscurity of androcentric scholarship that either relegated it to a backwater of ancient Mesopotamian kinship structures or else wrote off these two female characters in patronizing labels of female cattiness and jealousy. These feminist exegetes have been striving to read the text against the "patriarchal context of biblical literature" in order to detect the "strong countercurrents of affirmation of women...[which] undermine patriarchal assumptions."[47]

African American feminist scholars turn to this story because of the timely message they find there for African American women struggling to survive in white racist society.[48] African American theological readings of the Hagar story have developed in an interpretive stream sometimes independent from and at times in resistance to the dominant white exegetical literature (including white feminist exegesis). Black feminist scholars, not surprisingly, bring concerns of race to the forefront of feminist exegesis, reading this story in light of African American women's historical experiences of multiple oppressions clustered around racial discrimination. Black feminist and womanist readings significantly challenge the majority of white feminist theological uses of this biblical narrative which are dominated by the trope of patriarchy. What has resulted is a situation of competing dominant hermeneutical concerns— patriarchy versus racism.

While modern racial and gender categories apply only anachronistically to biblical texts, speaking of racism in the Bible requires more clarification than speaking of patriarchy in the Bible. Scholars have long documented evidence of oppressive acts and negative attitudes directed toward women as a whole in the Bible and have documented connections between those biblical passages and a history of institutional societal and religious practices that largely conform to modern understandings of patriarchal oppression. While differences in skin color are acknowledged in biblical texts, there is no historical evidence that racial discrimination as we might speak of it today occurred in the ancient cultures referred to in the Bible.[49] Slavery and antagonism between differing racial/ethnic populations are in evidence in the Bible; however, they do not seem to be racially linked but can be attributed to wars between tribal peoples, disputes over land, religious conflict, and such. Thus, we are not talking about the putative problem of whether white feminist scholars overlook evidence of racial discrimination in the Bible. The issue of racism and the Bible is a hermeneutical one, having to do with the concerns the theologian chooses to bring to her reading of the text.

In a context such as that of the United States with its trauma of the history of slavery and white supremacy, what is the effect of reading the Hagar-Sarah story primarily in terms of gender discrimination, such that Sarah's unjust actions toward Hagar (that some scholars would read via the trope of white racism) are downplayed or explained away as an outgrowth of patriarchy? What is the effect of reading Hagar's primary status as that of enslaved victim, such that her identity as responsible moral agent or co-sufferer with Sarah under patriarchy is downplayed or obscured? Other interpreters of the Sarah-Hagar story attempt to move beyond a hermeneutic of competing oppressions (i.e., patriarchy versus racism) in an effort to envision women's solidarity. In an age where calls for women's sisterhood are met with mistrust or cynicism, what is the effect of reading the Hagar-Sarah texts from a perspective suggesting the feminist utopian possibility that Sarah and Hagar were each more an agent of her own destiny than a passive victim of patriarchal oppression, and that Sarah and Hagar might even have been allies?

It turns out that current feminist approaches to the Hagar-Sarah story manifest a variety of concerns and assumptions, producing conflicting readings. Is Sarah most accurately depicted as an abusive slave mistress? Should Hagar be held responsible for any attempts she may have made to one-up Sarah? Might Sarah and Hagar have banded together in an ancient sisterhood? These are questions that historians will want to probe to determine if they have any historical merit. My concerns here are contemporary and theological. I want to assess how various current feminist readings of the Hagar-Sarah narratives construct the female subject in that story, with special attention given to women's agency. To this end, I have focused on eight important feminist interpretations of this story, mapping them along a continuum of themes related to women's agency. At one end is extreme victimization (virtually no agency); at the other end is the utopian possibility of an ancient women's subculture (almost unlimited agency).[50] At work at both ends are a number of implicit assumptions with troubling entailments about women's moral agency, oppressive power, and resistance to that power.

Scholars who present Sarah and/or Hagar as primarily victims (with little or no agency) tend to give what I call single-oppression-oriented reading. The oppressive force against them is categorized more or less univocally in terms of either gender oppression (which makes patriarchy culpable for Sarah's and Hagar's suffering) or race/class oppression (which makes Sarah primarily culpable for Hagar's suffering).[51] In privileging the problem of patriarchy, white feminist exegetes Danna Fewell and David Gunn (in a co-authored text) and Cheryl Exum tend to emphasize Sarah's and Hagar's gender victimization, relieving Sarah to a great extent of personal culpability in relation to her servant Hagar. The implicit assumption at work here is that oppressive power only represses agency (it never contributes to constructing agency), which has the troubling entailment that victims of oppression are absolved of moral responsibility in unjust actions toward others. Black feminist theologian Cheryl Sanders, who focuses on the story as a parable about racism, emphasizes how Sarah's actions are analogous to those of white slave mistresses in America; Hagar's resistance practices are depicted solely along the lines of an emancipation model. The implicit assumption here is that forms of resistance marked by cooperation with oppressive power are dubious, with the entailment that a hierarchy of resistance practices is suggested—namely, noncooperation is ranked higher than assimilation. At the other end of the continuum is Savina Teubal, who reads the Sarah-Hagar story against the backdrop of ancient matrilineal traditions that are independent from the Abrahamic covenant tradition. Teubal contextualizes the story in light of goddess religions at that time in such a way that she can argue for the utopian possibility of a nonpatriarchal women's religious subculture. Here we see the assumption that women can only resist domination by accessing positive women's power (such as sisterhood), with the troubling (very first-wave-feminist-sounding) entailment that women's resistance is contingent on overcoming conflictual differences among women.

In a midway position on this women's agency continuum (with its extremes of victimization and utopia), I place Phyllis Trible, Renita Weems, and Delores Williams.[52] These scholars complicate the notion of victim in relation to multiple, interacting oppressions. They eschew seeing oppressive power too univocally and see women's resistance practices as taking many forms. These feminist scholars are not averse to utopian thinking about women's coalitions without, however, losing touch with the nonutopian realities of present-day inequities that divide communities of women. Contrary to the ways in which women's moral agency is obscured (in the interpretations of Fewell/Gunn and Exum), presented too univocally (in Sanders's reading), or overinflated (in Teubal's utopian interpretation), in the readings of Trible, Weems, and Williams, agency comes to the fore in complex ways. The interpretations of the Sarah-Hagar narrative offered by Trible, Weems, and Williams help us see what a difference it makes to use this Bible story as a means of retrieving women's experience without the problematic assumptions mentioned above regarding oppressive power, emancipatory resistance practices, and women's alliances.

Constructing Sarah and Hagar Each as Victim or Oppressor

Fewell and Gunn exemplify a white feminist gender-focused standpoint. They use critical tools from literary theory, sociology, and anthropology, but also take Genesis 16 and 21 texts as a narrative whole. Thus, their approach is critical, but it marks the kind of break with traditional historical criticism that is much in evidence in literarily oriented biblical scholarship today.[53] They state that their goal is to "'redeem' the text, making it more palatable to a new world which is beginning to recognize a huge legacy of gender oppression (among the many oppressions to which patriarchal Western society has lent itself).”[54] However, no other significant type of oppression relevant to Hagar's suffering receives any attention in their text. Somehow, when Fewell/Gunn compare Hagar's and Sarah's situation, Sarah almost seems to come out worse in the end. In explaining how Sarah was battling the principle threat to her status in patriarchal culture—childlessness—Fewell/Gunn depict Hagar as a derivative victim of Sarah's catch-22 situation: “Sarai finds her voice and moves to ensure her own well-being... [with the result that] Hagar, like Sarai in Egypt, is confined to powerless silence.”[55] Hagar is Sarah's only defense, because Hagar can bear children for her mistress. Both Hagar's “arrogant” attitude toward her mistress upon conceiving (Gen. 16:4) and her subsequent fleeing from Sarah's abuse (Gen. 16:6-13) exacerbate Sarah's precarious position as barren “primary wife.” Fewell/Gunn argue that the events of Genesis 16 subvert the precarious triangle Sarah attempts to create between Abraham, Hagar, and herself, which would secure Sarah's position to some extent in a patriarchal household. Sarah's plan begins with exploitation of Hagar but, in the end, Sarah is the one who “feels violated” and becomes “the outsider.” Hagar, on the other hand, “temporarily usurps her place in the narrative spotlight” and gets more of “a glimpse of self-autonomy” than apparently Sarah ever gets.[56] Fewell/Gunn rightly point out how the pressures of patriarchal culture can cause women, who might have been allies, to turn against each other, competing for status as bearers of sons. Fewell/Gunn assign culpability for this to Abraham (“who sacrificed his first wife Sarah to strangers... , [and] sacrificed his second wife Hagar first to affliction and then to ostracism”) and ultimately to a patriarchal, possibly even “deranged and sadistic” God.[57] The implicit assumption at work here is that patriarchal oppression so eclipses women's agency that it largely absolves its female victims of moral responsibility. While Fewell/Gunn are justified in loudly protesting the text's entrenched patriarchy, the effect of their reading is that Sarah's moral agency disappears from view.

Exum's approach, like that of Fewell/Gunn, is to privilege gender oppression.[58] Although Exum recognizes that this situation is one of a “privileged woman's exploitation of her subordinate” (i.e., class oppression), she nevertheless concludes that the two women “make victims of each other”—Sarah by using and abusing Hagar, and Hagar by “apparently” coveting Sarah's position. Exum seems at times to portray the (barren) mistress and her (fertile) slave as standing on equal ground. She concludes that, in the end, while both women are victimized, Sarah seems to get the shorter end of the stick: “On a feminist reading, both women suffer: One is cast out, becoming the mother of a great nation excluded from the covenant; the other stays within the patriarchal hearth and almost loses her only child to the father."[59] Exum gives an incisive analysis of how androcentric narratives ideologically depict assertive women like Sarah as "mean-spirited, deceptive, and untrustworthy"—in short, a threat to "patriarchal social order."[60] Exum acknowledges that there are oppressions other than gender-related ones, specifically "[w]omen of lower status...are exploited for the sake of higher class women." However, she downplays class antagonism between women, arguing that it is largely orchestrated by patriarchy to prevent women "from gaining power by forming alliances."[61] Exum's analysis of patriarchal ideology in effect takes attention away from the fact that the Sarah-Hagar conflict was not a battle between equally empowered wives of Abraham but a battle between a mistress and her servant/slave (or at best between two unequal co-wives). Exum risks trivializing Hagar's oppression and exonerating Sarah by suggesting that either Sarah was more or less forced (by patriarchy) to act in the way that she did, or else she was just depicted as acting this way in an androcentric text. In the latter instance, we have a kind of *Who Framed Roger Rabbit* scenario where the vampish cartoon character complains: "I'm not really bad, I was just drawn that way." The Sarah character is seen as a caricature of an ancient misogynist author's mind who can be pitied for how she has been "drawn." According to Exum, Sarah and Hagar are victimized and forced into competition with each other by patriarchy that works to pit women against each other. The effect of this interpretation is to foreclose the possibility of feminist ethical critique of the moral agency of a character such as Sarah who is so utterly victimized and "drawn bad." Nevertheless, in feminist theological retrievals of women's experience of resistance to patriarchy in the Bible, female characters should not be passed over for moral critique, especially when their resistance is conducted at the expense of subordinate women.

Sanders, who also has a single-oppression focus, voices a strong black feminist standpoint. She sides exclusively with Hagar and finds no mitigating circumstances (e.g., gender oppression) for the behavior of Sarah, concluding that Sarah acted like a white slave mistress.[62] Sanders's approach, which she calls a "modern" interpretation of the Hagar story (I would classify her approach as an allegorical reading), does not pursue any historical-critical questions (e.g., the differing authorship of Genesis 16 and 21). This allows Sanders to focus instead on the moral relevance of the story told as a canonical unity for African Americans women today. While she states that her intention in her analysis of several biblical "African women" is to "challenge traditional assumptions held by white people and black men who may disregard sex or race as meaningful categories," her actual reading of the Hagar text privileges race oppression. How either Sarah or Hagar might be seen as resisting a discourse of patriarchy does not figure centrally into her interpretation. Sanders's reading highlights Hagar's "slave status, her distinctive racial identity, her sex, and her role as the single parent of a son who is predisposed toward violence."[63] While Sanders acknowledges the reality of patriarchy, she believes that Abraham abdicated his patriarchal authority and submitted to Sarah. Hence, Sarah's hostile actions toward Hagar are not seen as a result of her own victimization under patriarchy, since Sarah, according to Sanders, was in charge in her family unit.

Sanders demonstrates a powerful use of allegorical interpretation of the biblical text. There could be many contextual applications of Sanders's interpretation within the black church. Seeing Hagar's ability to resist Sarah as stemming from Hagar's "affirmations of the goodness of God, who intervenes on her behalf" would function pastorally as a message of God's power to sustain and liberate.[64] However, Sanders gives a narratively selective reading with some problematic assumptions. For example, she does not explore various complexities and ambiguities in the story. The complexity of Hagar's agency as she undergoes changes in her enslaved status becomes secondary to the message that Sarah is exclusively responsible for Hagar's suffering. (Abraham and God are largely excused from any culpability.) Each character in Sanders's reading is highly essentialized and typecast: Sarah is seen as evil, Abraham as submissive to his wife, Hagar as innocent victim, and God as good and powerful. (God's sometimes negative actions toward Hagar are not discussed.) Moreover, resistance is also narrowly conceived as that which is focused on emancipation from the forces of oppression. Sanders, in a comparative discussion of Hagar and Joseph (who is enslaved in Egypt but rises to prominence in Pharaoh's court), recognizes that each resisted enslavement in different ways; however, she characterizes Joseph's mode of resistance negatively as an "assimilation to the values of the dominant culture." Although she admits that Joseph's story "may be an inspiration" to black men today in white racist society, Sanders ultimately disapproves because Joseph paid a "price for personal affluence and success"—namely, "strained relations with his own people." Hagar's emancipation and reconnection with her cultural heritage, on the other hand, are seen by Sanders as an inspiration for black women today.[65] The assumption at work here is that resistance practices marked by cooperation with oppressive power bring dubious results; one may gain personal power but at the cost of cultural connection to one's own people. This is both a narrow view of resistance and a too univocal view of power.

Utopian Possibilities of Sisterhood across Difference

The interpretation offered by Teubal, who uses archeological and historical-critical tools to draw a very hopeful portrait about Sarah and Hagar, stands in contrast to the readings of Fewell/Gunn, Exum, and Sanders. Teubal searches behind the patriarchal exegetical depiction of the ancient biblical world and argues that the society of the ancient patriarchs of the Bible was likely marked by pockets of Mesopotamian matriarchal priestess culture in which women exercised considerable power. She posits that Sarah "held a position similar to that of ... the Mesopotamian *entu/naditu* priestesses" who brought her own religious orientation into line with her husband's worship of Yahweh.[66] This perspective casts the Hagar-Sarah relationship into a completely new light, regarding collaborative women's agency.

Contrary to what most other feminist exegetes argue, Teubal contends that Hagar was neither Sarah's slave nor Abraham's concubine. Had she been Abraham's concubine, she would have borne him more children, but the story implies that Sarah arranged for Hagar to conceive only one child by Abraham—a son, Sarah's heir. Had Hagar been Sarah's slave, she would have been depicted as performing menial tasks. Teubal points out that during the episode when Abraham hosts three visitors, it is Sarah who makes cakes for them not Hagar (Gen. 18:6). Teubal argues that being Sarah's maid also offered Hagar protection from unwanted sexual advances from Abraham or other males in the extended family unit. The fact that with the exception of the birth of Ishmael, Hagar remained childless, even suggests that Hagar, much more than a mere servant, was functioning in a role similar to "priestess-devotees."[67] A priestess-devotee would remain childless along with her priestess-mistress until that time when she might be given the honor of bearing the priestess' heir. The conflict that arises between the women is not due to Sarah's jealousy over Hagar's fertility but to Abraham's transgression of matrilineal customs. That is, Abraham apparently broke the agreement that Hagar would bear Sarah's heir and instead claimed the boy as his heir (Gen. 16:15), thus changing Hagar's status from Sarah's maid/devotee to Abraham's concubine.[68] Nevertheless, even with this change in status, Teubal insists that this is not a "handmaid's tale" as found in novelist Margaret Atwood's well-known story by that name. Hagar should not be viewed as "a poor slave thrown out into the wilderness empty-handed, the 'unwitting cause of Sarah's fury.' She leaves Hebron with her grown son, free to encounter a new destiny."[69] Hence, while some class differences separate Sarah and Hagar, Teubal downplays conflict between them—not because she privileges patriarchal oppression over class conflict but because she argues that reading Sarah's and Hagar's relationship through the lens of matrilineal and priestess-influenced culture reveals a relationship that could be seen as transcending class antagonism, as we know it today.

Utopian feminist writings have always played an important role in the history of the white American women's movement especially.[70] One might be tempted simply to subsume Teubal's utopian vision under a dominant white feminist rubric. For that reason, it is important to note Teubal's background. Teubal, a Syrian-born Jewish woman, was raised in Argentina and was also a self-identified lesbian who worked outside of academe developing Jewish women's spiritual rituals.[71] Given her background and the fact that she essentializes neither Hagar nor Sarah as victim or oppressor, one might expect a robust depiction of women's agency. To some extent, this is the case, because to attempt to keep matriarchal culture afloat in the presence of a tidal wave of patriarchy requires active women's agency and women's alliances. However, by emphasizing to the extent that she does the subtext of ancient women's solidarity, two significant aspects of women's experience relevant to contemporary women are overlooked in Teubal's utopian account: the particular kind of agency subordinate women develop when resisting victimization by elite women (often close to them); and the moral accountability elite women should develop in order to take responsibility for their complicity in patriarchal, racial, and class oppression of subordinate women (often close to them). Hence the assumption that resisting patriarchy requires women's alliances across difference, while not completely (politically) unfounded, can entail the expectation that to focus on women's differences is to subvert that feminist cause. It is precisely this very first-wave white feminist expectation that I want to expose for the way it elides difference and inculcates privilege.

Teubal's interpretation, a combination of feminist historical research and feminist utopian imagination, envisions the slim possibility that a culture might have existed where women were able at times to exercise significant power and form mutually beneficial alliances against patriarchal structures and customs. The political usefulness of her research is not simply in bringing to mind a possible women's ancient golden age but in suggesting that women might still attempt to carve out alliances and women-centered traditions for their self-protection and betterment. That things went awry between Sarah and Hagar is an unfortunate result of the clash of a diminishing matriarchal and prevailing patriarchal culture, but this should not detract from the fact that Hagar in the end continued the matriarchal customs. She left Abraham's household, returned to her people, and contracted a marriage for her son there. Thus, the Hagar story is one of a struggling but ultimately surviving matriarchal (possibly priestess) culture as it intersects with ancient Israelite history.

Teubal sees Sarah and Hagar as more or less relating peacefully with each other (when matriarchal customs hold). The very explicit assumption here is that women's ability to resist the incursion of patriarchal oppression is contingent upon women overcoming whatever ethnic or status differences separate them.

Constructing Women's Agency amid Multiple Oppressions

The readings of the Hagar-Sarah narrative by Trible, Weems, and Williams seem relatively free of the problematic assumptions discussed above. These three scholars are similar in that they address both gender and race/class oppression, and they resist essentialized portrayals of the characters in the Sarah-Hagar story.[72] Hence, women's agency and resistance practices are depicted with a great deal more nuance than in the previous accounts.

Trible's *Texts of Terror* gave one of the first scholarly expositions on Hagar's multiple oppressions: "Read in light of contemporary issues and images, [Hagar's] . . . story depicts oppression in three familiar forms: nationality, class, and sex." How did awareness of racial injustice and class antagonism enter into Trible's feminist scholarship? She explains: "Choice and chance inspire my telling"; it was "hearing a black woman describe herself as a daughter of Hagar"; it was "seeing an abused woman on the streets of New York," and so on.[73] Trible combines feminist justice interests with detailed rhetorical literary analysis (indebted in technique to Robert Alter), which highlights word usage implicating Sarah (and Abraham and God) for causing the suffering of Hagar.[74] Then in an allegorical move, Trible asserts: "As a symbol of the oppressed, Hagar . . . is the faithful maid exploited, the black woman used by the male and abused by the female ruling class, the surrogate mother, the resident alien without legal recourse . . . the divorced mother with child . . . the homeless woman." Trible is exemplary among white feminist exegetes in that she identifies her contemporary privileged position in relation to Hagar, allegorically understood: "All we who are heirs of Sarah and Abraham . . . must answer for the terror in Hagar's story."[75] Taken alone, Trible's reading, with its strong indictment of Sarah, could very well be placed closer to Sanders's reading. In fact when focusing on Hagar's suffering, Trible sees her as almost wholly victimized by her oppressors. Trible does not explore the significance of Hagar's resistance practices but finds primarily terror that must be mourned. Even the scene where Hagar names God is described as "fraught with ambivalence" and, in the end, "the circle of bondage encloses Hagar" who is largely a victim.[76] However, given the thrust of the rest of Trible's book and her other writings, I do not believe she means to discount the effects of patriarchy on both women or overlook women's agency. In an article on Sarah, Trible argues that in the end of the Hagar-Sarah story, Hagar finds some respite from her ordeal in Abraham's patriarchal household when she strikes out on her own (a perhaps utopian note in an otherwise somber picture). Trible asserts that Sarah, on the other hand, continues to be victimized by the patriarchal structures of that household—a victimization, it is important to note, that Trible does not use to absolve Sarah of moral agency vis-à-vis Hagar.[77] Hence we see an attempt in Trible's writings to do justice to women's multiple oppressions without obscuring women's agency.

Weems and Williams bring African American women's collective consciousness of multifaceted racist oppression to their readings of this story. Weems writes: "[W]e as black women appear, to some, to be reading too much of our own brutal history into the biblical story"; nevertheless, Weems explains, the Hagar story "is hauntingly reminiscent of the disturbing accounts of black slavewomen and white mistresses during slavery." Furthermore, though slavery was abolished almost 150 years ago, "those memories have proven especially hard to erase," and new reasons for resentment and distrust recur. "The truth is, very few black women manage to make it through adulthood without a footlocker of hurtful memories of encounters with white women."[78] These two theologians do not only use the story to indict white female racism and eulogize abused black women; their interest in this biblical text has a more complex, pastoral womanist thrust. While the pathos of the story may impel black women to lament for all the abused daughters of Hagar, Weems wants to make reading this story an opportunity for black women also to engage in self-critique, for even the exploited have opportunities to exploit. Weems admits: "I am painfully aware of this when I step across the floor recently mopped by the black janitress . . . [when] the white waitress who is the age of my mother calls me 'ma'm' . . . [when] the Latina maid tiptoes in to replace my soiled linen and make my bed." Weems speaks of this dynamic as "the potential to be a Sarai"—regardless of race.[79] In this sense, Weems is engaging in an allegorical interpretation of Sarah and Hagar, with Hagar symbolizing any oppressed woman and Sarah symbolizing any woman whose status works directly or indirectly to keep another woman subservient. Weems's interpretation suggests that a universalized message can be gleaned from the biblical text, but one should get to that message only after attending to (not eliding) its reminiscences of slavery when read in an American context. Williams combines allegorical interpretation and historical critical analysis in a hermeneutical approach she calls "identification-ascertainment." In the identification mode, "theologians discover with whom and with what events they personally identify." African American women identify with Hagar whom

Williams also reads allegorically as a black woman exploited by a white woman. In the ascertainment mode, "theologians engage the objective mode of inquiry" by which she means a critical inquiry into authorial intention, sociological setting, and so on—including a hermeneutic of suspicion about who is being silenced by the narrator. (Williams investigates the silencing of Hagar's Egyptian culture by the Hebrew narrator.[80])

Both these womanist theologians emphasize Hagar's complex agency and diverse resistance practices. Not content merely to label her a victim or a hero, Weems reads her part in the story with an eye to how victims must learn to transcend a mentality of victimization. Weems is quite direct and unflinching in her critique of Hagar: "Notice her pathetic sense of herself. In many ways, by acting as a passive victim throughout, she participated in her own exploitation."[81] Weems suggests that the reason why Hagar went back to Sarah in Genesis 16 was that she still conceived of herself as a slave. It took two tries before she could really claim her freedom—but even then, it was the *felix culpa* of Sarah's jealousy that gave Hagar the "shove" (brutal as it was) to get out and claim her own nonslave identity, with its freedom and responsibility.[82] Weems brings away a universalizing message: "At some time in all our lives, whether we are black or white, we are all Hagar's daughters"—that is, abused, lonely, in need of a "sister." Writing in 1988, Weems calls for an almost utopian multicultural (or perhaps it would be more appropriate, given the politics of that time, to say "Rainbow Coalition") attempt to build a "bridge over the memories of our scars."[83] Even with her reference to coalitions, however, she harbors no assumptions that resistance requires overcoming conflictual differences among women.

Williams focuses on the theme of African American women's survival. For Williams, this is a story not of liberation but of survival through a wilderness of surrogacy, homelessness, and economic and sexual oppression. She reads Hagar's story as modeling what happens in "many black American families in which a lone woman/mother struggles to hold the family together."[84] Williams is as forthright as Sanders in her indictment of how "white men and white women [work] together to maintain white supremacy and white privilege."[85] However, Williams avoids a narrow view on what constitutes effective resistance to that oppression. There is no assumption at work in Williams's text that emancipation is a superior form of resistance than other forms that African American women have been able to carve out. Her focus on survival allows Williams to display a wide range of resistance strategies from the dramatically liberating (e.g., Harriet Tubman) to the more subversively subtle.[86]

Even with their strong womanist standpoints, Weems and Williams do not turn a blind eye to Sarah's victimization. While they in no way try to equalize

Sarah's suffering under patriarchy with Hagar's slave exploitation, both Weems and Williams acknowledge that Sarah and Hagar are pawns in a patriarchal system. Weems speculates that if upper-class women faced this fact squarely, they might change their exploitative ways. "Sarai forgot that in a patriarchal society she and her female slave Hagar had more in common as women than that which divided them as Hebrew mistress and Egyptian slave-woman." One could almost say that "the only things which separated the two women were a couple of cattle and some sheepskins (which in today's language translates to a paycheck and a diploma)."[87] Williams echoes the theme of Sarah's and Hagar's solidarity in suffering under patriarchy, pointing out that "neither Sarah nor Hagar would inherit anything from Abraham should they outlive him."[88] By forcing widows to be dependent on their sons, the patriarchal system created rivalries among women. Ishmael's primogeniture was a threat to Sarah's and Isaac's future economic well being. The situation was ripe for Sarah to stoop to using whatever power she had to get rid of her competition: Hagar and her son. From this we can see efforts on the part of Weems and Williams to depict Sarah's and Hagar's multiple oppressions in complex ways that do not obscure their moral agency and survival practices—even those practices that may fall short of total liberation. As noted above, Weems even hints at the possibility of women's coalitions across boundaries of race and class but it is a subdued hope (Teubal's vision of women's alliances would be too rosy).

Scholars like Trible, Weems, and Williams, who come to the text with a visceral sense of race-related oppressions, a cultural memory of slavery, or a sensitivity to classism, will unavoidably see these patterns in this story. Trible, Weems, and Williams seem to avoid essentializing the story's characters. Both perpetrators and victims of exploitation tend to be interpreted with more nuance than in the single-oppression-oriented readings. Moreover, the attempt to address the multiplicity of women's oppressions seems to go hand in hand with insisting on a diversity of resistance practices, as well as exercising restraint in utopian visions of women's alliances. I endorse these impulses regarding the way women's agency is constructed textually and turn in the next chapters to how such impulses can be optimized. If I have illustrated sufficiently the drawbacks and limitations of single-oppression and utopian readings of this story, then the reader will now be persuaded about the problematic nature of the assumptions at work in those readings. Having identified these assumptions as problematic, the question becomes: how should we theorize the nature of power and women's selfhood so as to insist on women's moral accountability and encourage diverse resistance practices, without sacrificing attentiveness to difference? Chapters 3 and 4 take on the task of bringing together poststructuralist and postcolonialist theoretical perspectives on these issues. Before we turn to those complex and contested theories, we need to consider two obvious preliminary questions: Why not take a simpler route and go directly to women's experiences and personal testimonies of moral agency and resistance to oppressive power? Why not use ethnographic methods of directly retrieving women's experience so as to avoid the pitfalls of working with literary and biblical texts?

III. Feminist Ethnography: Now We're Seeing
Real Women, Right?

In a number of recent writings on feminist approaches to religious studies, ethnography has emerged as a central theme.[89] The reasons for turning to ethnography and the nature of ethnographically based theological writings differ greatly, depending on the scholar. For many feminist theologians of color, ethnography can be a means of advocacy. As womanist theologian Linda Thomas argues: "Not only should womanist scholars include historical texts and literature in our theological constructs and reconstruction of knowledge, but we should also embrace a research process that engages poor black women who are living human documents. . . . We must view books written about poor black women as secondary sources and employ anthropological techniques to collect stories and publish ethnographies of women who are still alive." In collecting testimonies and data about the material practices of poor black and other oppressed women, womanist ethnographers "would act as intentional agents in the control and distribution of knowledge" in support of sociopolitical changes.[90] Womanist sociologist Cheryl Gilkes demonstrates how literary, ethnographic, and ethical concerns can dovetail. In her ethnographic reading of *The Color Purple*, Gilkes argues that Alice Walker acts as an ethnographer who "provides unusually thick description" of African American culture in the Jim Crow south and who directs that description toward "prophetic critique" in a subversive vision of personal and political resistance to injustice and domination.[91] For Gilkes, Walker's text is an excellent ethnographic source not despite but because of Walker's prophetic (even "theological") intentions to spotlight literarily voices from a marginalized culture.[92] Cuban-born feminist theologian Ada María Isasi-Díaz argues for the appropriateness of ethnography within *mujerista* theology because its interview processes "have as their goal 'to learn from people, to be taught by them,' instead of just gathering information about them." Hence ethnographic writing can become the "vehicle for Hispanic women to develop their own voices."[93]

Like womanist theological uses of ethnography, Isasi-Díaz's *mujerista* ethnographic-based theology has an advocacy component. It is meant to uplift and empower grassroots Latina women, not merely to use their experiences for the theological pursuits of the researcher.

For some white feminist theologians, the turn to ethnography seems to be the logical progression of a historicizing and/or postmodern turn. In 1987, Sheila Greeve Davaney made the historicist argument that the appeal to women's experience is based on the faulty assumption that one can access a privileged feminist interpretation of reality that is "true" in contrast to the "male-constructed version of reality." Davaney proposes a pragmatic historicism, according to which "no particular form of experience, including that of women, will be able to claim ontological or epistemological privilege," and hence judgments about religious "truth" will have to be based on "pragmatic norms"[94] discerned via cultural analyses of "what practitioners actually do or say." She endorses a move from theology dominated by "exegetical, philological, and hermeneutical methods" to "ethnography of belief."[95] Mary McClintock Fulkerson's *Changing the Subject*, arguably the first poststructuralist feminist theological monograph, makes the case for why "woman" as a stable subject must be deconstructed, and demonstrated how this viewpoint enables one to find many more diverse spaces for women's religious performances of empowerment and agency. The heart of that text is her poststructuralist reading of the discursive performances of various groups of women—with ethnographic studies central for the data on one group (poor, rural Appalachian Pentecostal women). Fulkerson's current research project is her own ethnographic study of a southern Methodist congregation comprised of whites and blacks, disabled and able-bodied, working class whites and educationally privileged upper class whites.[96]

It would seem at first glance that a feminist theology rooted in ethnographic cultural analysis of women's experience would avoid many of the drawbacks to textually based feminist theology. There can be a sense of unreality and lack of political heft to some fictional portrayals of women's experience. Cheryl Gilkes's comments on Walker as a kind of ethnographer notwithstanding; Emilie Townes and bell hooks intimate that *The Color Purple* has a tendency in the direction of the privately idyllic.[97] Theologians working with the Bible have long recognized the challenge of the massive temporal and cultural divide between contemporary women's experience and often opaque ancient biblical texts. If it is true that many women's material religious practices tend to be less textually based—due in part to historical restrictions of women's access to literacy and formal study of sacred texts—then it would make sense to use ethnography to access "real" women's religious experiences. Moreover, ethnography would seem to be an effective way for the researcher to be confronted with difference literally face to face. However, the assumption that ethnography has finally allowed us less problematic, because unmediated, access to real women is an assumption that much current ethnographic theory would question. Moreover, that assumption actually obscures what happens methodologically when ethnographic data is used theologically. Not only is there no raw data on or unmediated anthropological access to women's experience, but the feminist theologian must unavoidably impose an interpretive paradigm of some sort on the ethnographic data in order to formulate a theological product. To attempt to refrain from the imposition of any interpretive framework would be to fall back to the idealism of detached and objective social science.[98]

I would stress that an ethnographic method per se is not a solution to problems of eliding difference, eclipsing agency, or idealizing women's alliances as discussed above. Ethnography is one more area where vigilance and theorizing are necessary in order to be attentive to difference when retrieving women's experience. In ethnographic as well as textual feminist approaches to this task, the scholar must be self-critical about the assumptions she inevitably brings to her research projects. I will illustrate my contentions using Isasi-Díaz's *mujerista* theological ethnography as a test case in relation to some critical points raised by white feminist Marian Ronan. As we will see, Ronan assumes the possibility and desirability of a putatively unmediated access to the ethnographer's informants. While Isasi-Díaz is herself at points ambivalent on these issues, I argue that her ethnographic-theological project is defensible, once we view it through the lens of standpoint theory proposed by black feminist sociologist Patricia Hill Collins. That said, I turn at the end of this section to the nature of current postmodern interrogations of any standpoint claim, including ethnographically based ones. Peering briefly into this current debate in cultural anthropology sets the stage for how I will deploy poststructuralist resources in somewhat dialectical relation to other current critical theoretical resources such as postcolonial theory.

Isasi-Díaz's *mujerista* theology focuses on the particularities of Hispanic women's experience via a two-part ethnographic inquiry into their "lived-experience" (*EL*, 62).[99] Lived-experience is a technical term Isasi-Díaz uses to signify intentional, self-reflective, or valued activity, not merely anything that happens to a person.[100] This lived-experience is the source and norm for *mujerista* theology. The first ethnographic task she identifies is to give descriptive presentations of Latinas' lived-experience in a way that is "as unmediated as possible" (*EL*, 62). (Ronan, as we will see, finds her unsuccessful in this goal.) Second, the ethnographer-theologian has the metaethnographic task of analyzing and synthesizing the data about Latinas' lived-experience in order to construe the overarching, significant or recurring themes of Latinas' religious ethos and worldview. These "generative" themes are, quoting Paulo Freire, ones with "'existential meaning, and, therefore, with greatest emotional content [which] . . . are typical of the people'" (*EL*, 70). Metaethnographic *mujerista* theological themes emerge by correlating Latina lived-experience with a wide spectrum of non-Latina theological and nontheological sources— church teachings, liberation theology, feminist writings, and so on. (Ronan will criticize the way she pursues her metaethnographic theological agenda.)

Isasi-Díaz does not pretend to have some objective, detached ethnographic position vis-à-vis her interviewees. She is upfront about her positionality as Latina theologian who must "straddle the academic and Latino worlds" and whose "praxis has to do with attempting to impact academia" (*EL*, xii). By virtue of her academic status, she is an "outsider" to the grassroots oppressed community of Latinas in the U.S. which she studies; yet as a Latina, she is also a part of this community (*EL*, 71). Her use of the first person plural possessive pronoun throughout her text ("Hispanic women . . . our . . .") underlines the fact that she sees herself as communally involved, along with the women whom she studies, in the process of "speaking our own word, naming our own reality, reflecting upon and making explicit our own religious understandings and practices" (*EL*, 2, 179).

Mujerista theology is a critique of those theologies that "reserve the title of 'theologian' to those who are academically trained" and hence obscure the voices of lay Christians (*EL*, 171). Isasi-Díaz argues that "grassroots Latinas are organic intellectuals" (borrowing Gramsci's term) and must be allowed to be "the subjects of the process of theologizing" not just its "subject matter" (*EL*, 176, 177; see 170). She claims that it is already part of Hispanic women's lived-experience to be active, critical "moral laborers . . . vitally involved in the process of evaluating existing moral norms of our communities, adapting them, and producing new ones" (*EL*, 196). The motivation, therefore, behind Isasi-Díaz's choice of an ethnographic approach is political advocacy. *Mujerista* theology intends to provide a forum for Latina voices largely absent from white-dominated theological discourse and male-dominated Latin American theology. Isasi-Díaz's goal is to foster "liberative praxis" by and on behalf of Hispanic women, allowing Latinas to become subjects of their own stories instead of being objects of study. A presupposition for this ethnographic method is that "people have and use 'practical rationality'" and that life is reflexively "self-descriptive"—that is, available for documentation in the "gestures, expressions, symbols, deportment" which create the social world the subject inhabits. The specific mode of data collection Isasi-Díaz followed was the interactive interview with individual subjects or in the context of weekend "retreats" with groups of Hispanic women (*EL*, 67). Isasi-Díaz recognizes that "filtering" occurred as she selected parts of interviews and transposed them to written form, translating (literally) from "Spanish, 'Spanglish' or *Mexicano* into English" (*EL*, 87); however, she believes her text gives a relatively unmediated picture of these Hispanic women's lived-experience "in their own words," as one of her chapter titles reads.

Isasi-Díaz does retain a distinction between grassroots theologians (her subjects) and "theological technicians" or professional theologians (such as herself) but says that "there is no such thing as academic *mujerista* theology on one hand and grassroots *mujerista* theology on the other" (*EL*, 177).[101] No distinction should be made between trained and untrained Latina theologians, insofar as who may be agents in the theologizing process; yet, it is the technical work of the academically trained ethnographer-theologian "to bring together multiple ethnographic accounts" in a metaethnographic interpretive synthesis which constructs the significant generative themes and broader commonalities of Hispanic women's lived-experience (*EL*, 68). *Mujerista* theology is thus an advocacy project with a critical stance regarding Latina women's oppressions and a scholarly project intended to produce a communally accountable and empowering constructive theological reflection.

Because ethnography is central to her project of recovering submerged and ignored Latina voices, any critique of that methodology would strike at the heart of her project. Marian Ronan's critical comments about Isasi-Díaz's methodology thus pose a serious challenge to her project. Ronan claims that "Isasi-Díaz blurs the distinctions between her own experience and that of her informants" in her quest to demonstrate that Latinas are agents of their own morality and self-worth. Ronan recounts that Isasi-Díaz questions her informants "about what a mother should do if she doesn't have the money to feed her child [which] . . . evolves eventually into an inquiry about what the subjects would do if they had to decide which of two babies to surrender to be killed."[102] Ronan contends that the issue of moral agency was in fact not a question for the informants but rather, Ronan speculates, a projection of Isasi-Díaz's own conflict with her "archbishop over the right of Catholics to dissent on the basis on conscience, an impasse which 'taught [her] first-hand much of what [she] argues here.'" From Ronan's perspective, Isasi-Díaz's ethnographic methodology is tainted from the start because it is apparently not objective enough. Isasi-Díaz's questions posed to her informants slant the discussions toward her own concerns and away from the issues that Ronan thinks would "preoccupy . . . economically deprived Hispanic women."[103]

Ronan raises an issue with which every ethnographer must grapple, since the way a question is posed can already anticipate a certain range of answers. However, I think Ronan is overly speculative when she infers that Isasi-Díaz was somehow working out her conflicts with rigidly Roman Catholic authoritarianism via her interviews with Latinas. It is clear from the interviews that Isasi-Díaz asked leading questions, but her informants took the discussions in their own directions as well. Inevitably, Isasi-Díaz's own personal life experience informed the kinds of questions she asked. That is unavoidable. I do not disagree with Ronan that Isasi-Díaz injected herself into the ethnographic process; I disagree with Ronan's negative judgment about that fact. In my view, Isasi-Díaz's theological ethnographic approach requires her to inject herself into the process if she is to meet her objectives of: (1) constructing a *mujerista* "narrative" that can empower Latinas and challenge society;[104] and (2) doing theological reflection that interacts with the Christian tradition in which she as a theologian is steeped, even if most Latinas have little existential contact with parts of that (elite, textual, and male) tradition.

Regarding the first objective, I would categorize Isasi-Díaz as having a Latina feminist "standpoint theory" approach to her ethnographic project, similar to the standpoint theory developed by black feminist sociologist Patricia Hill Collins, who explains the role of black feminist intellectuals speaking about black women's oppression. Standpoint theorists generally assert some kind of unified epistemic position of women in relation to some oppression affecting them as a group. Collins argues that the "experiences and ideas shared by African-American women...provide a unique angle of vision on self, community and society."[105] Collins insists that the experience of being black, female, and oppressed, however, does not automatically translate into black feminist consciousness or a normative epistemological standpoint. She affirms that oppressed black women cultivate vast resources of "'motherwit'" or "wisdom"; they are, to borrow Isasi-Díaz's Gramscian words, grassroots organic intellectuals. Nevertheless, Collins asserts, "subjugation is not grounds for an epistemology."[106] While African American women in the course of ordinary daily life may be said to share experiences and ideas that give them their unique and often wise perspective on life, those experiences and ideas require interpretation and "rearticulation" to form a standpoint. There is still a need for "specialists who participate in and emerge from a group [in order to] produce a...more specialized type of knowledge." It will be primarily (though not perhaps exclusively) "Black women intellectuals" who will produce a "specialized" black feminist standpoint that can "stimulate a new consciousness" among African American women.[107]

Collins unapologetically affirms the mediating and critically interpretive role of the black feminist intellectual vis-à-vis the experiences of ordinary black women. Collins neither overinflates nor underinflates the contributions of either group. The African American feminist intellectual has the theoretical tools to produce the specialized knowledge constituting a black feminist standpoint. That conceptualization, in turn, must be made accountable to and validated by the black women's community whose standpoint the black feminist intellectual has claimed to rearticulate. Collins's standpoint theory notion of specialized black feminist knowledge would seem to dovetail with what Isasi-Díaz implicitly suggests should be the methodological role of the professional *mujerista* theologian in relation to the Hispanic women's community (especially at the level of metaethnography). According to Collins, the black feminist researcher is in no way dispensable but performs a necessary task of constructing the standpoint of oppressed African American women. Likewise, the academic *mujerista* theologian is indispensable for constructing a Latina standpoint. Equally important, standpoint theory has the effect of shining a bright light on the social placement of the theorist, opening up the possibility for self-critical analysis. There is always the risk of elitism in highlighting the theorist's scholarly role, but it is a necessary risk if one is to move beyond the experience of oppression to an oppressed standpoint.

Regarding Isasi-Díaz's second objective of doing constructive *mujerista* theology, again, the scholar must insert herself into and direct the ethnographic process. It is in relation to the theme of conscientization that we see most strongly the theologically rich returns of her approach. Isasi-Díaz defines the collective conscientization of Latinas in terms of "the struggle *to be* fully," ethically and spiritually in relation to "the domination, subjugation, exploitation and repression that we suffer" (*EL*, 16, 17). A central part of this ethical and spiritual struggle is religious. Isasi-Díaz formulates the generative theme of conscientization by situating Latina religious experience in relation to the dominant Christian tradition, Latin American liberation theology and Hispanic cultural traditions. The religious aspects of Latinas' lived-experience have been poorly understood by the institutional church and scholars of religion. Isasi-Díaz, herself a Roman Catholic, comments on the lack of Hispanic women's experiential connection to what is central to much of traditional Christian doctrine and practice. For example, although Protestantism is making inroads into Hispanic culture, the typical Protestant view of the centrality of the Bible is foreign to the popular religiosity of Roman Catholic Latinas. "Most of us seldom read the Bible and know instead popularized versions of biblical stories" (EL, 46). Also, despite many liberation theological attempts to rehabilitate the figure of Jesus as the liberator of the poor, Isasi-Díaz comments that most Hispanic women's piety is not christocentric (see *EL*, 50, 74). There is a close, almost familial connection with God: "We argue with God, barter with God, get upset with God...use endearing terms for God" (*EL*, 39). However, in keeping with the syncretism of Hispanic women's popular religiosity, Isasi-Díaz explains that the term *God* does not necessarily "refer to one divine being but rather [is]...a collective noun that embraces God, the saints, dead ones whom we love, manifestations of the Virgin (not always the same as manifestations of Mary, the mother of Jesus), Jesus (not very similar to the Jesus of the Gospels), Amerindian and African gods, and so forth" (*EL*, 39 n. 17). She emphasizes that popular religiosity has played a positive role in "binding the different Latino communities together" and allowing "us to experience the sacred in our everyday lives" (*EL*, 49). Latina morality, while deeply religious, is not rooted in Roman Catholic (or Protestant) doctrine but in a typical Hispanic cultural practice: a deeply intuitive process of doing what "'[m]i conciencia me dice,' my conscience tells me" (*EL*, 141).

Isasi-Díaz juxtaposes this ethnographic description of Latina religious experience with official Roman Catholic Church teachings, Latin American liberation theology, and the work of a range of moral theologians. From this, she develops her own theological argument for how conscientization is enabled by the formation of a moral conscience. Borrowing from the work of Catholic moral theologians such as Bernard Haring and Charles Curran, she asserts that individual conscience is "'the natural yearning of the will and heart...for the true good'" (*EL*, 148; quoting Haring). Conscience is a natural function (natural law) congruent with but active apart from God's revealed law. Conscience is not a faculty of the person or a mere set of right decisions; rather, it is a more all-encompassing "awareness of oneself as an agent" who "'affirms and creates one's moral self in and through those decisions'" (*EL*, 154; quoting Curran). Communally, conscience is also agential; it is a function of the *sensus fidelium*—that is, the corporate agency of "'the body of the faithful as a whole, [who,] anointed as they are by the Holy One (cf. Jn 2:20, 29), cannot err in matters of belief'" (*EL*, 145–46; quoting from Vatican II's *The Dogmatic Constitution of the Church*). Both individual and communal forms of conscience, Isasi-Díaz argues, are thwarted by the institutional church's attempts to foster blind obedience—whether to Roman Catholic notions of papal infallibility or to Protestant notions of biblical authority.

Ronan's point about Isasi-Díaz's battle with Roman Catholic authority echoes through these theological remarks; however, unlike Ronan, I do not see Isasi-Díaz's constructive theological work happening at the expense of the task of retrieving the experience of her informants. While her critical interaction with the Christian tradition (including the Roman curia and various male theologians and ethicists) would be foreign to most Latinas' experience, Isasi-Díaz is doing the work of correlating Latina experience with the Christian tradition. *Mujerista* theologians "have paid attention to Latinas' stories because...we perceive that those stories are a *tela*, a cloth, out of which our own beliefs and self-understandings are made"—but not without the threads also of Roman Catholicism and academic theology.[108] Patricia Collins calls this the "outsider-within" aspect of feminist standpoint theory. The term outsider-within denotes the perspective of a woman of color whose job or societal role allows her to move within and often be intimately acquainted with dominant culture where she nevertheless remains a cultural outsider. (This outsider-within position has its roots in the history of African American women's domestic workers in white households.[109]) Collins suggests that African American women intellectuals take advantage of their outsider-within position in relation to predominantly white academe. Though an often lonely and stressful role, black feminist outsider-within scholars can "recenter the language of existing academic discourse" by "making creative use of their status as mediators."[110] Not only does this role allow the black feminist scholar to locate internal contradictions and conflicts in white racist society, but this role also contributes to her ability to bring critical analytic tools into the black community. Isasi-Díaz engages in similar mediating operations by reworking concepts from dominant theology, implicitly assuming something like an outsider-within position as a Latina scholar in the white masculinist academic world.

But Ronan may aver, is Isasi-Díaz giving us real Hispanic women's experiences? The answer has to be yes and no. Yes, we are getting Latinas' experience in some of their own words (I am not sure how much more real Ronan wants). But no, we are not only getting the stories of Isasi-Díaz's informants, we are getting a constructed *mujerista* standpoint. That is not only unavoidable; it is desirable, if Collins is correct. Isasi-Díaz does not have to represent all Latinas; no one can.[111] As a professional theologian, her task is to construct a *mujerista* garment, some parts of which are her informants' stories. *Mujerista* theological ethnographers, thus, are not holding up a mirror for real Hispanic women's experiences; they are seamstresses, skillfully crafting an interpretive ethnographic and theological product that is intended to be morally, politically, and religiously accountable to Latinas' experiences— even if some or many individual Latinas cannot relate to or fully understand that product because it speaks of matters outside of their experience.

Although Isasi-Díaz says she wants to give "unmediated" descriptions of ordinary Latinas' lived-experience (*EL*, 62), she does mediate and construct the experience she retrieves. For example, her chapter "In Their Own Words" gives a summary of each interviewee, detailing the nature of the ethnographic contact. Isasi-Díaz then presents, in dialogue form, each woman's views on various moral issues, though no such group conversation ever took place among all these women (some were only interviewed individually). Isasi-Díaz explains the format in her text by saying she wanted to find patterns in "the process they use in making decisions"—even though the women did not present their views within this framework and, moreover, "resisted dissecting their experiences" in this way (*EL*, 125).[112] This is evidence of how Isasi-Díaz's theological agenda was at work, even at the initial data collection stage, in order for her to achieve her stated goal of empowering Latina voices via a cohesive pattern of generative themes. My observation here is not the same as Ronan's charge that Isasi-Díaz illegitimately intervened and projected her own issues onto her informants. I am making a standpoint theory comment about the necessary intervention of the insider-outsider scholar. Thus, I see Isasi-Díaz's dual objective of empowering Latinas and doing constructive critical (theological) reflection as resonant with feminist standpoint theory—even if Isasi-Díaz's rhetoric of "in their own words" seems to point in the opposite direction.

Analyzing Isasi-Díaz's ethnographic theology in light of standpoint theory helps in two ways. It gives a theoretical warrant for what Isasi-Díaz actually does in her text, and it helps to expose the assumptions at work in Ronan's critique of her—namely, Ronan's assumptions about the desirability of the ethnographer's objectivity and of the unmediated presentation of the informants' own views. However, this standpoint theory point about the engaged role of the scholar, when applied to ethnographic method, sets us squarely in the middle of hotly debated issues in cultural anthropology, generally, and feminist ethnography, specifically. If feminist theology continues on the path of more ethnographic research, it would be beneficial to give more attention to these debates.

On the one hand, the standpoint theory view of the role of the scholar resonates with the current trend in cultural anthropology toward "reflexivity" on the part of the ethnographer. Dubbed the "reflexive turn," this approach recognizes the ethnographer's unavoidable "mediated vision."[113] Feminist cultural anthropologists have embraced this fact and attempt to establish reciprocity with their informants and to advocate on their behalf.[114] White feminist sociologist Mary Jo Neitz defends this stance: "Feminist researchers who study marginalized peoples ... often speak of giving voice to those who have no voice."[115] Neitz's comment echoes Isasi-Díaz's approach. On the other hand, postmodern theorists call this feminist ethnographic stance into question.

Australia-based, white feminist scholar Vicki Kirby gives a description of the "new" reflexive ethnography: "the ethnographer is now a caring ethnographer, sensitive, more hesitant, sharing, sympathetic, consciousness-raised." Kirby notes how some feminist new ethnographers who focus on women's experience try to exercise caution, not wanting to slip into a sense of false intimacy with their female informants with whom they still stand in an "imperial" power relation, and whose voice they still might distort. While she applauds that reflexive caution, Kirby argues that no amount of reflexivity in one's ethnographic writing or attentiveness to difference will get to the gist of the problem, which in her mind is the very modernist assumption that the individual's "voice [is] the mark of self-presence...[and] that voice is at one with itself." From her postmodern perspective, any mode of ethnographic writing is a process of "producing an object as knowable." Empathy is good, but it is not an experiential conduit to the real "voice" of one's informant, which is a very modernist way of conceiving of the self, dubbed by Kirby as "the dream of a sovereign subject."[116]

Kirby's postmodern perspective on the discursive construction of the ethnographer's subjects would seem to challenge Isasi-Díaz's standpoint theory approach that I have defended against Ronan's critiques. However, I have also indicated throughout this chapter that I intend to argue for a poststructuralist approach to selfhood. Is this an internal tension in my project? Are feminist ethnographer-theologians, or feminist theologians generally, faced with a choice between theories that promote the standpoint of marginalized subjects or postmodern theories of the discursive construction of subjectivity? Kirby's comments seem to point to such a choice; however, I would caution against viewing these two theories oppositionally. While I will spend considerable time in the next two chapters presenting a poststructuralist approach to subjectivity, I will argue in chapter 4 that postcolonial theories of an oppressed or "subaltern" standpoint remain of vital importance for feminist theology and should be used to balance and supplement poststructuralism.

This chapter's critical examination of textual and ethnographic approaches to retrieving women's experience has thrust us into the middle of a range of complex issues regarding how to theorize embodied sexed selves who are moral agents, how to theorize oppressive power and empowered resistance to it, and whether it even makes (postmodern) sense to speak of feminists' claims to have given voice to oppressed female subjects. What remains to be explored next are the full implications and payoffs of seeing women's selfhood as discursively produced. I can only state here the position I will present in chapters 3 and 4 that a poststructuralist approach to subjectivity affords a subtle way of analyzing the complex interworkings of privilege, power, and agency. After presenting a poststructuralist theory of embodied selfhood, I will demonstrate the payoff for doctrinal reformulations (of sin and creation in the image of God) and for reading texts like *The Color Purple* and the Hagar-Sarah narrative.

Although highly theoretical, poststructuralism need not be an academic distancing from women's material and everyday concerns. Some feminist theorists fear that too much poststructuralist analysis constricts the feminist theological throat and brings on a kind of academic women's "'self-erasure, an analogue to our obsession with thinness, ... a kind of professional/pedagogical anorexia.'"[117] Moreover, even if some postmodern writings do lose sight of and contact with actual oppressed women's experience, that problem is not solved simply by turning to ethnographically displayed real women. Ethnography is a vital methodology for feminist theology; it can contribute much that Isasi-Díaz, other theologians of color, and feminist new ethnographers generally want it to by way of documenting women's experience and breaking down the barriers of privilege between academic feminists and grassroots women through direct interactions. However, if poststructuralist scholarship needs something to neutralize some of its deconstructive acids, then I believe we may need to look elsewhere than just ethnographic methods. I will argue in the subsequent chapters for a feminist postmodern turn informed by other types of theory, including postcolonial and queer theories, as a way of developing a nuanced understanding of the complexities of selfhood, power, agency, and embodiment—in short, the factors that are actually at work in the experience of real women and are some of the most contested sites for feminist theorizing.

3

Reinterpreting Sex, Sin, and Desire

Feminist theology, it seems, cannot do without an appeal to women's experience. As we saw in chapter 2, feminist theologians use hermeneutic and ethnographic methods for retrieving women's experience in an effort to keep their theological formulations accountable to the communities of women they represent and to challenge dominant forms of theological discourse. Problems of various sorts, however, dog feminist theology's best intentions: eliding racial differences; ambivalence on issues of sexuality; obscuring women's agency, moral accountability, and resistance practices; and assumptions about the ethnographic process uninformed by current debates in cultural anthropology. Thus far, I have only been able to suggest that poststructuralist, postcolonial, and other theories offer some helpful tools for addressing these problems. In this chapter, I focus on the specific problem of theorizing sexuality and sexed identity in order to interrogate the assumption about natural maleness and femaleness, which has received little critical attention in feminist theology. Inevitably, what the scholar does not theorize adequately becomes a vacuum to be filled with views from dominant culture, which in the West are marked by longstanding influences from Christianity that have been particularly damaging for women and gender- or sexually marginalized people. Hence, a feminist approach to sexuality and sexed identity must take into account the legacy of how they have been viewed in the Christian tradition from the time of the church fathers to the present—in particular, the ways in which embodied selves have been caught up in a triangulation among three major issues: sex, sin, and desire.

As Augustine makes clear in his instruction on the difference between the venial sins of marriage (sex for pleasure) and damnable sins (fornication, adultery), even the lawful and honorable good of marriage (procreation) cannot be achieved without concupiscence, which he saw as a legacy of original sin.[1] For the church fathers, to be a sexual being is to be open to the temptations of inordinate or unlawful desire for another sexual being. Concupiscence, whether contemplated or acted out, was seen as a seemingly unavoidable sin for finite sexual beings. Feminists have noted how this theology of fallen libido has been damaging to women particularly because of the way in which "woman" has been targeted as the agent provocateur of men's sinful sexual urges.[2] Queer theologians have protested the labeling of all nonheteronormative erotics as unnatural desire. Since traditional theology's grouping of sex, sin, and desire has been so destructive to many Christians trying to find a more holistic approach to embodied spirituality, why continue to speak of those terms together? I do so, in part, because these themes continue to be interwoven in feminist theological writings in dialogue with that tradition. Feminist perspectives on these themes depart significantly from the patristic and later Christian tradition, and feminist theology has capitalized on the opportunity to redeem the category of sexual desire from its bondage to patristic anxieties about sexual libido and woman-as-temptress. Nonetheless, I detect an important insufficiency in feminist theological writings on the topic of sex: a deeply rooted and problematic assumption about a natural sex binarism.

This chapter will first discuss the sex binarism at work in feminist theological writings about women's creation in the image of God and about gendered sin. I argue that a sex binarism is problematic because of its link to heteronormativity (the notion that heterosexuality is the only legitimate form of sexual desire) and thus to heterosexism. I propose how to deconstruct that male-female sex binarism, in light of Judith Butler's poststructuralist theory of how selfhood (including gender and sex) is constituted performatively within a nexus of disciplinary cultural discursive conventions. In the second and third parts of this chapter, I apply this poststructuralist perspective theologically by reformulating the notions of sin and the *imago dei* in light of a theory of performativity. My poststructuralist approach has a number of payoffs (in addition to the immediate one of providing an avenue for ongoing feminist critical interaction with the Christian theological tradition): (1) it allows for the materiality of sexed bodies without a restrictive male-female sex binarism; and (2) it allows for hermeneutical nuances in feminist uses of women's literature like *The Color Purple* (with complex depictions of racial, gender, and sexual identity) or biblical literature like the Sarah-Hagar story (with complex familial and ethical relationships).

While this chapter makes constructive feminist proposals about sex, sin, and desire in a poststructuralist key, I am mindful that some feminist proposals in theology or philosophy of religion stand at odds with my approach. Here especially the discourse of desire looms large, at least for white feminist thinkers like Elizabeth Johnson and Grace Jantzen who argue, respectively, for women's ontological longing for divine mystery and for the divine horizon of women's deepest semiotic desires. Addressing their potential objections to my postmodern approach will open up a larger issue of how, in the process of rethinking sex and sin, the feminist theologian can rediscover not just women's embodied *jouissance* but the desire for the tradition itself.

I. Deconstructing the Sex Binarism in Feminist Theological Writings

Feminists appeal to women's creation in the image of God for many theological reasons. Some wish to combat vestiges of the largely sexist and dualistic notions in the early and medieval tradition of the originally perfect (male) soul.[3] Others make it the basis of demands for women's equality with men, which formed the political agenda of first-wave white feminist theology and which still pulsates throughout the writings of many white feminist theologians today. The affirmation of women's creation in the image of God is intimately related to their "struggle against the dehumanizing forces of patriarchy."[4] Many feminists of color promote the biblically based notion of women's creation in God's image because if "women of color can believe that we are also created in the image of God...and redefine ourselves not as other but as Godlike, then innumerable ways of lifting self-esteem and claiming the right to live whole, healthy lives can emerge."[5] The appeal to women's creation in the image of God has not always come easily. Womanist theologian M. Shawn Copeland notes the disturbing reality that in Christian theology generally, "although we recognize that the soul is without gender, we still doubt women's *full participation* in the *imago dei*."[6] Yet much is at stake in making this appeal successfully. White feminist theologian Elizabeth Johnson asserts: "As women's experience of their own worth is articulated today, ownership of the *imago dei* doctrine is occurring at a foundational level.... If women are created in the image of God, without qualification, then their human reality offers suitable, even excellent metaphor for speaking about divine mystery."[7] On the whole, feminist views of creation promote a nonhierarchical, non-gender-biased view of the creator God, a wholistic approach to spiritual embodiment, the created equality of the sexes, and a nonanthropocentric, eco-friendly attitude toward nonhuman species and the cosmos. Womanist Patricia Hunter sums up the implications for women of a creation-oriented theology: "If all God created was very good, including humankind, then all women, regardless of ethnicity, class, varying abilities, or sexual orientation, are part of God's very good creation."[8]

I affirm the attempt to combat the tradition's patriarchy, racism, androcentric hierarchy, and mind/body dualisms that oppress women (and men); however, it is also important to reflect critically on feminist appeals to sex-differentiated creation. For most feminist theologians, humanity's maleness and femaleness are seen as a biologically based, God-given duality and a self-evident good for the continuation of the species—in contrast to the supposedly more culturally complex formations and conventions of masculinity and femininity (that is, gender). There is an unmistakable sex binarism at work, even when every attempt is made not to "polarize the human couple into a binary pattern."[9] To challenge the notion of dual sex creation would appear to undercut a principle (i.e., creation in the image of God) that feminist theologians everywhere have held dear. However, many feminists are beginning to question the price that is paid for an uncritical acceptance of this male-female sex binarism—namely, heterosexual privilege—even if unintended. Mary Fulkerson has noted "the deployment of the heterosexual binary" in the writings of Ruether.[10] I would like to examine this issue further: first, in relation to the biblical creation accounts that form the explicit or implicit subtext for feminist appeals to women's creation in God's image and, second, in feminist theological discussion of gendered sin. Having unmasked the sex binarism in these writings, I will then argue for why a natural sex binarism is problematic and how one can avoid it by conceptualizing selfhood in a poststructuralist way.

Some feminists conclude that the two creation stories read together yield the insight that "the image of God is reflected in a community of persons, in a humankind that is created male and female" for whom "being like God can be achieved only by the gift of self to others and the reception of the gift of self from others."[11] Other feminist theologians wish to affirm sexual embodiment, correcting a long-standing tendency in Christian thought to associate sexuality with the sin of concupiscence. In an effort to endorse the created goodness of sexual bodies, Catherine LaCugna argues that "[s]exuality lies at the heart of all creation and is an icon of who God is, the God in whose image we were created male and female (Gen. 1). Sexual desire and sexual need are a continued contradiction to the illusion that we can exist by ourselves."[12] Feminist theologians resist interpreting the story of creation as "a binary pattern of sexual complementarity" because of "its hidden theme of domination" and argue instead that "[i]n both creation stories mutuality is the key."[13] This critique is directed toward the complementarity aspect, not the binary sex notion itself. Thus, many feminist theologians stress that being created in the image of God entails the embodied fact of sex-differentiation, which they interpret to mean that humans achieve their fullest capacity for reflecting God's goodness in unitive, mutual relationality (sexual or social) between male and female persons.

Positive as these statements are for affirming nonhierarchical, mutually dependent human community and sexuality, they entail a disturbing male-female sex binarism that can be traced to the Genesis creation narratives. Rebecca Alpert, a lesbian feminist rabbi, argues that the Genesis account of creation "introduces a rigid binary identity" that inculcates "painful and prejudicial societal attitudes" toward intersexuals, lesbians, gays, transgendered individuals—in short, anyone who deviates from the "compulsory heterosexuality" entailed in the biblical call to become "one flesh" (Gen. 2:24).[14] Are such problems entailed even when (1) the Genesis text is not cited specifically; (2) an appeal is made only to male/female creation in the image of God in Genesis 1:27, and texts like the aforementioned Genesis 2:24 or 1:28 ("and God said to them, 'Be fruitful and multiply'") are downplayed or avoided; and (3) the feminist writer in no way endorses and even explicitly rejects such prejudicial views? I would answer yes in all three cases. Regarding case 1, the Genesis creation narrative functions as an unavoidable subtext to any (Christian or Jewish) appeal to creation in the image of God, even when the Bible is not specifically quoted. Regarding case 2, appealing to the notion of natural, God-created maleness and femaleness contributes, as I will argue below, to an ideology of normative reproductive heterosexuality from which heterosexism follows. Regarding case 3, without an explicit understanding of the connection between the notion of binary sex and assumptions about compulsory heterosexuality, the best of intentions to combat heterosexism will be hampered.

Sex and gender also emerge as important issues in feminist discussions of sin located in theological anthropology.[15] It has been noted that theological anthropology as a distinct doctrinal locus "is relatively new to the theologian's agenda," having received much of its impetus as Christian theologians endeavored to respond to the secularism in the Enlightenment's turn to the subject.[16] An important figure in this stream of modern theology is Søren Kierkegaard, whose existentialist starting point typifies an anthropological approach to sin found in later thinkers such as Reinhold Niebuhr.[17] Feminists who approach sin in critical conversation with Kierkegaard or Niebuhr also stand in this theological anthropological stream of thought. Valerie Saiving made a ground-breaking proposal in 1960 to reformulate sin in light of women's experience of diffuseness or lack of self.[18] In this same vein, the 1980s saw a number of feminist attempts to break free of the male-oriented Niebuhrian paradigm of sin and highlight women's experience, most principally in Judith Plaskow's *Sex, Sin, and Grace*.[19] Feminist theologians persist in viewing sin-talk as a crucial way to address human failings and structural evils and to envision how to live hopefully and productively in light of them. Kierkegaard's writings are explicitly being retrieved by a number of current white feminist scholars who find in his discussions of sin an anthropology they believe has great potential for gender equality and for addressing more fully female and male experiences of sin. I will identify the nature of the sex binarism at work in some Kierkegaardian feminist discussions of gendered human failings, with special attention given to how assumptions of natural binary sex differentiation contribute to discursive regimes of normative "naturalized heterosexuality" that function prejudicially toward sexualities that deviate from that norm.[20] Borrowing from Judith Butler's poststructuralist theory of how selfhood is constituted performatively within a nexus of disciplinary cultural conventions, I will propose a theoretical approach to sexed and gendered selfhood that can deconstruct the sex binarism at work in feminist theological writings—both those appealing to the *imago dei* and those addressing gendered sin.

Kierkegaard identifies two types of sinful ways of responding to the inability to synthesize "infinitude and finitude":[21] the despair of weakness and the despair of defiance. Though the despair of weakness (one form of which Kierkegaard describes as "not to will to be oneself") is culturally identified as a feminine trait, in contrast to the defiantly masculine "despair to will to be oneself," both sins are intermeshed and found in women and men.[22] Neither weakness nor defiance (theo)logically predominates. Kierkegaardian feminists approve of the way Kierkegaard maintains a fruitful "dialectical tension" between the two kinds of gendered sin.[23] They conclude that there is a "complementary wholeness" in the way he specifies that the path to overcoming sin requires implementing the opposite mode of being (in an attitude of faith): the person caught in the despair of weakness needs masculine self-assertion, and the person caught in the despair of defiance needs feminine self-giving.[24] They find a positive kind of androgyny in his view of selfhood that "includes both masculine and feminine modes of relating" because this "common structure of selfhood" could potentially foster "a fuller development of individuality and relatedness in both sexes" which avoids damaging hierarchies.[25] Some feminist interpreters of Kierkegaard conclude that sexist statements of his such as "'the woman actually relates to God only through the man'" should be interpreted as Kierkegaard reflecting societal gender conventions that he "personally wished to avoid" and that his deeply held belief was that "'the distinction man-woman vanishes'" in relation to God.[26]

I have a number of reservations about the Kierkegaardian anthropological model, not the least of which is a male-female binarism.[27] The Kierkegaardian feminist appeal to binary sex differentiation is part of an effort to promote an androgyny model of selfhood where masculine and feminine gender attributes can be combined. This approach is based on the assumption that gender is culturally constructed, as compared to sex, which supposedly is not. One writer comments: "[W]ithout negating sexual differences, one can ultimately look beyond them to a common model of selfhood not defined by gender."[28] That is, gender stereotypes are seen as open to cultural redefinition, but sex is seen as a self-evident bodily given. Sex differentiation is, in other words, natural: "[o]ne of the things that we inevitably are ... is male or female."[29]

I would argue that however much one tries to stress equality in the Genesis account or however much one tries to complicate male and female selfhood (e.g., saying that men can despair in "womanly" weakness or women can despair in "manly" defiance), one still has not adequately addressed the assumed natural male-female sex differentiation structure. Why is the assumption about a natural sex binarism so problematic? Isn't it enough to show that gender is culturally constructed and hence open to resignification? An increasing number of feminist theorists are contesting the viewpoint that gender fluidity is enough, and central to their critique is Judith Butler's deconstruction of natural male-female sex differentiation.[30]

Butler uses a poststructuralist approach to material selfhood in order to deconstruct the idea, so dear to Western (biblically shaped) culture, that sex is a natural attribute. Early feminists such as Simone de Beauvoir, began a hard-fought battle to gain acceptance for the idea that "'[o]ne is not born a woman, but, rather, becomes one.'"[31] The notion is now broadly accepted that gender (masculine and feminine) is culturally constructed. Butler pushes feminist thinking to another (poststructuralist) level, arguing that "'sex' is as culturally constructed as gender."[32] That is, there is no natural sexed subject prior to the discursive regimes that subject bodies to certain gender-specific regulations and that promote certain sexual practices and affectivities. These discursive regimes do not just influence persons who stand in some way outside of discourse; they regulate self-knowledge and "contour the materiality of bodies."[33] In our culture, the dominant discourse of heterosexuality constructs male and female sex as opposites that attract. That is, man is constructed as the male sex who desires the female; woman is constructed as the female sex who desires the male. Sexed bodies, in other words, are seen as "'a cause' of sexual ... desire." According to this view, any other form of desire is a noncoherent sexuality, an unnatural inversion of a putatively natural heterosexuality. Butler argues the exact reverse: that the so-called cause (sex) is actually "'an effect,' the production of a given regime of sexuality."[34] Heterosexuality is a pervasive cultural regime whose hegemony is a factor of its multiple, localized disciplinary mechanisms (terms borrowed from Michel Foucault's thought, to which I will return below). The discourse of heterosexuality is dispersed in a myriad of societal institutions (advertising, education, religion, medicine, and so forth) and shapes our understanding of natural/unnatural in order to produce normalized subjects who conceive of themselves as having a coherent heterosexual identity secure in the intermeshing of biology and libido. Butler uses Foucault's theory of discursivity to decenter the assumed coherence of sex and sexuality as cause and effect; she further analyzes their perceived naturalness in terms of performativity.

Performativity is a notion Butler derives by combining Foucault's view of discursively constructed identity with the theories of speech-acts philosopher J. L. Austin and deconstructive philosopher Jacques Derrida. Butler argues that a "performative act is one which brings into being or enacts what it names" (Austin's classic example of a performative utterance is the vow "I do" which constitutively inaugurates a marriage). Derrida takes this idea of words constituting a reality in an intertextual direction. Inherent to any discursive performance is the "*citation* and *repetition*" of (con)textual convention; when one acts, one is "citing" previous "texts" (with texts meaning not just writings but any signifying activity).[35] Hence, to be discursively constructed is to be "performatively constituted."[36] Performativity is not analogous to theatrical or dance performance—if one is presupposing an actor or dancer apart from the "stage" of discursive relations. Performativity means the way things are constituted in the saying/doing. It is not performance as play-acting.[37] A poststructuralist focus on the performative is meant to deconstruct philosophical assumptions about a pre-given "doer [or play-actor] *behind* the deed."[38] Agency is not defined in terms of a core self prior to cultural and linguistic structures to which one might attach certain attributes (e.g., will, intention, freedom, etc.); rather, agency is constituted in a process of negotiating multiple cultural discourses about such attributes. The poststructuralist theorist engages in "the difficult labor of deriving agency from the very power regimes which constitute us" and form our understanding of ourselves as centers of will, intention, freedom, and so forth.[39] The agential power of the postmodern subject is analyzed in terms of performatives (i.e., bodily performative acts) situated in terms of societal conventions that one both cites and resignifies in one's utterances or actions. (There can be both complicity and sometimes "parodic" resistance to those conventions.[40]) Men and women can be spoken of poststructurally as embodying particular societal conventions of maleness and femaleness when performing their sex, gender, and sexuality. Performativity theory emphasizes that the sexed body has no substantial "ontological status" but rather is constituted in performative acts.[41] Thus, the notion of discursive performance reinforces the poststructuralist critique of the idea that sexuality is naturally caused by a pre-given sexed body.

What is the payoff for looking at selfhood poststructurally? Hermeneutically, it allows for reading practices that can exhibit significant nuance on issues of sex, gender and desire. When we bring Butler's poststructuralist theory of performativity to bear on *The Color Purple*, Celie's black lesbianism is read not as a natural identity but rather as an identity constructed and performed in relation to discourses of race, family, religion, and so on. A poststructuralist way of construing sex, gender, and sexuality may come the closest to capturing what Alice Walker is narratively theorizing in the following conversation between Celie and Mr. ———:

> Mr.——— ast me the other day what it is I love so much
> bout Shug. He say he love her style. He say... Shug act more manly
> than most men. I mean she upright, honest.... Just like Sofia.
> ... I tell him. You not like this. What Shug got is wom-
> anly it seem like to me....
> Sofia and Shug not like men, he say, but they not like women
> either.
> You mean they not like you or me.[42]

Celie loves an "other" whose gender shifts and whose sexual desire is multiple. Shug, the object of Celie's and Mr. ———'s desire, is both manly and womanly but like neither men nor women. Furthermore, this gender description is applied to both Sofia, who is (performatively) heterosexual, and Shug, who is (performatively) bisexual. In this way, Walker can be read as interrupting the "causal relation among sex-gender-desire," thus destabilizing the heterosexually linked man-woman binary.[43] Celie's desire cannot, in this instance, be seen as an inversion of natural heterosexual desire. With the breakdown of the naturalized heterosexual paradigm, Celie's lesbianism must be renegotiated as well. That is, her lesbian identity is not natural but performative. One could counter with the observation that within the story Celie's sexuality seems quite stable and natural (as opposed to Shug's, which is more fluid and changing). Even after Celie reconciles with Albert, she seems quite set and secure in her lesbian identity. Here we must clarify that the notion of performativity does not necessarily mean one is incapable of a perduring identity performance. It merely signals that all identities are contextually situated and performed within a nexus of discursive relations—including discourses of natural sexed selves.

There are also constructive theological benefits from a theory of performativity. In the section that follows, I will apply this theory to the two theological loci discussed above: sin and the *imago dei*. I will first propose a poststructuralist reformulation of sin that avoids the sex binarism that lurks in the Kierkegaardian notion of sin. Then I will argue in part three for recuperating (via performativity theory) the feminist appeal to women's creation in the image of God so as to avoid the same problematic sex binarism.

II. Performative Sin

I want to propose a poststructuralist reformulation of sin from a theological anthropological starting point, in order to demonstrate how one could avoid the sex binarism problem I analyzed in Kierkegaardian feminist writings, while still making a constructive theological proposal about the nature of sin. After presenting the notion of sin in terms of performativity theory, I will test my thesis that approaching sin from a poststructuralist perspective is theologically and ethically illuminating by applying this approach to the Hagar-Sarah story.

If selfhood is constituted and reconstituted performatively, and if sin (very formally) is an act of the will that impedes one's relationship with God and one's neighbor, then sin poststructurally conceived would be the self choosing to engage in discursive relations in distorted ways that impede godly performativity. It is difficult to find the appropriate overarching metaphor for this spiritually distorted discursive relationality. For the sake of argument, let me call it a "narrowing" of relationality. This sinful discursive narrowing can be thought of as happening in two aspects: as undue cooperation with disciplinary power and as underdeveloped cooperation with disciplinary power, to use a Foucauldian notion that I will explain below.[44]

Both undue and underdeveloped cooperation with disciplinary power must be understood against the backdrop of Michel Foucault's theory of how selves are constituted through relations with disciplinary discursive regimes. Much of Foucault's work investigates how individuals and whole communities have been regulated in a myriad of ways by cultural discourses. Discourses of medicine, jurisprudence, sexuality, religion, and so forth constitute powerful forces determining the true, the right, the normal. These discourses and their mechanisms of implementation do not merely impinge on the individual as a "pre-given entity which is seized by the exercise of power. [Rather] the individual is the product of a relation of power exercised over bodies...movements, desires."[45] The individual is constituted as a subject by being "subjected to" the apparatuses of truth-conveying power discourses, referred to in a kind of Foucauldian shorthand as power/knowledge (the title of one of Foucault's books).[46] Foucault's point about power is that even in the midst of a subjugating process, an agential subject is being produced. Individuals "are always in the position of simultaneously undergoing and exercising...power. They are not only its inert or consenting target; they are always the elements of its articulation" and, hence, there follows the possibility if not the actuality of what he calls an "insurrection of subjugated knowledges."[47] These knowledges are marginalized discourses that emerge to resist society's dominant discourses. Thus, related to the notion of the discursive constitution of subjects is the notion that power is not only coercive but also productive: "Power must be analysed as something that circulates....[Moreover] there are no relations of power without resistances."[48]

Foucault analyzes some classic normalizing disciplines with a focus on particularly oppressive power/knowledges in institutions of past centuries: prisons, hospitals, and insane asylums, as they were then called. However, one should also think of discourses that shape us with what we hope would be less frightening institutional manifestations: academe, religion, childrearing, sports and exercise, patriotism, and so forth. A normalizing disciplinary power can and does entail levels of "pleasure" for the subject who is being performatively normalized. Foucault explains: "If power were never anything but repressive, if it never did anything but to say no, do you really think one would be brought to obey it? What makes power...accepted, is simply the fact that it...induces pleasure, forms knowledge, produces discourse."[49] My use of the term "cooperation" attempts to get at this often misunderstood aspect of Foucauldian power theory. That is, power is not simply imposed. It produces something: a subject whose agency is constituted in the process of interacting performatively with power/knowledge.[50]

Given this analysis of power relations, there would seem to be a temptation (as the theologian might say) to maximize one's pleasure in cooperating with a particular discursive regime with the result that one's identity performativity mimics to an extreme the disciplinary power with which one has unduly cooperated. We can describe this performativity in terms of what has classically been called sin against God. For example, undue cooperation with any of the power/knowledge regimes mentioned above (e.g., academe, religion, patriotism) makes what (religiously speaking) should be a relative good (the pleasure of scholarship, a practice of piety, or love of country) into the supreme good. Not only is the relation among relative goods disordered, but what should be the supreme good (allegiance to God) is supplanted by another allegiance. Undue cooperation with a discursive regime can also be seen as a sin against one's neighbor. An undue pursuit of any of the three disciplinary discourses listed above might yield something like this: an ivory tower academic, a religious fanatic, or a xenophobe. The performativity in these examples entails the risk of an abuse of power with repressive (sinful) effects on others, such as (respectively): the less educated person one treats condescendingly, the nonbeliever one condemns, the foreigner one viscerally mistrusts.

This construal of sin as undue cooperation with a disciplinary power presupposes the notion mentioned previously that power circulates, so that the cooperation cannot be simply explained away as unavoidable coercion or cultural brainwashing. Some feminists have referred to Foucault's notion of the disciplined "docile" body as descriptive of the way women are dominated and victimized by the mechanisms of patriarchal culture with which they are forced to cooperate.[51] If one analyzes power only in this way, one could not call undue cooperation with disciplinary power a sin; it would be an instance of being structurally sinned against.[52] However, if one concurs with Foucault's observations that the normalizing process necessarily entails (except in cases of extreme domination) some circulation of power, then agency (not just victimization) is constituted. Moreover, one can speak of a morally accountable agent. After all, North American society may pressure a woman toward, for example, obsession with weight loss, but (with the exception of very dominated docile bodies where the obsession degenerates into anorexia or other eating disorders) no one is really forced into Weight Watchers. One can choose to submit unduly to a normalizing regime such as this. One has the choice to broaden one's discursive relationality in order to avoid letting the "pleasure" of cooperating with dieting become a narrow, rigid obsession that is destructive to self and others. A broader, more fluid relationality could counteract a tendency toward undue cooperation with a particular disciplinary discursive regime because one's performativity in one discursive context would be counterbalanced by negotiations with other power/knowledges, both dominant and insurrectional. The obsessive dieter would benefit from widening her discursive relations to include medical discourses of healthy body weight. These might help, but feminists would argue that medical discourses do not go to the root of the problem. One needs to contest the patriarchal male gaze that insists on sculpting the female body as thinly and docilely as possible, thus inscribing her body with conventions of femininity (gender) and female allure (sexuality). To address the oppressive effects of that male gaze, one would need to include insurrectional power/knowledges, such as critiques of the dieting industry from thealogical, womanist and other circles.[53]

The other aspect of sin is the flip side of the first: underdeveloped cooperation with disciplinary power. This is also a kind of narrowing of relationality. In light of what has just been said about the first aspect, the question arises: why should discursive underdevelopment be labeled sin? Wouldn't resistance to the dominant discourses of our sexist, racist, consumerist, violent society be laudable? Yes, of course. However, underdeveloped performative cooperation with power/knowledge is not resistance; it is in fact the avoidance of the conditions for resistance—namely negotiation with power relations. Resistance arises only in and through normalizing discursive processes. Insurrectional discourses do not happen outside of discursive relations with dominant discourses; they happen as a result of relational interactions where control, discipline, and normalizing are in effect. Hence, to leave relations with a disciplinary discourse underdeveloped would be to miss the opportunity to enter that power/knowledge loop. It would be to evade power/knowledge in that context and thus avoid the conditions necessary for resistance practices to emerge.

This construal of sin as underdeveloped cooperation with disciplinary power makes no sense if one is operating with the notion that power is bad, that it only corrupts, that it is what my oppressor has taken from me. I have argued that power is not simply something one group or institution possesses but is something that, to some extent, is dispersed in a network of mechanisms, institutions, and technologies (many of which may well be dominating). Leaving relations with a normalizing regime underdeveloped would be to stall the circulation of power. This constitutes a temptation of a different kind. Underdeveloped cooperation with certain kinds of disciplinary power can be a tempting evasion of what Foucault calls technologies of "care of oneself"—that is, taking responsibility to know oneself in relation to others, in particular, to know what one's ethical agency should be towards others. That knowledge then affects the way "an individual acts upon himself in the technology of self," with whatever responsibilities that entails.[54] Parenting provides one example.

Think of a mother in a very patriarchal household who is erratic in setting limits for her children and communicating about appropriate behavior, whose most prevalent response to her children's misbehaving is "wait until your father gets home." One could say that she has left underdeveloped her cooperation with the disciplinary discourses of parental authority that specify the importance of maternal as well as paternal authority. (Correlatively, she can be seen as unduly cooperating with patriarchal power/knowledge.) One can imagine that somewhere in her societal interactions, this mother has been exposed to the normalizing effects of maternal authority discourses as they might be disseminated by the media, school officials, social service agencies, church pastors, childrearing manuals, and so on. Her underdeveloped cooperation with those discourses is an agential choice, resulting in a sin against others—namely, her children who are instilled with patriarchal notions of parental authority. The voices of victims of abuse within patriarchal family models would function as an insurrectional discourse relevant to this mother's parenting flaws.[55] This example also illustrates sin against God, if one sees inadequate development of her own power and authority as stunting her ethical and spiritual development. With the exception of, for example, a battered wife or a woman whose own childhood might have been one of abuse that thoroughly scarred her, one can speak of a morally accountable agent who has the ability to widen and more fully develop her parental performativity in relation to other dominant and insurrectional discourses, thus enabling her both to care for herself and her children with the proper exercise of power.

My categories of sin may sound like they echo Kierkegaard's. Underdeveloped cooperation with disciplinary power may sound like the womanly despair of weakness, and undue cooperation with power/knowledge may sound like the manly despair of defiance. However there are several important differences. First, Kierkegaard's two modes of sin are (according to some interpretations) hierarchically related gradations of selfhood; whereas my categories are not. For Kierkegaard, womanly despair is a factor of less self-consciousness and reflects his psychologically based opinion that women have a less "egotistical concept of the self" and less "intellectuality" than men. Woman's natural devotedness, Kierkegaard continues, is a good thing, but "take this devotion away, then her self is also gone."[56] Hence the feminine despair of weakness (in men or women) reflects a less formed self, compared with the more highly developed self-consciousness reflected in the manly despair of defiance. In my approach, on the other hand, underdeveloped cooperation is as agential as undue cooperation. Both are different aspects of a narrowly performing subject, not indications of greater or lesser degrees of selfhood or self-consciousness.

A second way my approach differs from a Kierkegaardian model is that mine does not trade on gender or sex binarisms. For Kierkegaardian feminists, the path to overcoming sin is to rectify an imbalance between two types of sin with the aim of transcending gender and promoting androgynous selfhood. As I argued above, this androgyny mode complicates gender roles at the price of reinscribing a sex binarism. There is no sex binarism in a poststructuralist approach to sin because maleness and femaleness are one of many identity markers that are negotiated performatively. Sex is not differentiated binarily as something we naturally "inevitably are."[57] Furthermore, overcoming sin is not about balancing opposites at all—a third way my proposal differs from a Kierkegaardian one. The most religiously faithful response to both undue and underdeveloped cooperation with disciplinary power is the same: appropriately wider discursive performativity. Undue and underdeveloped cooperation are both aspects of overly narrow discursive relationality. Hence, breadth of performativity of the needed kind puts the subject in a position potentially to avoid sin, understood poststructurally as undue pursuit of, or underdeveloped relations with, power/knowledge.[58]

Discursive breadth in and of itself cannot be said always to prevent sin; nothing theologically speaking can make that claim. This brings us to a final important aspect of sin: sin's inevitability. A modern existentialist construal of finitude and sin (like Kierkegaard's) accounts for sin's inevitability in terms of the tensions experienced by the self caught between two poles of being.[59] The drag of finitude cannot coexist harmoniously with the loft of infinitude— hence anxiety and its inevitable resolution in sin for all humanity.[60] Post-structuralism views human subjects culturally and is suspicious of the essentialisms in ontological explanations of the inevitability of sin. In human culture every relation is a power relation with its own history of effects. Although power is not evil in and of itself, the dynamic of ubiquitous power relations can be said to be a condition for human failings. For some reason (and here I would invoke the theological category of inscrutability), human discursive relations, which have the potential for an equitable exercise of power under communal "rules of law [and]...ethics," inevitably devolve to some degree into oppressive uses of power.[61] The best rules of law humanity can construct cannot protect against all misuses of power. In a more theological mode, we can say that sin's inevitability is a result of the recurrence of subjects continually entering into power/knowledge relations in a distortedly narrow way. Historically, to some degree, every discursive performance has fallen short and will inevitably fall short of God's goodness and glory. However, unlike Christian existentialism, which grounds sin's inevitability ontologically, mine is a theological claim based on a (poststructuralist) reading of the consistent pattern of human practices. Hence I do not have the basis for arguing for sin's universality, but I can ground my claims for the pervasiveness of sin in real life manifestations of evil (which appear to be, for all intents and purposes, personally and publicly ubiquitous).

By way of an illustration, let me apply this theory to the Hagar-Sarah narrative, discussed already in chapter 2. First, I would insist that Sarah and Hagar are mostly sinned against structurally in ways that cry out for an insurrection of subjugated knowledges. Some apparatuses of power make overt resistances difficult if not impossible; however, to some extent, Sarah and Hagar can be seen as having agency (and for most feminist interpreters, this

is a desirable interpretation). Thus, their behaviors and attitudes can be analyzed in terms of the theological anthropological categories of sin I outlined
above: undue and underdeveloped cooperation with various discursive regimes.
Sarah sins against her neighbor, so to speak, in unduly pursuing the pleasure
of her performativity as mistress in Abraham's household, which functions
as a disciplinary power over Hagar, with whom she "dealt harshly" (Gen. 16:6).
Sarah, in her narrow discursive relationality, does not engage any insurrectional knowledges (e.g., sisterhood within patriarchy or the injustice of in-
dentured servitude), which might have fostered in her some empathy for
Hagar. In relation to God, Sarah leaves underdeveloped her cooperation with
the discourse of divine promise that she will bear a son (18:12). She does not
widen her discursivity to embrace this promise in faith but, instead, remains
docilely focused on a discourse of barrenness. Her undue cooperation with
that discourse contributes to her lack of openness to the mysterious ways
God plans to realize the Abrahamic covenant through her own offspring.

After she bears Ishmael to Abraham (16:4), Hagar apparently sins by
undue cooperation with the patriarchal discourse of mothers-of-firstborn-sons
as it relates to the Abrahamic covenant. By giving birth to a son first, she and
not Sarah is the one manifesting the inauguration of God's covenantal promise
to Abraham regarding his (patrilineal) unlimited progeny (15:4, 5). She unduly
cooperates with this discourse and, as a result, looks "with contempt on her
mistress" (16:4). Hagar is later given a divine promise that her own (presum-
ably matrilineal) progeny will be numerous and that Ishmael's nation will be
great—independent of the Abrahamic covenant (16:10; 21:18; cf. 21:13). That
divine discourse is the basis for a potentially powerful subject position as God-
namer and receiver of God's promise. This is an identity that even Sarah
and Abraham did not have the power to annul and could have functioned as an
insurrectional knowledge that might have enabled Hagar to feel more secure
about God's providential care for her despite the mistreatment she suffered.
It seems, however, that Hagar leaves underdeveloped her cooperation with
this power/knowledge because, in her brief time of relatively elevated status
as mother to Abraham's firstborn son, she seems to have succumbed to the
temptation to "lord it over" Sarah. It is not until she is cruelly cast out into
the desert with Ishmael that she launches into courageous performativity of this
subject position.

A possible complication of an account of sin in terms of performativity
theory alone is a debilitating relativism. If identity performances are fluid
and multiple, sin as the distortion of our performativity of godliness would be
multiply defined as well. This would seem to undercut what a feminist doctrine
of sin has traditionally wanted to do—that is, specifically name and protest the

sinful acts and structures that distort the image of God in women and men and throughout creation. Surely it would be ethically inadequate to suggest that Sarah and Hagar are equally responsible or culpable in the effects of their sin toward their neighbor. That is why it is vital to situate a story like this one in terms of social sin so that one can name structural oppression, as I will argue in the next chapter. As we will see, this allows the theologian to analyze three factors: (1) the extent to which Sarah's identity performances carry more oppressive force than Hagar's; (2) when it makes sense to essentialize Hagar as "victim"; and (3) how Hagar's experience can be retrieved as a "subaltern" standpoint, without however losing sight of her discursive construction.

III. A Performative *Imago Dei* and Desire for the Divine

For the many feminist theologians who share the view about the importance of the doctrine of women's creation in the image of God, it would be methodologically devastating to lose possession, so to speak, of that doctrine due to problems of a pervasive sex binarism. I argued in the previous section for a theory of nonbinary, performative sex identity. In what follows I will propose how a feminist commitment to women's creation in the image of God can be situated within that theory of performativity and reformulated so as to function as an important criterion for the wide discursive performativity necessary for godliness. I will then respond to two feminist positions that would seem to present a decisive challenge to a postmodern performative approach to the *imago dei*—namely Elizabeth Johnson's Rahnerian theological anthropology and Grace Jantzen's proposal for the divine horizon of a feminist ethics.

If the self is constituted in the context of multiple performative acts in relation to cultural discourses, then the image of God would be the graced possibility for godly performativity in every discursive relation. To say that our humanity is created in God's image means that our performativity has the possibility of being "an icon of who God is."[62] If all aspects of human performativity (including gender, sex, and sexuality) can be iconic of who God is, then excluding any discursive relation from what is seen as reflecting God's image would render an incomplete *imago*. Since our discursivity is fluid and multiple, we have a lifelong project of performing the image of God. This poststructuralist concept of performance need not conflict with the deeply held Christian beliefs that the *imago dei* is a gift of the Creator and that growth in godliness is only possible by grace. To reconceptualize the *imago dei* in terms of identity performance is not to say that salvation or justification before God is the individual's accomplishment. My poststructuralist reformulation simply resituates the notion of the divine gift of the *imago* to the human person in a way that does not invoke notions of a pre-given human subject.[63]

What would it mean concretely and overtly for the believer to perform the image of God? The answer to that question will necessarily differ widely. Each individual would negotiate her particular way of performing God's image as it is construed by the religious community with which she associates (and there may be widely divergent interpretations of it). That is, each community's construal of the *imago dei* becomes a discursive regime that functions as a convention for religious conformity to God's will. As the believer cooperates with or resists aspects of these community-specific discursive conventions, they become constitutive of her religious selfhood, so that she is performatively constituted in part by relations of power (and grace, the theologian will want to add) with the discourse of creation in the image of God. The believer performs her faithful religious identity while also discursively negotiating her various subject positions as, for example, a woman, a caucasian, a mother, a factory worker, an immigrant, an artist, and so on. The discourse of religious faithfulness to the *imago dei* would need to intersect with discourses of sex, race, family, labor, national origin, and such, so that the believer could endeavor to embody godliness in all aspects of her life.

Having argued for a performative view of sin and the *imago dei*, we can now bring these two notions together. Referring back to my argument in the previous section that overcoming sin requires the *proper* breadth of discursive relationality, we can say that the discourse of the *imago dei* functions as an important criterion to inform what is godly and ethical performativity in every discursive relation. Given this poststructuralist definition of sin and the image of God, redemption would logically be what rectifies distorted, narrow performativity of God's image. As with performative notions of sin, a performative notion of redemption will be variously instantiated, depending on the ecclesial context of the believer. Redemption governed by Lutheran discourses of imputed righteousness will be differently performed by the believer as compared to redemption governed by Roman Catholic discourses of cooperative grace or Eastern Orthodox discourses of *theosis* or liberation theological discourses of Christ's liberating praxis. Construing these various schemes of redemption from a poststructuralist perspective reveals that all of them function analogously—that is, they serve as the discursive conventions with which the believer negotiates so that she can perform her identity as a sinner-redeemed-in-Christ. Assessing whether any such religious identity performance adequately reflects the *imago dei* is a task incumbent on each believer and believing community—a task hopefully undertaken with breadth of discursive relationality.

How can this reformulation of the *imago dei* assist feminist theologians wishing to avoid a sex-binarism in their appeals to women's creation in God's image? Viewing selfhood performatively deconstructs the notion that to be created in the image of God means having been given some putatively natural femaleness (or maleness); rather, femaleness is seen as a performed effect of discourse and not the cause of natural desire for its opposite (maleness). If one can break the assumed causal connection between sex and desire (sexuality), then one can affirm sexuality as divinely blessed without any entailments of normative, privileged heterosexuality. In the poststructuralist reformulation of the *imago dei* I have just outlined, human sexuality can be affirmed as part of what it means to be created in the image of God—that is, we as embodied beings have the possibility of godly performativity in the way we negotiate our gender, sex, and sexuality. Some individuals' religious performative identity will include the pleasures and constraints of heterosexual maleness and femaleness (among other conventions), but a performative theory of the *imago dei* does not entail notions of naturalized, normative heterosexuality. Reconstructing the *imago dei* performatively thus decenters heterosexuality and allows the theologian to theorize that many sexualities have the possibility for performatively reflecting the image of God.

Let me now address some limitations and possible objections to a poststructuralist approach to sin and the *imago dei*. While this approach arguably clears theoretical ground for feminist appeals to gendered sin and women's creation in the image of God that are relatively free of a sex binarism (and hence, free of entailments of compulsory heterosexism), that does not mean that poststructuralism is all we need to combat heteronormative discourse in the Christian tradition. The Sarah-Hagar story again serves as an example. This story, not surprisingly, plays out in a context of normative heterosexual reproductivity. My feminist poststructuralist approach to construing sin in that story did not destabilize that regime, nor was I able to theorize any sexual identity outside of compulsory heterosexuality. Here we see a limitation of poststructuralism. To destabilize more fully the discourse of compulsory reproductive heterosexuality, one would need a hermeneutical strategy specifically oriented to reading past the story's heteronormativity—a strategy often referred to as "queering" a text.[64] This hermeneutic destabilizes heterosexuality not by finding historical evidence of nonheterosexual identities (often impossible to do especially in many ancient texts) but by reading homo- and/or gyno-eroticism into a text like the Bible, thereby unsettling contemporary assumptions of what is sexually normative and what is "deviant" (a dictionary definition of "queer"). Queering the Bible has been classified as a type of reader-response criticism and is related to a feminist hermeneutic of suspicion and remembrance.[65] The Bible, from a queer perspective, is read sometimes as a "text of terror" (referring to Phyllis Trible's book by that name) and other times as a "friendly text" with stories about characters that can "function as queer ancestors of faith."[66] It is beyond the purview of this chapter to queer the Hagar-Sarah story;[67] however, given that I have argued so adamantly against the implicit heterosexual privilege in the feminist appeals to the Genesis accounts of creation, I would be remiss not to indicate at least that a queer hermeneutics would entertain the (insurrectional) possibility that Sarah and Hagar—like Ruth and Naomi, for example—could function as queer ancestors of faith.[68]

Objections to my proposal may come from a number of Christian theological circles. Some might argue that binarily sexed bodies are an order of creation and that my reformulation of the *imago dei* and sexuality in terms of a theory of discursive performativity, therefore, threatens this belief.[69] In other words, the theory might be seen as freighting an agenda that is not compatible with certain Christian faith claims. Here I would draw a distinction between using the theory of performativity to analyze the discursive formations of any religious belief or practice, versus using it (as I am) to reformulate the notions of sin and the *imago dei* in order to deconstruct heterosexist binarisms. The theory used in the first case is a neutral tool of analysis and, in principle, could be used by any theologian to analyze Christian practices discursively. However, I take an advocacy stance that feminist theology would be well served by viewing sin, the *imago dei*, and sexuality performatively. Doing so militates against narrow discursive relationality and avoids implying that the *imago dei* is connected to natural sex differentiation with its entailments of compulsory heterosexuality. My use of the theory is therefore paired with a stance opposing any interpretation of the biblical account of creation in God's image as God-ordained binary sex.

A different objection to my performative approach to the *imago dei* might be that the poststructuralist notion of performativity does not go far enough in articulating the conditions for the possibility of human godly performativity—meaning, I do not present the ontological and epistemological bases for women's desire for and participation in the mystery of God. For example, Elizabeth Johnson, drawing from Karl Rahner's view of the human person as a self-transcending mystery, asserts that "a human being is primordially 'spirit in the world'" who is structurally oriented toward "fathomless mystery as the very condition for the possibility of acting in characteristic human ways.... In the experience of oneself at... this prethematic level whence our own mystery arises, we also experience and are grasped by the holy mystery of God."[70] Johnson supplements this transcendental analysis of the religious conditions for our existence as humans with a theory of religion that sees religious symbols not simply as a "projection of the imagination" but as expressions emerging "from the deep abyss," as Rahner would say, of "our encounter with divine being" (*SWI*, 46, 47).[71] Referencing thinkers as diverse as Paul Ricoeur and Martin Buber, Johnson argues that "images with the capacity to evoke the divine are in some way *given* in the encounter which at the same time brings persons to birth as persons" (*SWI*, 75; emphasis added). Johnson takes this approach in an effort to affirm that religious symbols issuing from women's depth encounter with the divine should be taken seriously as expressions of religious truth. What we can know and express linguistically of this depth experience is always mediated by the conditions of our "location in time, place, and culture" (*SWI*, 7); hence, Johnson explains (following Paul Tillich), religious symbols, as contextual mediations, may grow old and tired and "die" when they lose their "power to bear the presence of the divine" to a new cultural situation (*SWI*, 46). New religious symbols emerge because human creatures continue to "participate to some degree in... the dynamism of existing which God in essence is" (*SWI*, 114) Women, as spiritual human beings oriented ontologically to the mystery of God, articulate their experience of God in new symbols. Women's experience is a "lens" that helps us to see what makes for "the promotion of true humanity," which we all share as creatures of God (*SWI*, 31). In this way, she establishes via a theological anthropology why women's religious discourse is not just an arbitrary or trendy affixing of new names upon God but rather a profound naming of "the mystery of God in whose being we participate" as image and likeness (*SWI*, 67).

Johnson's position reflects a classic theological theme that to say one is created in the image of God is not a statement about the knowability of God but a statement about how humans are "united to God as to an unknown, savoring God only through love" (*SWI*, 108). This is theological discourse about desire more than knowledge. Johnson might argue that a performative approach to the *imago dei* is insufficient because it makes no claims about the innate human experience of the call of God's mystery that causes our hearts to be restless until they rest in God. What causes desire for God is a complex and important theological issue to raise. However, having raised it, one enters a philosophically contested field where spiritual desire is seen either as a given (in some essential prethematic experience) or produced (in and through culture). This is the familiar essence-culture philosophical debate (here, in a theological mode). I cannot resolve that debate (nor would I want to).[72] While my sensibilities tend toward a postmodern cultural constructivist position, I do not reject out of hand ontological approaches, because their claims have functioned in powerful ways in theological circles historically. Ontotheologies have given us discourses of realism, mystery, darkness, and desire that post-modern theologians cannot discount, since those discourses infiltrate much first-order Christian practice—whether everyday devotional prayer or full-blown mysticism. Discourses of ineffable mystery invoke the reality of desire for the holy and often have the power to impel the most disaffected believer to stay (and stay even contentedly) within a partly or even overwhelmingly alienating tradition. As a theologian I remain open to the believer's first-order claim to have had an ineffable experience of specifically divine love. Never-theless, whether it is philosophically intelligible to speak of a prethematic experience of, or desire for, something is open to considerable debate. Current postmodern philosophy tends toward skepticism of any prelinguistic experi-ences that we could ever claim meaningfully to know. To posit, as Johnson does, that humans qua human are constituted by the experience of the tug of specifically divine mystery is a theological claim. Such a claim is based on a belief in humanity's innate God-connectedness, which Johnson takes as a theological premise. Even if there is a God-oriented structure to human con-sciousness, that structure is epistemologically ambiguous to us—and perhaps theologically ambiguous as well, given Christian teachings about the fallen-ness of creation.

Grace Jantzen and I share a critical stance toward an ontologically oriented account of women's desire for the divine. Nonetheless, Jantzen's proposal dif-fers significantly from mine in that she uses a predominantly psychodynam-ically influenced philosophical approach to argue for a feminist "imaginary" outside of "the traditional masculinist religious symbolic."[73] I approach women's spirituality poststructurally in terms of the ways in which women negotiate with a masculinist religious tradition in order to open up possibili-ties for the production of new religious desires (including insurrectional ones) that might widen patriarchally disciplined performativity. In the next two chapters, I will present arguments for and examples of my approach to nego-tiation with the Christian tradition. In what follows, I will analyze Jantzen's compelling though ultimately internally unstable proposal in *Becoming Divine*.

Jantzen employs the postmodern psychoanalytically based theories of French feminists Luce Irigaray and Julia Kristeva to argue for how women can tap into a female semiotic, whose *"jouissance"* challenges the "phallocentric" symbolic of the Christian tradition.[74] Central to Jantzen's approach is a Kris-tevan distinction between the symbolic ("what we normally think of as lan-guage and cultural system") and the semiotic ("'a psychic modality logically and chronologically prior to the sign, to meaning, and to the subject'") (*BD*, 195). That psychic reality is rooted in material experience—particularly and significantly, gestational growth in the womb and early stages of infant development related to the mother's body. The symbolic phallus is oppressive because it represses the maternal semiotic; nevertheless, Kristeva argues, the semiotic breaks through in transgressive symbolic expressions (poetry, art, etc.) that constitute an irrepressible "welling up from the semiotic [that] has the 'capacity for letting jouissance come through'" (BD, 197; quoting Kristeva).

Jantzen is critical of French feminist semiotic theory because it implies that attaining subjecthood requires submitting to "the (paternal) symbolic as that which imposes rationality and order on the (maternal) semiotic, which is chaotic and undisciplined energies and drives" (BD, 199). That is, the individual must pass through the phallic symbolic to attain cognition. Jantzen redefines the categories of symbolic and semiotic not as polar opposites but as dialectically related, in part because she sees the maternal semiotic as funding its own rationality and symbols, which apparently can emerge separately from and as a challenge to phallocratic symbolic patternings. This suggests that symbolism is no longer an exclusively phallic realm and that there is a feminine discursivity in some sense independent of masculinist discursive systems. As a factor of the resistance of the maternal symbolic to the phallocratic symbolic, there is the possibility of the construction of a feminist "imaginary" that can subvert masculinism.[75] Jantzen's constructive feminist imaginary focuses on the concept of "natality": the "fundamental human condition" of being born of a woman, having a unique embodied, unrepeatable narrative, sharing in a web of human relationships, feeling oneself obligated "to the world into which we were born" (BD, 144, 152).[76] Out of a revaluing of the experience of natality comes a feminist ethics of responsibility to all other human beings who are born (and by extension all things that exist) and a feminist religious imaginary that "draws us forward in becoming divine for and with one another" as fellow natals (BD, 99).

Jantzen presents this as an incarnationalist perspective that reveals the truth repressed in Christian theology. "Because 'unto us a child is born,' the door is open to develop a new religious imaginary which will enable sexuate becoming, the flourishing of our natality" (BD, 17). By flourishing, Jantzen means a symbolic alternative to the traditional notion of salvation whereby one needs to be rescued from the human predicament by a divine savior. By contrast, for Jantzen, "an imaginary of natality expressed in an idiom of flourishing, would lead in quite different directions, opening the way to a divine horizon which celebrates alterities and furthers the aim of the divine incarnation of every woman and man" (BD, 157). Divinity is thus an imaginative projection of our deepest semiotic experience of and desire for all natal flourishing. This point recalls Irigaray's projectionist theory of religion, which, Jantzen explains, is not meant reductively to suggest atheism (BD, 89).

Because the projection issues from the most basic, real and universal experience of natality, which we all share and all need to be whole, we do not simply project the divine (as an illusion), we desire the divine as the real horizon for our flourishing.

Jantzen offers an ambitious reworking of phallocentric philosophy; however, there are problems in the way she tries to secure natality as a source and norm for her feminist ethics. Natality is the norm that, even in a pluralistic world, can guide us to act with "empathy and...respect for" any fellow natal. Jantzen affirms that "where natality is celebrated, totalitarianism becomes impossible" (BD, 150, 148). In addition to natality as a norm, Jantzen wants to secure natality as a positive material source for our desire for the divine and our universal ethical responsibility to others. There is something about our experience of natality that—if we can reconnect with it—disposes us to welcome fellow natals in a way that brings "god to life through us" (BD, 272). Given her reliance of the work of Kristeva, who gives considerable attention in some writings to maternal experience,[77] one might expect Jantzen to argue for the goodness of natality based on the spiritual experience of nurturing motherhood (and there are some moments when Jantzen seems to do this). However, I take her at her word that she does not want to go in this direction because it risks romanticizing and stereotyping women as mothers and nurturers—a problem she notes in the work of Kristeva.[78] I believe Jantzen would agree that natality under the material conditions of our phallocentric world is never unambiguous and would not necessarily function as a consistent norm for welcoming fellow natals. Actual gestation, birthing, and caring for infants could equally produce ethnocentric, even xenophobic, protectiveness in order to guarantee the survival of my child or the children of my clan. However, Jantzen could be taken as proposing natality simply as a norming *ideal* for ethicists and philosophers of religion to debate the meaning and application of today. I would welcome entering into such a debate on this very rich though, I would argue, also ambiguous ideal.[79]

Regarding natality as a source, however, I do not see how Jantzen avoids an internal tension that renders her project unstable. In an effort apparently to avoid a romanticizing of motherhood, Jantzen proposes using Kristeva's Lacanian "techniques" but with a "small shift," whereby she secures the unambiguous goodness—indeed the divine horizon—of natality semiotically. That is, Jantzen defines natality not in terms of a phenomenology of motherhood but as, in part, a reality independent of and prior to any phallocentric symbolic: natality is, at its most fundamental level, the process whereby "the fusion or healing of the rift between...symbolic and semiotic, word and flesh..., human [and] divine" takes place (BD, 203). This methodological move is vital for establishing natality as the source of our desire for God and love of others. Nevertheless, it is not at all clear how she can appeal to natality's prelinguistic, semiotic aspects and remain true to her stated intentions to avoid ontotheology and instead construct an ethics rooted in "the material and discursive conditions within which subjects are formed" (*BD*, 146). Hence when we analyze the way Jantzen approaches the concept of natality as a source for feminist ethics, we see an internal tension. If she were to argue for the life-affirming and spiritual aspects of actual gestation and birth, which would present natality as a positive material source of ethical responsibility, she would romanticize motherhood. In order apparently to avoid this, she instead argues for natality as a semiotic reality of divine-human integration, which presents natality's unambiguous goodness at the cost of obscuring the material and discursive conditions that constitute us as subjects.[80]

The poststructuralist philosophical orientation I have been advocating would not conceptualize natality or human desire for the divine prethematically or semiotically but discursively. In the next two chapters, we will explore how the concept of desire is discursively constituted in relations of power. "Where there is desire, the power relation is already present.... [It is] vanity ... to go on questing after a desire that is beyond the reach of power."[81] Like power, desire is something quite neutral; it can be good or bad or even good and bad at the same time. Like power, it is relational. One always has desire-relations within the context of power. As constituted in discursive relations, desire is in part produced because it is disciplined and repressed. Desire is produced via intersecting discursive relations, including normalizing ones. There is never any category of desire for the divine generally; it is always specific to culture and history. Christians have spiritual desires in part because of the way they are normalized by means of various religious discourses: harmatiologies and practices of penance produce sinners desiring to be saved; doctrines of creation produce creatures longing to have God's image restored in them; preaching and bodily experiences such as baptism produce believers who desire to be born again; and so on.

What might a Christian feminist poststructuralist approach to desire for the divine look like? It would inevitably mean negotiating with the disciplinary force of the Christian symbols, creeds, doctrines, and biblical texts. Whereas to Jantzen's eyes this approach might seem thereby to reinforce a phallic symbolic and suppress a feminist imaginary, I would argue that only by negotiating with the disciplinary force of the phallic Christian tradition (with all its history of promoting sexism, gender hierarchy, body/soul dualisms, misogyny, etc.), can one construct desires and practices in relation to it that are both pleasurably compliant and imaginatively and subversively resistant.

To pursue this line of thought, I propose delving further (in the following chapter) into Foucault's notion of power to see whether and to what extent the poststructuralist approach I am advocating does serve a wide range of feminist interests and objectives. Once we have a firm grasp on the nature and workings of power from a poststructuralist perspective, we can explore in chapter 5 the possibilities and fruitfulness of feminist negotiations with the disciplinary power of the Christian tradition.

4

Theorizing Power

The issue of power surfaces throughout feminist theological writings, particularly at those points when discussion turns to how women suffer from oppressive power formations and power inequities. The tendency is to assume that the nature of oppressive power is self-evident (that is, it corrupts and dominates) and that theorizing about power generally would be redundant to accounts of women's experiences of disempowerment and resistance. There is a pervasive (and not altogether unfounded) dualism at work here: institutional power is either oppressive and bad or liberating and good. Let me give two examples of typical white feminist rhetoric on power. In Ruether's midrashic "The Kenosis of the Father" in *Sexism and God-Talk,* she has God the Father muse: "The kings of earth that bow down before me in their temples cry that I am their only Lord.... By calling me Father, Lord, and Ruler, they claim the power to rule the earth.... The rebelliousness that [they] experience among their menservants and, even worse, their maidservants, points to this other reality. Perhaps ... [t]here is another power outside Our rule."[1] Power, in Ruether's text, is presented dualistically as either dominating or liberating, idolatrous or spiritual, a lie or the truth, breeding violence or spreading "Shalom."[2] Carter Heyward echoes this starkly dichotomous view of power when she asserts that "[u]sing *power-with* others is good. Using *power-over* others is evil."[3]

My investigations into a poststructuralist approach to selfhood in chapter 3 began to theorize power as something other than simply good versus bad and as more than simply repressive when disciplinary. In this chapter, I will explore further how this theory of power complicates the claim that one should strive to access a liberating form of power that stands in stark contrast to oppressive, evil power. I will argue that a poststructuralist approach to power provides an effective tool for addressing both oppressive societal structures (e.g., racism and sexism) and oppressive cultural formations, including the kinds of Christian symbols that feminist theologians have criticized as oppressive.

In part one, I analyze the views about power in feminist discussions of structural oppression or "social sin." I will argue that there is a tendency among feminist theologians to inscribe potentially restrictive essentialisms about women as victims in relation to systems of oppressive power construed too monolithically. Central to my discussion will be Michel Foucault's poststructuralist theory of the disciplinary and productive effects of power and Gayatri Chakravorty Spivak's postcolonial notion of strategic essentialization. Seeing how these two theories can balance and supplement each other will help us reconceptualize social sin in an effort to retain the ethical and political force of appeals to an oppressed standpoint, but without static essentialisms. Part two focuses on two symbols in traditional Christian theology that feminist theologians have regarded as having particularly onerous effects on women—the cross and Jesus as the (male) Christ. Some feminists depict the cross and Jesus' maleness as irretrievably bad symbols of violent and sexist dominating power. Those feminists who challenge this extreme critical estimation of these Christian symbols argue that it is possible to recuperate a gyno-friendly mode of power in the cross and in Jesus' humanity. Again, we can see a dualistic approach to good versus oppressive power. I will attempt to carve out theoretical space for a more nuanced understanding of the disciplinary power of these Christian symbols and how they might be deployed for women positively in what Foucault calls technologies for the care of the self.

I. Power in Feminist Discussions of Social Sin

Many feminist construals of sin have insightfully focused on social hierarchies, power imbalances, and discriminatory attitudes and practices—and how all these are factors in women's exploitation. A problem affecting some of these discussions is a tendency to imply more or less static oppressor-oppressed categories that essentialize women as victims in relation to some totalizing domination. One finds this tendency in Ruether's classic first-wave white feminist construal of sin as the projection of "group egoism," in particular, "the dominant male group ego" that manifests itself in the social sin of sexism.[4] Ruether emphasizes that women are not just oppressed but can passively cooperate with forces of domination and can oppress others by being "racist, classist,...manipulative..., dominating toward children," and so on. However, she adds, when women become oppressors, the real culprit is the "overall system of distorted humanity in which ruling class males are the apex."[5] Under this patriarchal system, women are not really oppressors but rather are misguidedly "cooperating in their own subjugation."[6] In other words, women are ultimately cast in an essentialized role of victim in relation to hegemonic structural evils like sexism, even when they sin by degrees of participation in this androcentric group egoism. Ruether toys with some notions that could lessen the essentialism of women as exploited victims when she comments that oppressed women can also engage in "covert resistance"; however, she suggests that covert resistance is an undeveloped feminist consciousness and falls short of "real feminist thought and practice."[7]

A different but analogous essentialism is suggested in Delores Williams's womanist appeal to "demonarchy," a term she coined in an early writing in order to highlight that black women's oppression in "*white-controlled American institutions*" is different from "patriarchally-derived-privileged oppression" where white women are subjugated but also receive certain privileges (albeit male-controlled) because of their race.[8] Demonarchy is a complicated term. It is extremely effective rhetorically for emphasizing the overt and insidious workings of white supremacy as well as for breaking through white feminist scripts of evasion of racism ("my ancestors never had slaves," "some of my friends are womanists," "my parents were discriminated against because of their ethnicity," etc.). However, as a term of analysis, demonarchy runs the risk of essentializing African American women in the role of oppressed in relation to a hegemonic structure viewed too univocally. Analogous to what Williams says of the term patriarchy, demonarchy "leaves too much out."[9] For example, demonarchy does not have the nuance to address class differences and hierarchies among women of color.[10] Or it may bring attention to the structural sin (in the tradition of black liberation theology) of the "defilement of Black women's bodies" but is less effective for understanding the dynamics of what Williams calls "individual sin"—that is, the agential ways in which "Black women also participate in sin when they do not challenge the patriarchal and demonarchal systems in society."[11] When she invokes demonarchy, Williams runs up against the problem (as we saw with Ruether) of how to theorize morally accountable personal agency in relation to oppressive social structures.

There are vital insights in both Ruether's white feminist account of the social sin of sexism and Williams's womanist account of the social sin of black women's oppression. My critique is not directed toward their claims that evil as a social reality "transcends us as individuals" and that liberation from such evil must emerge from "shared community struggles" against structural oppression.[12] However, those claims will, in many cases (but with important exceptions), be better served by decentering oppressor and oppressed positionalities and by relying on a nontotalizing view of power. In arguing below for a poststructuralist approach, I am not suggesting that poststructuralism should be alone in the "tool box" that the theorist uses for analyzing the nature of power and oppressed identities. Feminist theologians have cultivated a rich methodological tool box for analyzing the intricacies of women's oppressions and liberating resistances. Some black feminists employ historiographical and sociological methods, such as Patricia Hill Collins's method of tracing African American women's "culture of resistance."[13] Some *mujerista* and Latina feminist theologians employ a cultural studies approach to understanding the particular challenges of negotiating *mestizaje* and "borderland" identity as marginalized Latinas in white, English-speaking North America.[14] Gender analysis is used pervasively and continues to be fundamental to feminist understandings of both patriarchal oppression and the revaluation of feminine power and women's spiritualities. Many feminist theologians from the two-thirds-world and elsewhere bring a postcolonial perspective to their analysis of the destructive impact of colonization and imperialism on non-Western women and indigenous women of the Americas.[15] These and other theoretical tools can and often should also be used in tandem with poststructuralist ones—a methodological approach illustrated in Kelly Brown Douglas's multidimensional analysis of the disciplinary effects of white racist sexual stereotypes, in which she combines some Foucauldian notions with other nonpoststructuralist (historical, sociological) investigations of the roots of heterosexism in the black church.[16]

In the previous chapter, we began to investigate a theory of discursive power regimes, which postulates that individuals are constituted in relation to various power/knowledge systems. The discursively constituted individual is not just an "inert or consenting" object but is to some extent also produced as a subject. Hence, with the exception of extreme domination, power is not only coercive but also productive: "power must be analysed as something that circulates."[17] This theory of power has positive applications for decentering the essentialism of a dominator-dominated dualism because it enables us to go beyond the truism that everyone is to some extent both oppressor and oppressed—a truism that, taken alone, could suggest the dangerously relativistic notion that all oppressions are equal. My use of poststructuralism to decenter the label "oppressed" is not focused on exposing how subjugated persons in some set of power relations may be dominating subjects in another; rather, I want to focus attention on how power/knowledge presupposes a relationship with an other who is "an acting subject" and who, therefore, as we will see below, is a subject with potentially insurrectional knowledge.[18] One never speaks simply of power but power relations. Hence, according to this theory, the oppressed person is also always an agent to some extent, and the oppressor is not the sole possessor of power.

A critique that white feminist liberation theologians, womanist theologians, and others might raise is this: emphasizing the notion of an oppressed subject who acts will lead us politically astray, given the extent of the unjust structures that oppress whole communities of women, people of color, the poor, and so on. Ruether speaks of the "universal cultural structure" of sexism that posits female nature as inferior to male nature, and Williams speaks of how the "American national conscience is thoroughly saturated with the idea of . . . *white racial narcissism*."[19] They are correct to indicate the repressive intensity and insidious pervasiveness of the societal and institutional mechanisms of sexism and racism. Neither theologian, however, would want to imply that these oppressions constitute a totalizing monopoly crushing all forms of resistance, since both Ruether and Williams point to a history of resistance to racism, sexism, and classism. Here, Foucault's genealogical approach to history is helpful in accounting for how structural oppression can be seen as pervasive yet nonmonolithic and nontotalizing.

"Genealogy" is Foucault's term for the type of analysis of history that traces power from its localized and "infinitesimal mechanisms." No predominant trajectory of the movement of power or its centralization is presupposed; indeed, what is uncovered is a complex and "unstable assemblage of faults, fissures and heterogenous layers" of historical events where power relations are in evidence. Genealogical investigation is oriented to uncovering not only an "endlessly repeated play of dominations" but also the breakthrough of resistant power/knowledge.[20] Genealogy unmasks: (1) how putatively monolithic power structures are disseminated in local social and institutional networks (some feminists call this a microlevel analysis of power, helpful for analyzing complex, context-dependent social/legal problems like flirting versus sexual harassment); and (2) how broad-ranging cultural meanings are inscribed on psyches and bodies to create macrolevel power/knowledge regimes, which are then used to label whole groups of subjects as, for example, delinquents, insane, and sexual deviants.[21] From this genealogical perspective, what liberation theologians call social or structural sin could be analyzed for how those structures of domination subjugate on micro and macrolevels. Furthermore, because this theory also exposes how power circulates (nearly) everywhere, it would not thereby essentialize women as victims of these various subjugating "isms." Quite the contrary. Genealogy's interest in subjugated knowledges can open up possibilities for perceiving the disruptive emergence of women's liminal identities and transgressive practices.[22]

This poststructuralist appeal to the circulation of power, however, must be held accountable to the realities of unremitting structural oppression. Although some, or even many, oppressed individuals can be seen as positively accessing subject-forming power, nevertheless, the overall disciplinary effects of certain power/knowledge mechanisms on whole communities of people require the theologian to affirm that an advocacy or standpoint invocation of the labels of "oppressor" and "oppressed" are often rhetorically appropriate because they are politically necessary. Resources for addressing this issue can be found in the work of Gayatri Chakravorty Spivak, a multidisciplinary feminist scholar and translator of Jacques Derrida, who brings the postcolonial term "subaltern" into critical interaction with postmodern thought. Subalterneity (defined as designating "nonelite or subordinate social groups") is a notion Spivak derives from her interaction with the Subaltern Studies Group, a collective of contemporary historians from her native India who are committed to retrieving the suppressed history of peasant resistance in colonial India. On the one hand, she reads the work of these politically engaged historians "against the grain" by deconstructing the peasant subject in order to see more discursive complexity than what is suggested in these historians' claims about a unified insurrectional consciousness and revolutionary solidarity.[23] On the other hand, Spivak resists a complete deconstructionist erasure of the revolutionary subject and retains the *"figuration* of the peasant or subaltern consciousness" as a kind of "theoretical fiction to entitle" an emancipatory reading of Indian colonial history.[24] Spivak describes this figuration of the subaltern as "a strategic use of positivist essentialism in a scrupulously visible political interest." Strategic essentialization, in other words, allows for the "insistence upon the subaltern as the subject of history" but also clarifies that this is not a strictly standpoint epistemological or identity politics claim.[25] Spivak uses postmodern and postcolonial theories together so that the revolutionary Indian peasant is posited as a politically strategic trope in relation to the poststructurally understood constructed nature of the political agent. I would argue that something like the notion of strategic essentialization is needed in addition to poststructuralism for the task of theorizing oppressed women's selfhood and agency. Hence, in specific situations, appealing to an oppressed standpoint is necessary when oppression creates subaltern subjects for whom the circulation of power has been effectively cut off.[26]

Spivak provides a category that affirms what is strategically essential for womanists to claim about the ongoing and debilitating oppressions suffered by whole communities of African American women, men, and children. Williams's term demonarchy can be interpreted (as Spivak does with the rhetoric of the Subaltern Studies group) as "an interventionist strategy" on the part of the womanist theorist who reads back into history the presence of a generalized hegemonic force (demonarchy) that provokes a collective consciousness of resistance among a particular oppressed group (African American women). This is not a luxury according to Spivak: "the unified consciousness of the subaltern must inhabit the strategy of...historians."[27] To say it is a political strategy is not to eclipse the reality of oppression; it is to acknowledge, as Williams and other womanists in fact do in their historical and sociological analyses, that demonarchy is not one thing but a widely dispersed and historically changing network of white racist mechanisms ranging from enslavement to exploitation of wage-labor to racist eugenics, and more.

The category of strategic essentialization can also be used to see feminist appeals to women's experience in a new light. Focusing on an example from chapter 2, Cheryl Sanders's allegorical understanding of Hagar's enslavement under Sarah can be seen as an inteventionist hermeneutical strategy. When Sanders's interpretation is recast as a strategic essentialization, it allows for the emergence of a strong womanist standpoint meant to bolster African American women's struggle to survive in today's racist society. As we have seen, womanist and other scholars have strongly argued against (and rightly so) any interpretation of the story that might explain away Sarah's mistreatment of Hagar or ignore the power imbalances between them. The postcolonial notion of strategic essentialization allows the theologian to highlight differences in the material effects of the oppressions women suffer. When Sanders names Sarah's behavior as sinful oppression, using the story allegorically to draw connections to "white slave mistresses who abused their female slaves" in American history and to hold up Hagar today as "an inspiration to black mothers living in a society that would deny them access to power and material provisions for their children," we can name strategic essentialization at work.[28] By essentializing the status of Hagar rhetorically as more victimized than victimizer, one can make ethical judgments about Sarah's actions so that the gravity of Sarah's participation in the structural oppression of Hagar comes clearly to the fore. Yet, by seeing Hagar's essentialized victim status as provisional and strategic, one can still affirm Hagar's performative agency and hence her need to combat passivity and take responsibility for her own relationship to God.[29] If Hagar's allegorical positionality as oppressed black slave woman were to be seized upon as a definitive identity politics, that would perpetuate a statically essentialized view, which would in the long run be unproductive. However, in order to draw ethical distinctions between the actions of individuals with differing positions of power, the feminist theologian may be obliged to freeze-frame women's identity performances, so to speak, in a strategically and provisionally essentializing way in order to name the sin and structural oppression for a specific ethico-political purpose. In a situation of both injustice and moral ambiguity such as that depicted in the Sarah and Hagar story, this approach to conceptualizing sin (both personal and social) seems a particularly apt way of naming sin and assessing moral accountability, while avoiding overly essentialized victim or victimizer roles.

Spivak's strategically essentialized notion of subaltern consciousness is analogous to Ada María Isasi-Díaz's generative notion of Latina women's conscientization (discussed in chapter 2). Spivak's method of situating a particular revolutionary standpoint within a broader understanding of how particular historical subjects are socially and discursively constructed could be effectively used by Isasi-Díaz to situate *mujerista* generative themes within the context of the social and discursive construction of Hispanic women's experience. Moreover, any essentializing of Latina women's standpoint, which Isasi-Díaz needs to do to some extent in order to construct generative themes, would be linked to a specific historical resistance activities related to Latina women's oppression, making the essentialization a strategic one.

Strategic essentialization in *mujerista* (or any other marginalized) theology cannot be transferred to white feminist theology without important provisoes attached. After Spivak coined it, the term "strategic essentialization" circulated widely in postcolonial and Western feminist circles. In subsequent years, however, she considered abandoning strategic essentialization because of the way the term has been used, especially by white first-world feminists looking for ways to bring back together the sisterhood that they perceived identity politics had rent asunder. (Of course, many feminists of color would insist that the liberal notion of sisterhood always was a white feminist myth.) Spivak notes the disturbing tendency in white feminism to essentialize without a concrete political strategy cognizant of difference. She mentions, for example, how first-world white feminists were appropriating experiences of women from the two-thirds-world, creating versions of their experiences that "become more real than the original culture."[30] That is, first-world white feminists tend to produce an essentialized identity of oppressed two-thirds-world women (with which they then try to link to their own oppression) that is disconnected from the political context in which that identity served a particular strategic, possibly revolutionary function. This kind of nonstrategic essentialization becomes a romantic appropriation and recolonization of the other. Because of these tendencies, any feminist theology today would need to insist on very specified strategic essentializations—for example, essentializing done by feminists of color in the context of the concrete political interests of their subjugated group or subgroup. Such essentializations would have to be provisional and politically well defined so that their use would not lead to a kind of romantic recolonization on the part of white, first-world feminists.

II. Disciplinary Discourses and Technologies of Care:
The Cross and the Maleness of Jesus

Thus far I have proposed a poststructuralist approach to the notion of power in relation to widespread oppressive systems such as racism and sexism as a way of deconstructing restrictive dualisms of oppressor versus oppressed. I have also proposed a postcolonial perspective on how oppressed communities claim essentialized identities in a politically strategic way. Now we turn to the situation of oppressive power within Christianity. What do we do when Christian symbols function oppressively? Doctrinal and ecclesial reforms have always been vigorously pursued by feminist theologians; however, it is to be expected that—feminist theological reformist hopes notwithstanding—not all oppressive aspects of Christian faith symbols may be able to be reformed or excised. Two very thorny issues for feminist theology have been the cross (or atonement theory) and the maleness of Jesus as savior. Some post-Christian feminists might argue that any christology at all is deeply phallocentric and necrophilic, and they shake their heads at women's willingness to continue to try to rework such symbols. Christian feminist theologians usually criticize post-Christian feminist critiques as undervaluing the reforming potential inherent in the tradition. Despite their disagreements, these Christian and post-Christian feminists share the same assumption: unless the symbol can be understood and experienced as gyno-friendly, it has no place in a feminist worldview. Basically, this is a very either/or approach: if the religious symbol does not empower, it is oppressive; if it is oppressive, women must change or reject it. I will argue that an either/or approach to the cross and Jesus' maleness assumes a too restrictive view of the power exercised by those symbols. I will argue for understanding the power of those Christian symbols in terms of a disciplinary discourse that need not exclude the possibility of also functioning as a technology of care—a Foucauldian notion that will receive extensive comment below.

Understanding the Cross as Discipline and Empowerment

The more vocal majority feminist theological opinion asserts that the cross traditionally interpreted (especially through doctrines of the atonement) is oppressive and disempowering for women. The minority opinion tries to retrieve positively the notion of sacrifice (as exemplified in Jesus' death) for women's experience. I will argue that both groups rely on problematic views of power—the former has a too negatively caricatured notion of disciplinary power and the latter retains the power of the cross but only at the cost of downplaying the ambiguous or outright terrifying aspects of cross symbolism.

Many white feminist theological writings exhibit a deep concern about the symbolism of the cross as the locus of salvation: Joanne Brown and Rebecca Parker argue that the notion of a divine Father sending his Son to suffer and die on a cross is an image of "divine child abuse" and promotes "an abusive theology that glorifies suffering"; Carter Heyward concurs that appeals to a salvific cross sacralize violence; Darby Ray suggests that some atonement theories amount to a kind of deification of unilateral power.[31] Asian American theologian Rita Nakashima Brock argues that the maleness of a sacrificial Christ hero infantilizes women, making them dependent on a (male) hero to save them from, ironically, a brokenheartedness resulting from the physical, psychic, emotional abusiveness of the patriarchal family structure.[32] Delores Williams sets atonement theories in the context of the oppression of black women in America—in particular the ways in which enslaved black women were forced to act as sexual surrogates and the ways in which they continue to sacrifice themselves in a culture that devalues their race and gender. She rejects classic atonement theories on the grounds that the symbolism of Jesus' sacrificial and substitutionary death on the cross provides dangerous theological justification for black women's surrogacy.[33]

Many feminist theologians adamantly reject any doctrinal formulations that propose the cross as an atoning sacrifice where someone died on behalf of sinners in order to effect their salvation. They reject the violent imagery of the cross as well as the notion that redemption is transacted for the individual sinner who remains, for all intents and purposes, passive in the process. To the extent that the cross is acknowledged as a powerful Christian symbol, it is viewed as a terrifying sign of how the righteous are often persecuted by forces of injustice. The cross is invoked primarily as a protest against injustice; it in no way is interpreted as a vehicle for sacrificial or substitutionary redemption conferred on the otherwise passive and infantilized sinner by a God-Man savior.

Only a few feminist theologians argue for a positive function of the symbolism of the cross as sacrificial—and even then it is often a very selective retrieval. Mary Grey suggests that the stories of female martyrs in the early church could and should be interpreted within a paradigm of sacrificial redemption.[34] She is cognizant of feminist critiques of sacrificial and substitutionary atonement language and in no way wants to promote women's self-sacrifice. Hence, after a brief discussion of how the cross might be read positively, she takes the more common feminist position on Jesus, arguing that his death points back to "his life values"—namely, "the dynamic of mutuality in relation."[35] Ultimately, Grey promotes a christology where the cross is tragic not redemptive.

Womanist theologian JoAnne Terrell goes further, arguing that the symbol of Jesus' death on the cross, however much we recoil from its bloody violence and surrogacy implications, is an important symbol to retain. She also cites the example of church martyrs, but her primary argument is more current and personal. Terrell's viewpoint grows out of her attempt to do theology that is accountable to the experience of African American women, such as her mother, who was a victim of violence. Her mother stayed in a situation of domestic abuse in an attempt to shield her children and was subsequently killed by her partner. Terrell describes her mother's death in the same way as she describes Jesus' death on the cross and the deaths of the early church martyrs: "the surrender or destruction of something prized or desirable for the sake of something considered as having a higher or more pressing claim."[36] She is not glorifying the fact that some African American women have limited life choices so that the only choice some women can envision turns out to be a lethally self-sacrificial one. Terrell is aware of other feminists' concerns about symbols of sacrifice and blood atonement. She is in specific dialogue with Williams on surrogacy issues for African American women. However, she insists that crucifixion imagery should not be abandoned altogether. In an effort not to depict Jesus' sacrificial death as a surrogacy model for women (especially black women) to follow, she argues four points: (1) atonement happened uniquely *"once for all"* in Jesus' death (hence no one should be asked to copy that kind of self-sacrifice); (2) his sacrifice was voluntary (whereas her mother was forced into a position of self-sacrifice); (3) God does not relish blood sacrifice (Jesus' or anyone else's); and (4) the meaning of the cross can only be understood in light of the incarnation—"there is a divine-human dynamic in the story" (which makes it unique). Because God is present uniquely on the cross, "the crucifix is a supreme reminder of God's *with-us-ness*." Redemption is an effect of divine solidarity in suffering and empowerment through resurrection.

Terrell argues that despite all the problems of violence and surrogacy, there is "power in the blood" of Jesus in the form of redemptive "release from... self-alienation and social alienation."[37] Not only is this, to Terrell's mind, the theologically correct position to take, but it honors the moral and spiritual significance of African American women's self-sacrifices—which, in some ways, do mirror the kind of sacrifice Jesus made.

I agree with the theological intuitions behind Terrell's reappropriation of the tradition in light of particular African American women's experiences. Terrell acknowledges that the cross, for all its problematic surrogacy symbolism, functions to form agency—even if in very ambiguous ways. This presents a dilemma. How can the cross both oppress and save? Terrell responds to this dilemma by deemphasizing the cross's negative aspects and reemphasizing how the cross can be refigured as, at its core, antithetical to the type of surrogacy that oppresses African American women. In other words, she insists that the cross, correctly understood, is a positive form of power. I am arguing for a different approach to the power of Christian symbols. I suggest viewing the cross poststructurally, especially in terms of Foucault's notion of technologies for the care of the self because this theoretical approach provides a lens that is able to capture the ambiguity—and even the oppressiveness—of Christian symbols, like the cross, while still recognizing their empowering function.

Not all postmodern theorists would agree with me that Foucault's theories provide a helpful way to retrieve cross symbolism. Postmodern biblical interpreters (mostly white) have emphasized the negative disciplinary force of the cross read poststructurally. Deborah Krause exegetes the garden of Gethsemane scene as an unveiling of the "overwhelming will of the phallic Father." According to Krause, this text functions as a kind of disciplining power/ knowledge that polices the minds and bodies of the disciples by its account of how the will of their teacher (Jesus) is subsumed into that of the Father. It is a terrifying "curriculum" for students to witness their teacher "castrated."[38] Stephen Moore depicts an equally disturbing picture when he situates the cross against the backdrop of Foucault's description in *Discipline and Punish* of a man executed in 1757 France by being burned with sulfur and then having his body drawn and quartered. Moore notes how executions such as this followed a logic not of retribution or reform but of restoration of the "'power and integrity of the [king's] law'" by means of "'the ritual of atrocity.'"[39] Moore shares liberal theology's embarrassment over the violence of sacrificial atonement metaphors in the New Testament but worries about the tendency of other liberal exegetes (like Rudolph Bultmann) to excise the "savage" (read: Jewish) elements of propitiatory sacrifice from the New Testament text. In

addition Moore argues that a liberal, demythologizing reading of the crucifixion obscures the power dynamics in the text whereby believers are meant to
be disciplined by a symbolism of torture. "'Do you not know that all of us who
have been baptized into Christ Jesus were baptized into his death?' (Rom. 6:3).
Paul refuses to separate torture from reform."[40] A Foucauldian approach,
Moore insists, lays bare how such biblical discourse is meant to produce docile
Christian bodies—and has for centuries done so effectively. Since forms of
power are most dangerous when one does not detect their mechanisms for
coercion, Moore makes the case for shining a bright poststructuralist light
on crucifixion language in the New Testament in order to expose how the cross
is a "spectacle of atrocity inseparable . . . from the spectacle of docility, 'the quiet
game of the well behaved.'"[41]

Krause's and Moore's Foucauldian reading of the discourse of atonement
and the spectacle of the passion would seem to reinforce why so many feminist
theologians reject the cross as a dangerous symbol. Haven't women's bodies
been policed by misogynous religion for too long? Why retrieve a symbol
system that could arguably be called torture? My poststructuralist answer
comes in the form of a counterquestion: can the Christian ever really leave it?
The point poststructuralism tries to make is that there is no stepping outside
of the cultural discourses that form us. There is no place outside of language
where we can start over with a clean slate, so to speak. The reason why nonpoststructuralist thinkers advocate doing so is that they are trying to resist or
overturn oppressive cultural and political systems and empower people to
liberate themselves and develop new linguistic and cultural patterns. I believe
that this view of power is unhelpful because it suggests that I will never be
empowered unless I reject everything about my oppressor and access a different, "good" form of power. I have been arguing for a less dualistic viewpoint:
power is disciplinary and productive. Agents are constructed in the process of
negotiating with disciplinary power/knowledges. The mechanisms of policing
discourses may squelch certain emancipatory practices, but they also contribute to forming agents who can create alternative knowledges and practices,
even insurrectional ones—though never without some ambiguity.

Poststructuralists like Moore focus on the construction of docile bodies
in Foucault's writings on prisons. However, we get a different perspective
when we look at Foucault's later writings on technologies for the care of the
self where he explored the discursive bases for ethics and practices of piety.
Focusing on ascetical practices of the ancient Greco-Roman world and medieval monastic Christianity, Foucault studied those "technologies of the self
which permit individuals to effect . . . a certain number of operations on their

own bodies and souls, thoughts, conduct and way of being, so as to transform themselves [into]...a certain state of happiness, purity, wisdom, perfection."[42] Whether one is talking about Stoics or early church monks, self-disciplining practices are part of a technology of moral, bodily, and spiritual improvement—not just docility. When one looks at what Christian ascetics did over the years, it is not something that most people of the day, and certainly not people now, could completely endorse as religiously warranted and healthy. Yet these practices created discourses that have formed generations of Christians to see themselves as agents of their piety, responsible for their innermost thoughts and impulses and accountable to God and their neighbor, and as participants in a larger web or body called "church." The rich Christian tradition of spiritual confession and religious autobiography from Augustine to Jarena Lee is in part linked to self-disciplining discourses such as those of redemption and atonement.

Daniel Bell offers one way of viewing Christian doctrine and practice as a technology for the care of the self.[43] My proposal parallels some of his views, but I carefully distinguish my use of Foucault from his on several points that are pertinent for the feminist concerns I have addressed here. Bell describes Foucault's recent work on "governmentality" (his theory of how people in the modern state are formed, disciplined, subjugated, and constituted as subjects by governmental and nongovernmental power networks). Foucault explains that the modern state is not just a set of mechanisms for totalitarian rule but also exercises "pastoral power," a heritage of the influence of Christianity on the rise of the Western modern state. Taking his lead from Foucault, Bell argues for a return to this religious source. He argues for the positive social impact (in relation to the ills of, e.g., capitalism) of seeing the church as a place for implementing pastoral technologies that can reorient individuals' disordered desires toward God. His views emerge out of a debate with classic atonement theories. In contrast to Anselmic interpretations of Christ's sacrificial death making satisfaction in light of God's requirements of justice, Bell argues that the "atonement is identified not with a propitiatory sacrifice in the name of justice, but with the self-giving of the Son to the Father as an act of recapitulation that provides humanity with a positive means of return to its Creator." Namely, the sinner finds in Christ's death on the cross "the gift of love as obedience and praise to the Father" who has graciously forgiven the sinner.[44] The cross, thus interpreted, can become a disciplinary discourse by which old desires (e.g., desires for acquisition that systems like capitalism exploit) can be healed and reoriented toward a spirituality of gratitude to God and an ethic of forgiveness toward those who have done us wrong.

There are a number of questions I would want to raise in relation to Bell's critique of liberation theological views on spirituality and ethics,[45] but I will focus on his application of Foucault. Bell begins with Foucault's paradigm of the pastoral technologies of care of the self; however he ends up in a therapeutic paradigm. The predominant metaphor Bell uses is healing. Disordered desires are healed by means of the correct understanding of Christ's death on the cross. In being forgiven by God in this way, one is enabled (healed) to forgive others. Bell has effectively and conveniently abandoned the disciplinary aspect of the cross as a policing power/knowledge. According to Bell, the cross does not really *discipline* one's desires, it heals them therapeutically so that one's desire is now for God. I agree that a power/knowledge discourse could produce therapeutically oriented effects; nonetheless, I object to Bell's completely therapeutic move that seems to ignore the fact that the cross does also function in a disciplinary (and hence repressive) fashion. Bell drops the disciplinary metaphors because he wants to present the cross event as only an unambiguously positive symbol in the believer's life. For Bell, the cross seen as repressively disciplinary is simply a wrong-headed interpretation of the atonement.

I would argue that the cross is a much more ambiguous event for the Christian community. The historical tradition's multiple and often conflicting metaphors for and theories about Christ's death on the cross seem to suggest, at the very least, a kind of theological undecidedness regarding the meaning of the cross. If the cross is ambiguous, then interpreting it as therapy is too simplistic. The claim that the cross heals is one kind of Christian discourse that is meant to discipline the believer by creating in her a self-awareness of her sin-sickness and a desire to be healed. This church discourse may be extremely effective and appropriate in certain pastoral contexts. However, one must be mindful that while the cross may produce desires, it also polices. It can empower but it can also render docile. This poststructuralist approach to the power-formations of the atonement seems to ring more true to the experiences of Christians over the millennia. Moreover, this approach allows me to respond to the concerns that feminist critics of cross symbolism and atonement theories have voiced.

It is true that the imagery of sacrifice on a cross can be psychologically destructive for some individuals or whole communities affected by an unjust use of power and violent abuse. When the cross is invoked in such a way that it renders victims docile in the face of abuse and oppression, that discursive practice should be classified as domination that annihilates agency, not power/knowledge. Telling battered women to take up their cross and remain in abusive situations or telling patriarchally brokenhearted women to rest their burdens on a male hero savior does not rise to the level of the production of power/knowledge in discursively constituted agents. Disciplinary power/

knowledge, on the other hand, is that which constructs agency in part by the formation of desires to comply with that discourse. I have in mind the pleasures that are produced, for example, when one participates in singing "O Sacred Head Now Wounded" at a Good Friday candlelight service. This hymn can be said to normalize listeners with a discourse of Christian guilt as well as to elicit pleasures of a corporate experience of spiritual regeneration and, quite frankly, beautiful hymnody. Terrell also points out the combination of repulsion and fascination evoked by various iconographies of the cross.[46] A poststructuralist approach to the symbolism of the cross can acknowledge its real repressive effects without precluding the possibility that redemption can still occur in ways that are empowering for the very subjects who are negotiating and even complying pleasurably with troubling atonement discourses or crucifixion imagery.

The advantage of approaching the cross in this way is that the feminist theologian can acknowledge how Christian selfhood is constituted by this symbol's sometimes pleasurable technologies—without having exegetically or theologically to reformulate the cross by fixing its meaning. Bell sees the cross positively by fixing its meaning as therapy. Feminists who take a liberation theological approach to the cross fix its meaning negatively as a kind of protest sign—a symbol of how righteous prophets, such as Jesus, are often persecuted or killed. In this way, the cross is retained within a Christian feminist canon of symbols only insofar as it is read as a protest against injustice. My approach sees the cross as a much more open-ended, potential religious technology of care. In answer to Bell, I would argue that exposing the crucifixion's repressive aspects does not mean that the cross may not also produce some subjects who will be therapeutically healed. Or, in answer to liberationist feminists, acknowledging the repressiveness of the cross does not mean that many women cooperating with its discourse will thereby be stripped of all agency and rendered unable also to resist the destructive aspects of its policing. I would argue that it is better to acknowledge and name the sometimes oppressive disciplinary nature of the cross in order to make space for experiences of pleasure, technologies of care of the self, and insurrectional resistances that can arise in relation to its oppressive power. Terrell is somewhere between liberationist feminists' and Bell's approaches. On the one hand, she points to the surrogacy implications of the cross and affirms womanist critiques of atonement theory. On the other hand, she argues that Jesus was a unique, divine, and willing surrogate; hence, the cross retains a positive meaning for women today, when read correctly. In holding on to the negative and positive meanings of the cross, the notion of power is left unclear. My poststructuralist approach to power offers an analysis of how a Christian symbol can function negatively and positively by viewing that symbol as a discursive technology that both polices and constitutes subjects who can apply that disciplinary symbol to themselves in ways that make possible an experience of transformation and spiritual growth.

Even if feminist readers find this theoretical perspective on the cross to be fruitful, it may be that the symbol of a male savior does not seem amenable to this approach. How could it be useful for women to constitute their subjecthood via a discourse of a divine salvific God-Man? In the following section I will address this very pertinent feminist question about Jesus' sex—a question I will complicate in light of gay and queer theological voices on this issue.

The Maleness of Jesus: Beyond the Either/Or of the Androcentric or the Erotic Body

A central concern voiced by first-wave white feminist theologians was the maleness of Jesus. Ruether formulated this concern in the form of a provocative question: "Can a male Savior save women?"[47] Her answer to this rhetorical question was no, and she proceeded to reconstruct redemption in ways that would intentionally decenter Jesus' maleness. For Ruether, Jesus is representative of redeemed humanity. His prophetic message and praxis of liberation for the poor and oppressed exemplify what is redemptive for women and men today—that is, a way of living that reverses sexist, classist, racist and other hierarchies and ushers in a new world order of equity among people and ecological well being. His sex, ethnicity, geographical location, and so on are incidental to his message. Many other feminist theologians offer similar descriptions of how Jesus, as depicted in the gospel stories, modeled a kind of liberating, survival, or healing praxis. Williams emphasizes how Jesus' wilderness experience and ministerial healing speak to African American women's historical struggles in a kind of wilderness of slavery, economic oppression, the degradation of their bodies in white racist society, and sexism in the African American church. Jesus' maleness was not a necessary component of his ministry. The experience of survival in the wilderness and the call to ministry are possibilities for anyone, including and perhaps even especially African American women of faith who, like Hagar, have called on God as they struggled for survival in many wildernesses in American history.[48] Darby Ray emphasizes how Jesus' life of nonviolent resistance to injustice, which continued even in his death, is exemplary for the church today. Jesus' sex is incidental to how "the righteousness of his cause" is revealed in "the moral persuasiveness of his praxis."[49] A number of feminist theologians describe redemption as entailing a particular kind of deep psychic, emotional, and social mode of being, variously described as relationality (Grey), mutuality (Heyward), and erotic power (Brock).[50] The maleness of Jesus is in no way decisive for his effectiveness in modeling this mode of being. In fact, the patriarchal or ethnocentric bias he exhibited in some encounters with women demonstrates that Jesus achieved healing relationality almost in spite of his maleness.[51] Many feminist theologians have explored non-male symbolic depictions of Christ. Some feminists invoke the image of "Christa" (referencing a sculpture by Edwina Sandys of a woman on the cross).[52] Jacquelyn Grant decenters Jesus' traditionally Eurocentric whiteness and explores the notion of Christ as a black woman.[53]

All the above-mentioned theologians take a representative approach to christology. Seeing the male historical person of Jesus as only representative of God's redemptive message renders his maleness incidental. What is important is not the sex of Jesus but what he said and did, which can be followed, replicated, and even surpassed today by Christians (and perhaps even other spiritually exemplary individuals). For this type of christology, feminist theologians usually take on the task of arguing for, based on a reading of the gospels, a particular kind of liberatory or healing praxis, which can be translated into a redemptive message for contemporary women. A representative approach to Jesus circumvents the imposition of a sexist symbol on women by accessing the power of gender-neutral or gynocentric symbols of salvation. Here we see a stark dualism between the oppressive power of the male savior symbol and the positive power of alternative feminist symbols of redemption.

The first christologies proposed by explicitly gay (white) theologians also tended to have a representative, liberationist approach to the issue of how Jesus saves, locating redemption in Jesus' practices of compassion, justice, and openness to socially marginalized people. In an early work, Robert Goss echoes feminist liberation theology when he argues that "it is not Jesus' maleness that made him the Christ. It is his *basileia* practice of solidarity with the oppressed...that made Jesus the Christ."[54] Out of deference to feminist critiques of sexism, Goss wants to decenter Jesus' masculinity but not in ways that would obscure issues of embodiment and sexuality. Gay theologies depart from the demasculinizing tendencies of feminist interpretations of Jesus in order to explore the sexual component of the erotic relationality of Jesus' redemptive practice and to argue that the desexualization of Jesus in the Christian tradition is not life affirming. This general tendency in gay theology can be seen in Goss's writings. Goss conducts a genealogical analysis of Christian history, tracing the constructed nature of Jesus' asexuality and arguing that as christology was "Hellenized, ontologized, spiritualized, depoliticized, and ecclesialized...the human person, Jesus, was neutered [and] his sexuality diminished into celibate asexuality."[55] Goss attempts to recover the fully sexual male humanity of Jesus and suppressed practices of homodevotion to him in church history and the present day.[56] Goss outlines a threefold project: "to deshame Jesus' inherent sexuality"; to recover the history of male erotic contemplation of Christ's body; and to address the stigma of anal intercourse in a gay men's sexual practices by contemplating the erotic spirituality of "the [penetrated] body of Christ in the bodies of other men."[57] There has been little response from the straight feminist community.

Marcella Althaus-Reid's queer approach departs from feminist liberationist christology in a different way. She argues that feminist reimaging of the Christ via female metaphors is not disruptive enough of the "heterosexual gaze." Her "indecent" approach to christology challenges feminist theology by pushing feminists to see beyond metaphors of female gendering of the Christ symbol—as, for example, Christa—to the necessity of a more thoroughgoing "obscene" christology. Indecent theology attempts to transgress all fixed gendered and sexed ways of thinking that cause people to be policed not only by compulsory monogamous, procreative heterosexuality but by anatomically impossible and sexually repressive symbols such as Christ born of a virgin. Althaus-Reid takes an ostensibly negative term such as "indecent" or "obscene" and makes it a badge of merit for theological method (akin to the way Mary Daly has retrieved negative labels for nonconformist women—such as hag, witch—and made them feminist badges of honor and empowerment). Naming something as indecent or obscene for Althaus-Reid means to render visible, via a scandalous or blasphemous rhetoric, the truly obscene thoughts and desires that are covered over with a veneer of decency. The Black Christ is an example of obscene African American christology "because it uncovered [obscene] racism under the guise of a [decent] white Jesus"; Christa (the female figure crucified) is likewise read by Althaus-Reid as obscene in the way it confronts and disrupts the oppressive "heterosexual gaze... still fixed on the shape of the breasts, the youth of the body and its sexual desirability."[58] This interpretation of Christa differs from that of the feminist theologians mentioned above for whom Christa is the evocative gynocentric icon opening up constructive theological reflection about female metaphors for Christ. For Althaus-Reid, that feminist reverence for Christa iconography does not go far enough to disrupt what she finds oppressive in dominant Christology— namely, the suppression of lust in Christian discourse generally and the specific theological exclusion of "invisible desires contravening the 'normative vision' of heterosexual difference." Althaus-Reid explores several indecent (and hence liberating) interpretations of Jesus as male: "Take for instance the claim that Jesus was "a 'friend of sinners and prostitutes.' Does this statement not imply that he shared his life with sinners and prostitutes? What sort of sinners:... sexual deviants?... Jesus must have had something of the sinner and the prostitute too within himself if he enjoyed their company."[59] Althaus-Reid is not romanticizing prostitution; she speaks extensively about how poor women's bodies are exploited sexually in the market economy of global capitalism. She is trying to point out the way in which Christian discourses group together people such as prostitutes, homosexuals, transvestites, and so on, labeling them as sinful in such a way that their economic and material needs are ignored and their sexual practices are called "indecent." The "sinner and the prostitute" become for Althaus-Reid a metonym of the sexually ostracized and economically exploited people with whom Jesus can be theorized as feeling at home.

Both Goss and Althaus-Reid retrieve Jesus' maleness by making his sexuality hospitable to the sexually marginalized. They do not situate their retrievals of a male Jesus in opposition to feminist concerns about androcentrism since they are deeply supportive of those concerns. An erotic, queer male Christ is assumed to be nonsexist. In order to evaluate this type of positive retrieval of Jesus' maleness, one needs to interrogate critically the primacy granted by queer theology to the notions of the erotic and lust, since no concept is innocent. Are Goss and Althaus-Reid giving the sexually erotic an overly inflated value? I agree with Kathleen Sands, who states in her appreciative critique of Althaus-Reid's book, that sex is a good, but it doesn't do everything. In fact it doesn't need to do anything good at all; it might be sufficient to situate the concept of sex as something that does no harm within an overall political feminist strategy of combating sex discrimination or homophobia.[60] Althaus-Reid has responded and agrees that an indecent theology that aims at affirming sexual desires should not be exclusively a theology of eros but should demand "less of sex and more of politics."[61] Althaus-Reid wants to "unveil the sexual ideology of systematic (even liberationist) theology"; part of this project is to show that sexual practices often have many meanings.[62] They may be about sexual desire but they may also be about politics and economics. Thus, in Latin America, indecent theology functions as a discourse of political resistance in light of right-wing totalitarian dictatorships, heteronormative liberation theologians, North American voyeuristic theologians writing about the Latin American poor, and sexual and economic exploitation that accompanies globalized capitalism. The degree to which Althaus-Reid continues to de-escalate the liberatory power she attributes to her notion of an erotic Jesus will determine the degree to which she avoids a dualistic view of power (where the liberatory power of the erotic is opposed to the oppressive power of the anti-erotic Christian tradition).

Gay and queer theological construals of Jesus' maleness and sexuality play an important role in exposing the desexualizing tendencies in feminist theological writing. They also explore how Jesus' sex and sexuality can be retrieved as positive symbols that are transgressive of repressively androcentric and heteronormative views of sex, gender, and desire. Whereas most (straight) feminist theologians attempt to avoid or downplay Jesus' maleness because of the patriarchally oppressive entailments of his male incarnation, gay and queer theologians turn to Jesus' male body as an affirmation of embodiment and, by implication, eroticism, pleasure, and a politics of justice.

Hence, we have a theological point of tension in current writings on Jesus' maleness. If one embraces Jesus as an embodied sexual, male being, it is difficult to escape the genitally aware identity that is central to gay men's homoerotic spiritualities. If one suppresses Jesus' maleness and diverts the theological gaze from his genitals to his nonsexually marked message and praxis, then one escapes the phallic Christ at the cost of a desexualized, even neutered Jesus. It would seem that the only way out of this conundrum is to accept the symbol of Jesus' male body as both oppressive and liberating, as dominating and empowering. Neither straight feminist theologies nor gay and queer theologies have found a way to theorize this. Foucault's theory of power is again instructive here, revealing that straight feminist theologies on the one hand, and gay and queer theologies on the other, are two sides of the same coin on the issue of Jesus' male body. Because these theologians have tended to promote the notion that only a liberating, positive construal of Jesus' maleness is helpful and appropriate, they inculcate a dualistic notion of the power of religious symbols—namely, only that which can be experienced as liberating is good power; all else is unjust, oppressive power. Since feminist theologians find Jesus' incarnational maleness to be an insuperable obstacle to women's spirituality and ministerial vocations, they reject giving it any important soteriological role; instead they redeem his maleness by making him an exemplary (though largely nonsexual) male prophet, liberator, and co-sufferer. Gay and queer theologies foreground Jesus' male body and his sexuality because not to do so, they assert, would be to remain theologically captive to the prejudice that sexual pleasure is somehow antithetical to divine incarnational presence and socio-political liberation.

When one looks at Jesus' maleness poststructurally, one sees a discourse that can both discipline and liberate. To the extent that it disciplines, it also produces knowledges and desires that constitute subjecthood. The notion of Jesus as the incarnate Son of the Father may be a discourse of domination for some women that leaves no room for gynocentric agency and pleasure. However, I would venture to say that for many women, the discourse of Jesus' maleness also produces forms of subjecthood and empowerment. How else can one account for the hugely rich discourses of, for example, medieval women mystics whose near erotic heterosexual adoration of Jesus' male body empowered them to do great feats of piety, transgress rigid social boundaries, and even challenge patriarchal church authority at the highest levels? This spirituality is not unambiguously gynocentric—despite some French feminist claims that medieval women mystics are examples of *jouissance* and women's agency.[63] Nevertheless, the example of medieval women's spirituality does testify that women's compliance with androcentric, phallocentric, heteronormative discourses of Jesus' maleness cannot be said only to reduce women to patriarchally oppressed victims.

If the maleness of Jesus cannot be said (poststructurally) only to discipline, neither can it be said only to elicit liberatory pleasure—despite the growing literature of homoerotic devotion to Jesus' body.[64] To the extent that Goss uses Foucauldian theory, his writings suggest this as well. Goss references Foucault to expose genealogically the orchestrated construction of Jesus by dominant theology as a celibate, asexual male. Goss makes the case for how new insurrectional (queer) knowledges about Christ and sexuality can emerge (the bi-Christ, the transvestite Christ, etc.).[65] However, Goss pulls back from a consistently poststructuralist perspective when he claims that queer imaginative reconstruals of Christ "break boundaries of compulsory heterosexual construction of Jesus the Christ" and "cut the Christ from the moorings of dominant, heterosexist and patriarchal theologies."[66] These comments seem to suggest that one can effectively step outside of, or free oneself from, the policing of dominant discourses in order to construct a new, queer christological imaginary (as Jantzen would say) independent from them. While I would dispute this perspective on poststructuralist grounds, Goss' comments do reflect the direction taken in some theology and philosophy of religion where scholars use Foucault's views to criticize much of the tradition and to advocate on behalf of sexually marginalized groups. I see the value in this approach; yet I am arguing for the advantages of an approach that holds open the possibility of using dominant discourses, such as those of Christianity, as technologies of care, even on issues of sexuality and desire. I believe my approach serves many feminist and queer theological interests in relation to the maleness of Jesus specifically and regarding negotiations with the Christian tradition generally. In order to make my case, we need to probe more deeply into Foucault's (not always easy to decipher) writings on sexuality, power, and liberation.

I contend that Foucault's writings, especially his later interests in the ethical dimensions of technologies of care of the self, are illuminating because of the way he came to greater clarity on the limits of talk about sex and sexuality in relation to power and liberation. White British scholar Jeremy Carrette, on the other hand, concludes that Foucault's writings as a whole can have only limited ongoing usefulness for theorizing on how to resist dominant forms of the policing of sexuality and sexual practices—what Foucault spoke of in earlier writings as "'fascism in the body.'"[67] Carrette argues that the late Foucault's attempts to combat such fascism via explorations of technologies of care of the self (particularly Christian confessional and ascetical practices) are problematic. Carrette claims that queer theory effectively takes up Foucault's anti-fascism baton by promoting notions of "polymorphously perverse" desire and a "diversity of truths" about sex and sexuality.[68] While this queer perspective may be one way of combating fascism of the body, it is problematic for the same reason that feminist views of structural sin are problematic: a too dualistic view of oppressive power (fascism of the body) versus liberating power (polymorphously perverse desire). I have been attempting in this chapter to show the drawbacks of this viewpoint. As I read him, Foucault points us in a different and less dualistic long-term direction on the issue of sex, liberation, and power.

Foucault argued that as a result of mechanisms as diverse as the traditional Christian confessional and the modern psychiatrist's couch, sexuality has been passed "through the endless mill of speech" and meticulously examined (theologically, medically, sociologically, etc.); every wayward sexual inclination or practice has been and can be catalogued and hence disciplined.[69] The emergence of so-called deviant sexualities is, in part, a result of the power relations of those policing mechanisms. That policing is a double-edged sword of both repression and pleasure—the pleasure of bringing one's deepest sexual longings to speech, even if the result is to have those longings pathologized or condemned as religiously aberrant. This is a genealogical point, not a prescriptive one. Foucault is not suggesting that one should seek out repressive power relations in order to maximize the pleasure of having one's sexual identity (or identities) exposed and named. His point is that, from an historical perspective, sexual identity is a power/knowledge that arises from the imposition of disciplinary discourses. The policing of sexuality by religious and medical specialists in the modern period especially has entailed the goal of finding the truth about one's desires and bringing them to speech. Thus, the construction of sexuality in the modernist West has been inextricably linked to the notion that "the discovery of one's true sex is the discovery of one's true self," ruled by the dominant discourse of normative heterosexuality.[70] Hence, an effective policing mechanism of heteronormativity was the linkage: true sex equals true self. Foucault was deeply and personally committed to challenging "deployments" of sexuality constrained by heteronormativity. However, he did not think that the agenda of liberating new sexualities and new desires could break the back of heteronormativity because that agenda would feed into the modernist policing tool of linking truths of the self with truths about one's sexual desires—hence his provocative statement that talk about "sex is boring."[71]

Foucault saw much more liberatory promise in investigating discourses of selfhood that do not attempt to discover truth about the self at all. That may be one reason for his interest in his later writings in ancient Christian ascetical and confessional practices, whose goal was not discovery of the true self but surveillance and transformation of the soul. The believer practiced technologies of renunciation of the *sinful* self not technologies of discovery of the *true* self, which (as the pastoral literature of the day insisted) is known only to God. The truth was that one could never really know the truth about one's self—that is, whether one's soul was in the grip of the devil or not. Hence, the pastor's task was not to discover the sinner's true self but to help the sinner keep the devil at bay: "For Christians the possibility that Satan can get inside your soul and give you thoughts you ... might interpret as coming from God, leads to uncertainty about what is going on inside your soul. You are unable to know what the real root of your desire is."[72] James Bernauer also interprets Foucault as insisting that for the early Christians, "the truths of the self were always precarious" because "[t]here could be no firm allegiance to a positive self, for there was no truth about the self which could not be utilized by the False One."[73] Policing of sex and desire played a large role, but there was no linkage between the truth of one's concupiscence and the true disposition of one's soul. Even the sense of victory over bodily desires could become a tool for the devil to instill the self-deceptive sin of pride.[74]

Foucault's study of Christian asceticism led him not only to the notion of technologies of care of the self but also to ethics. The two were interrelated in a way that is perhaps surprising to some of Foucault's readers. Foucault was interested late in his career with the notion of a practice of freedom based on an ethics of personal conformity to moral codes. He saw ethics as "a process in which the individual delimits that part of himself that will form the object of his moral practice ... [which] requires him to act upon himself, to monitor, test, improve and transform himself."[75] Foucault asks the rhetorical question: "How can one practice freedom? In the order of sexuality, is it obvious that in liberating one's desires one will know how to behave ethically in pleasurable relations with others?"[76] His implied answer is: not necessarily. Foucault was certainly not advocating for a set of laws to "intervene in our ... private life."[77] He was exploring, shortly before his death, the positive ethical value of a very ancient principle: the notion of a "*rapport à soi* [literally a relation to one's self or self-understanding] which I call ethics, and which determines how the individual is supposed to constitute himself as a moral subject of his own actions."[78] The freedom to explore multiple desires could be part of a practice of an ethical *rapport à soi*, but Foucault injected a strong note of skepticism or realism regarding this idea. Any new exercise of freedom, including sexual freedom, "opens up new relationships of power, which have to be controlled by [ethical] practices" appropriate to that form of liberty.[79]

Carrette argues that the queer pursuit of multiple desires must entail a critique of "the imperialist regime of theology." Christianity, in the name of orthodoxy, makes "claims for a single (orthodox) truth about salvation [that] anchors an ideological oppression of a single (heteronormative) sexuality."[80] In other words, Carrette believes that liberation from heteronormative sexuality is related to liberation from Christian orthodoxy. While I agree that the Christian tradition does function to police sexuality heteronormatively, I disagree that the tradition is as monolithic as Carrette portrays it. Moreover, if ethics is something Carrette values along with the multiplication of theological and bodily desires, the practice of an ethical *rapport à soi* becomes even more imperative. That type of *rapport à soi* only comes about in negotiation with (not in a putative release from) the cultural discourses (such those of the Christian tradition) that seem to permeate the mind and flesh of most Westerners with mechanisms of conformity and uniformity. I have only stated here that I think Carrette is mistaken to see the tradition (with its orthodox thrust) as simply antithetical to the queer project of complicating desires and identities (a project I affirm). In the following chapter, I will try to argue the case that one can negotiate with the tradition—even at its most orthodox, creedal core—in the mode of a technology of care that can potentially liberate multiple desires.

The question of how to interpret Foucault on sexuality and desire will probably remain an open one among scholars of poststructuralism.[81] However, I think a strong case can be made that if the theologian begins with a Foucauldian notion of subjecthood, Christian identity should be seen theologically as constituted in part via the church's disciplinary discourses (such as Jesus' maleness, his death on the cross), which will be to some extent repressive. Feminist theology has tended to respond to this repressiveness by arguing (based on an appeal to women's experience) that it is necessary to excise what is oppressive in Christian teaching. This feminist approach assumes that the believer can step outside of the oppressive discourse (that has in part constituted her subjectivity). I have argued that one can only ever negotiate with—not reject—the repressive technologies that have formed one as a subject. If discipline and punishment, however, were the end of the story, then we would have a system of domination not salvation (and indeed, critics of atonement theory come close to suggesting this). I am inviting feminist theologians to remain open to theorizing how even repressive Christian symbols can also become technologies for care of the self. The cross (meaning, the passion narrative, its long iconographical and liturgical legacy in the church, its role in theological formulas) works to police the believer's self-image and spirituality in ways that have often been repressive yet can also be productive of agency and spirituality, as Terrell so evocatively demonstrates. The male body of Jesus, traditionally and widely understood, renders many female (and queer) bodies docile. If, however, the believer can apply that disciplinary symbol (and others also) as part of her *rapport à soi*, then she can constitute her own moral, spiritual, and sexual agency in vigorous negotiation with the Christian tradition. This is not liberation, but it is a worthwhile project of constructing oneself as an ethical subject in relation to (what Carrette calls) Christian orthodoxy with, nevertheless, the possibility of insurrectional knowledges and multiple desires.

5

Negotiating with a Disciplinary Tradition

In the previous chapter, I argued for an approach to the disciplinary power of oppressive Christian doctrines and symbols whereby they could become technologies of care of the self for the believer. Images and doctrinal formulations that feminist theologians judge as patriarchal and misogynist do work to police the believer's self-image and spirituality in ways that may often be repressive; yet they, like most power/knowledge regimes, are also to some extent productive of new and potentially insurrectional subjugated knowledges. Policing discourses can be appropriated by the believer as a technology of care to constitute herself as a subject with spiritually enlivening performativity (to bring Butler's terminology back into play) and ethical responsibility towards others. For the average believer, this cooperation with the tradition happens in ad hoc and organic ways, with varying levels of self-reflection. For the feminist theologian, who as a result of her training most likely has a more fully developed critical grasp of the complex interlocking mechanisms and disciplinary force of the dominant tradition historically and in the present, negotiation with the tradition presents new challenges.[1] How can the contemporary feminist reformist theologian continue to remain engaged with the Christian tradition, whose texts, doctrines, institutional history, and even conservative evangelical demographics today may create roadblocks for the reforms she feels impelled to make in the name of women's experience? To use a Wesleyan metaphor, how can the heart of the feminist theologian be warmed by scripture and doctrines that are benevolently patriarchal at best and misogynist at worst in their disciplinary thrust? The Christian feminist theologian needs to find ways to negotiate with the classic textual sources of the tradition—for example, its classic creedal formulas and the New Testament text, which will be the two foci of this chapter. I will first argue that it is only through engaging the complex disciplinary dynamics of these textual sources that the feminist theologian (who may also be drawn to many other philosophical, artistic, cultural, and religious resources) has the possibility of rediscovering desire for the tradition itself. In the next part of this chapter, I will propose using a rule theory of doctrine to show that even the writings of feminists who are hostile to the Christian creedal tradition can be seen as maintaining an implicit regulative connection to it. Once this connection can be established, the door is open to envisioning not only productive negotiations among feminists who differ but also negotiations with the tradition's disciplinary creedal discourses.

I. Engaging the Nicene/Chalcedonian Doctrinal Tradition

The creeds of the Christian church are many and encompass the earliest confessional formulas of the New Testament (e.g., 1 Cor. 15:3–5), the Apostles' Creed, the creeds of Nicaea and Chalcedon, and later confessions, catechisms, and conciliar decrees (Heidelberg, Westminster, Trent, etc.). Feminist theologians from various communions critically engage different sets of creedal or confessional formulas (referencing christological, incarnational, and Trinitarian notions), many of which trace their origins authoritatively back to Nicaea and Chalcedon. However many feminist theologians find themselves in an uneasy and even outright hostile relationship with the creedal tradition.

Kelly Brown Douglas articulates from a womanist perspective what many feminists may feel when doing theology in the shadow of Nicaea and Chalcedon. She ponders the issue of christological doctrine specifically, asking: "Are womanists doing Christology?...No, if doing Christology means that the Nicene/Chalcedonian traditions must provide a norm...for what we say about Jesus as Christ."[2] Douglas admits to having been raised reciting the creeds but insists that they have not affected her theology and that of most other womanists:

> Born and raised an Episcopalian, I could perfectly recite the
> Nicene creed, but I did not know what that had to do with Jesus be-
> ing the Christ.... Though I no doubt have been influenced by

> its claims ... it does not ... have any normative significance as
> womanist theologians attempt to articulate Christ's meaning for
> the Black community.[3]

She testifies to the ecclesial influence of the creeds but denies that they have any normative role in womanist theology.

There is a sense among many feminists that the traditional doctrinal formulations for God, Christ, church, and so on are outdated and illegitimate from the perspective of contemporary women's concerns. Even those feminists fully committed to doing doctrinal theology admit that the church's Nicene/Chalcedonian formulations are "both sexist and idolatrous," perpetrating an "androcentric theological dualism."[4] Feminists have typically responded in one of three ways: (1) to reject the tradition entirely on the basis that Christianity at its core and feminism are incompatible; (2) to reinterpret the symbolic meaning or essence of the creeds, leaving behind the so-called husk of their masculinist formulaic language; or (3) to treat doctrinal subjects such as christology—without referencing, for example, the Nicene/Chalcedonian tradition explicitly as a warrant or norm. I believe all of these options represent losses of various kinds for Christian feminism.

Daphne Hampson exemplifies the first of the three feminist responses to Nicaea/Chalcedon. In answering the question of "whether feminism is compatible with Christianity," she zeroes in on christology as the sticking point. High christology, according to Hampson, implies adherence to the Chalcedonian formulation that Christ "was fully God and fully human, these natures existing in one person"—namely, the male Jesus. Since a male person becomes integral to the Godhead, Christianity is "logically biased against women" and contradicts her most basic definition of feminism as the "equality of women and men." Hence feminism is logically incompatible with Christianity. Christianity's identity has historically mostly been based on its creedal formulations, propositionally understood as rooted in the foundational revelation from God. From this perspective, if you change the content of the original creeds, you change the religion. Hampson is aware of low christological positions that "wish to speak of [Christ's] uniqueness in some other way than the classic two natures."[5] However, revisionary feminist low christologies (such as Rosemary Ruether's) that deemphasize Jesus' maleness, divinity, and uniqueness appear to Hampson to be not properly Christian.[6] Hence, she finds feminism and Christianity to be incompatible either because the androcentrism of its propositional creedal orthodoxy conflicts with core feminist values, or because the feminist-inspired reformulations of those classic dogmas no longer appear to her to fulfill even the minimal definition of Christian.

Rosemary Ruether represents the second feminist position listed above. She has responded to Hampson by arguing that Hampson's claim that Christianity is fundamentally and unchangeably patriarchal is based on a "notion of static past historical revelation." Ruether asserts that feminists are doing Christian theology as long as we "use scripture as foundational memories with which we enter into dialogue as a contemporary community . . . adding new experiences in sermonic commentary, in order to open up . . . lifegiving futures."[7] For Ruether, Christianity is bounded by the historically established past "memories" (scripture, creeds, rituals, etc.) but it must and does continue to change and expand its meaning. "A religious tradition remains vital so long as its revelatory pattern can be reproduced generation after generation." Christian doctrines are part of a hermeneutical circle: out of the original "breakthrough" religious experiences of the earliest Christians emerged individual and communal symbols which became codified (into scriptures, creeds, liturgies).[8] These normative symbols are not static but are in turn continually reinterpreted in light of new breakthrough experiences. Hence Ruether is able to bypass the christological formulations of Chalcedon by reinterpreting Christ of the gospel narratives as a paradigmatic prophetic symbol of "liberated humanity."[9] Contemporary women's experience of Jesus (based on a return to the gospel texts) funds on-going revelation; this in turn produces new feminist doctrinal expressions that appear to be, for all intents and purposes, independent of the creedal tradition.

The debate between Ruether and Hampson stalemates because each insists on incommensurable definitions of what Christianity is and what doctrine is. The question of the nature of doctrine must be set, in part, within the context of the well-known debates that have swirled around George Lindbeck's *The Nature of Doctrine*.[10] To use Lindbeck's categories, Hampson works with a propositionalist theory whereby doctrines "function as informative propositions or truth claims about objective realities." Ruether tends toward an experiential-expressive theory of doctrine, which "interprets doctrines as noninformational and nondiscursive symbols of inner feelings, attitudes, or existential orientations."[11] A third approach to doctrine is a regulative one, which sees doctrines not as propositional truth claims or symbolic expressions of religious experience but as formal rules for how correctly to speak about God and the things of God. Those rules (analogous to grammatical rules one must learn to speak a language correctly) are derived in part from the classic creeds such as Nicaea and Chalcedon. I suggest that this third approach affords the best theoretical orientation for promoting dialogue among feminists who differ theologically and for promoting fruitful feminist negotiation with some streams of the Christian tradition. Let me demonstrate by giving an example of a pair of creedal formulas viewed regulatively and then showing how those doctrinal rules are instantiated in the writings of two theologians (Delores Williams and JoAnne Terrell). We will first see how a regulative approach detects the normative role of Nicaea/Chalcedon in an otherwise very revisionary and low christological proposal. This allows us then to imagine how regulative aspects of creedal disciplinary discourses may be utilized as a feminist technology of care.

An example of a soteriological formula interpreted regulatively would be the following: (1) "the principle of maximal salvific dependence" which specifies that "one should ascribe the greatest degree of [the sinner's] dependence upon Christ that is consistent with a real role for persons"; and (2) "the principle of maximal salvific difference" which specifies that "one should affirm the greatest degree of difference...[before and after being saved by] Christ that is consistent with remaining a continuous person."[12] The first principle of maximal dependence shows the importance of holding in theological tension the notion that Christ alone can act salvifically on behalf of another with the notion that persons must be seen to have "roles to play" in the process. That is, Christ alone saves, but persons must be seen as intentional actors to some extent in order to give meaning to, for example, the apostle Paul's exhortations such as "present your bodies as a living sacrifice."[13] The second principle of maximal salvific difference shows the importance of holding in theological tension the notion that people can undergo profound spiritual transformations (to the point of feeling born again in Christ) with the notion that the born-again Christian is still materially the same person ("the old man must be linked to the new man" in a real way[14]). These can be seen as the rules animating and reflected in a diversity of church statements across confessional lines that might seem to be irreconcilable. The first rule of maximal salvific dependence has been differently affirmed in Roman Catholic and Protestant formulas. The Council of Trent posits an infused grace that enables the sinner to be transformed and cooperate with God's prevenient grace.[15] The Westminster Confession, on the other hand, speaks of humanity as being completely passive yet being graced to respond freely to God's effectual call.[16] Both creeds arguably adhere to the same formal regulative principle mentioned above that prevents an eclipse of either divine grace or human agency in talk of redemption (notwithstanding their divergent emphases and vocabularies, as Lindbeck would say).[17]

But is Kelly Douglas correct that some feminist theologians, especially perhaps womanists, are not interested in norming their christological talk by way of Nicaea and Chalcedon? As I discussed above, a third way feminists relate to the creedal tradition is to do theology with no normative reference to the creeds. I would argue that even if a theologian does not explicitly ref-erence the creeds normatively, one can (and should) still draw the grammatical connections. Let me give two examples from womanist theology. Delores Williams, although she has a low christology and claims that Chalcedon is not theologically normative for womanists, can be construed as negotiating regulatively—even if not overtly—with the classic creedal rules of faith.[18] By this I mean that she instantiates the two regulative principles outlined above—maximal salvific dependence and maximal salvific difference—albeit in a dis-tinctively contemporary and womanist key.

Williams believes that "the story of black Christian women's fortitude cannot be accurately told without Jesus, whom these women have historically regarded as their helpmate on their journey."[19] That is, African American women's survival depends on asserting and fostering the independent strength of black women to do for themselves, so to speak, and initiate their own liberation—yet always "only with God by her side."[20] This reflects the first rule stated above about salvific dependence. Williams ascribes the greatest degree of dependence upon God and Jesus that is consistent with affirming womanist agency, given the particularities of African American women's oppressions from slave times to the present. The second rule is reflected in Williams's comments on sin. Williams is critical of traditional teachings on sin that, along with white racist attitudes and practices, have inculcated destructive feelings of unworthiness in black women historically. Williams's hope is that all African American women will undergo liberation from the social sin of "defilement." She realizes, however, that the structures of black women's defilement are continuous in our culture and the impact of those structures on black women's bodies will not disappear completely even though black women do experience in Jesus "liberation from 'unworthiness' to a state of 'somebodiness.'"[21] Recall that the principle of maximal salvific difference is meant to show that while one becomes a new creation in Christ, one is still concretely living in the same body and must contend with the "old man." Williams simply brings a social sin perspective to this issue when she affirms that even when black women are transformed in Christ they must contend with the effects of ongoing institu-tional oppressions (i.e., the "old man" structurally and socially understood). An African American woman who has become "somebody" in Christ still must combat racist structures that attempt to reduce her to unworthiness. Williams thus shows how the second rule about change and continuity would be in-stantiated within the context of a discussion of the structural sin of the racist defilement of black women's bodies. To my (regulative) reading, her vocabu-lary is contemporary and womanist but the formal grammar is traditionally Christian.

Construing Williams's writings on redemption in terms of rule theory allows one to see how she stands within a particular grammatical stream of the creedal tradition and is, in effect, negotiating critically with (not just leaving behind) its regulative principles and vocabularies. If one took Hampson's (propositionalist) viewpoint, Williams's soteriology does not rise to the status of Christian theology because she does not reiterate even a low christological affirmation of Jesus' uniqueness, not to mention a two-natures high christology. Hampson might conclude that Williams is on her way down a feminist road away from Christianity. It might seem as if Ruether's experiential-expressivist hermeneutical circle makes ample room for a womanist "breakthrough" experience (Ruether's term) in dialogue with the tradition's foundational memory. This is a possible way of situating Williams within the Christian tradition. However, I see experiential expressivism as less a negotiation and more an attempt to live in parallel universes, so to speak. Contemporary expressions of divine-human meaningfulness are posited as upholding the religious essence of the creeds, but those contemporary symbols are only loosely connected to the language and logic of the creeds, if at all (though usually a biblical emphasis is maintained to some extent[22]). As Julie Hopkins states: if the resulting "spirituality is deep enough to embrace all aspects of life...then the theological controversies surrounding the nature of 'Christ' can respectfully be circumvented."[23]

While an experiential-expressive approach may have strong pastoral applications for women searching for a relevant feminist spirituality, it does not constitute enough of a negotiation with the tradition. This is not the same as saying that feminist experiential-expressivist theologians are not within the Christian tradition, as Hampson implies. I am not interested in setting boundary markers. My point has to do with finding the best means by which a disciplinary discourse (which the creedal tradition arguably is) can become a technology of care. As I have argued in chapter 3, one can only resist a power/ knowledge by engaging it to some extent; likewise, one can only appropriate the Christian creedal tradition as a technology of care to the degree that one has engaged it regulatively.[24]

How can a regulative use of the creedal tradition become a technology of care for feminists today? I want to answer that question in relation to Williams and Terrell (the latter's christology was developed in part in a critically appreciative debate with Williams). Comparing the regulative approaches of Williams and Terrell illustrates my proposal for how the Christian creedal tradition can become a technology of care for religious performativity today. As I noted in chapter 4, Terrell recognizes, in agreement with Williams, that traditional atonement formulations about how "Jesus Christ died 'for our sake'" have had the effect of "highlighting the surrogacy motif."[25] Terrell, however, insists that the notion of the sacrifice of Jesus, who is affirmed as incarnationally divine, has functioned importantly in African American spirituality[26] and continues to be important for womanist theology—despite the fact that the imagery of the cross does reinforce troubling themes of surrogacy and violence. Terrell, in other words, feels the full disciplinary impact of a bloody cross but is able to take that symbol and see not just violence but noncoercive and sacramental self-sacrifice that is meaningful in light of African American women's suffering.

The reason, I suggest, she is able to transmute such an arguably oppressive surrogacy symbol into a spiritually significant symbol is because, in part, she reads the tradition regulatively. Here we see an important similarity to and divergence from Williams. Not only does Terrell instantiate (like Williams) the two above mentioned formal regulative grammars of soteriology (salvific dependence and salvific difference[27]) but she also appropriates some of the creedal tradition's vocabulary (unlike Williams). For example, Williams categorically rejects any meaningfulness to the language of sacrifice and the imagery of a bloody cross. Terrell, on the other hand, wishes to appropriate, in a new context, the symbol of blood sacrifice. She argues that an incarnational perspective makes it possible to affirm "that there is something of God in the blood of the cross." When that imagery is combined with a reading of the Hebrew Bible showing how "Yahweh reveres and does not require blood," it is possible to see her mother's bloody death (and by extension all African American women's suffering) sacramentally: "Jesus' own life and *sacramental* example [affirms]...women's blood as sacred." Terrell's retrieval of the crucifixion symbol goes above and beyond her appropriation of formal soteriological grammars. That vocabulary of redemptive blood functions as a powerful technology of care that speaks to the reality of African American women's lives where tragic self-sacrificial choices sometimes are made with lethal consequences. Terrell mourns and protests but also wants to honor those tragic choices. The spiritual performativity fostered by her theology is not one of docility in the face of oppression and abuse but rather one of "moral and creative agency" to mourn, protest and honor black women's sacramental suffering.[28]

I am not arguing that Terrell, by virtue of her ability to retrieve both classic regulative grammars and vocabularies, creates a superior technology of care or a deeper spiritual performativity than Williams. Williams's call to follow the ministerial practice of Jesus and the survival performativity of Hagar in the wilderness suggests an equally powerful, though very different, religious performatively for many African American women. The point here is not hierarchy but difference between two womanist proposals, both of which can be linked to each other not only by a common womanist commitment but a common (implicit and explicit) regulative link to the creedal tradition. With reference to one set of doctrinal rules, we have seen how negotiation with the tradition is ongoing in feminist theology (in this case, womanist theology). If feminists can see even very revisionary feminist theological formulations as regulatively connected to the tradition in dynamic and creative ways, then the impetus is there not to reject the tradition (propositionally), circumvent it (experiential-expressively), or ignore it (with the claim that it does not "have any normative significance" in one's theology[29]). There is sufficient good reason to highlight these kinds of regulative connections in feminist constructive theology, not just because that gives one reason to see how the creeds the Christian community worldwide recites are relevantly at work in feminist theology, but because it may allow feminists to see new possibilities for technologies of care and of spiritual performativity in relation to a heavily disciplinary tradition.[30]

II. Negotiating with Exclusivist, Masculinist, Colonialist Biblical Texts

The creedal tradition and the biblical text came into being historically in interrelated ways. The early church's reading of the Bible—or what would become the Bible, especially the newly emerging gospel narratives about Jesus—was influenced by the still-evolving rule of faith, which in turn was used to norm interpretation of scripture.[31] Nevertheless, reading the text was always more than just a regulative affair, since scripture reading came out of a largely Jewish and Hellenistic textual environment where various methods of interpretation were routinely employed. Hence biblical interpretation "emerged as a literary genre as early as the time of...Origen," and one can begin speaking from the third century to the present of a textual activity that is linked regulatively to the creeds but could and should engender more meanings than what the creeds outline. From the patristic period forward, the church recognized that the Bible was a rich text with many possible proper meanings, requiring interpretation.[32] Feminists today stand in a long, multifaceted hermeneutical tradition in relation to the Bible and must argue for the validity of their readings of scripture alongside many others. They must contend not only with the androcentrism of the biblical text itself, but also with the phallocentrism of the rule of faith, and the patriarchy and misogyny of the history of ecclesial and exegetical interpretations of the Bible.

There are several ways feminists have coped with the biblical and particularly New Testament text in light of women's concerns. Some have taken a post-Christian stance, rejecting the text as thoroughly patriarchal, misogynist, exclusivist, or homophobic. However, most (even very revisionary) feminist theologians continue to engage the text in some capacity in relation to their feminist theological proposals. Most feminists have a so-called canon-within-the-canon approach that posits some core texts or themes as having a liberatory message or as pointing to gyno-friendly early church institutional structures. These feminist theologians try to recuperate the gospel picture of Jesus and the nascent Christian communities as, to some extent, worthy of feminist attention. The assumption underlying this move is that some minimal hermeneutical basis must be established to keep Jesus positively in the picture in order to counteract the heavily patriarchal dogmatic appropriation of his memory. A widespread feminist assumption is that enough of the gospel texts portray Jesus as linked to a message of liberation, community, justice, and compassion. I have been positively influenced by feminist attempts to find resonances in the New Testament text that are consonant with women's experience. However, I want to show the limitations of this prevalent feminist approach, which cannot, to my mind, generate negotiations with the text that resist sufficiently the legacy of misogyny, heteronormativity, christological exclusivism in the church's and the exegetical guild's uses of the New Testament. Whether or not an argument can be made convincingly for some liberative core feminist message (let us not forget Mary Daly's now famous quip that a feminist New Testament would make a very thin pamphlet), the received canon and its history of interpretation are thoroughly conditioned by that legacy. In what follows I will discuss drawbacks of traditional feminist hermeneutical methods and propose an alternate method that opens up new avenues for women's creative spiritual appropriation of arguably oppressive biblical texts.

My focus text is John 4:1–42, the story of Jesus and the Samaritan woman at the well. I chose this text most obviously because its central female figure provides an opportunity to reflect on women's experience directly in relation to the biblical text (and the growing number of articles and monographs on this text is evidence that many other feminist scholars share this sense). Feminist interpretations of Jesus and the woman at the well can be classified in roughly two categories. Some white feminist exegetes attempt to bolster the status and reputation of the woman in relation to a submerged theme of egalitarian women's roles in the early church. For example, Elisabeth Schüssler Fiorenza, Sandra Schneiders, and Janeth Day argue that this biblical text supports a theme of women's missionary authority in the early church.[33] Others, such as those working from a postcolonial perspective, treat this story as a "text of terror" (to use Phyllis Trible's phrase) because of the way it exemplifies a colonizing of native spaces or because of its sexist and racist uses in the first-world church against certain immigrant women of color.[34] All these readings of the text can be seen as critical responses to the mostly male and/or hegemonically first-world exegetical guild that has been largely silent on the text's inherent sexism and the history of its oppressive uses in the church and colonizing uses in the two-thirds world.

Much feminist energy has been devoted to responding to male exegetical impugning of the Samaritan woman's morals. Schneiders objects to the way one male exegete calls the Samaritan woman a "tramp" or the way another paints her as a loose woman trying vampishly to seduce Jesus. Schneiders argues that the reference to the woman's past and present male partners is a political allegory.[35] Nigerian-born exegete Teresa Okure denies that Jesus was trying to confront her with her past, and Janeth Day argues that the multiple husbands issue must be understood in light of the culture of first-century Palestine that left women with few options for controlling their marital status, hence it is unfair to prejudge them according to modern standards.[36] Korean American scholar Jean Kim writes about how this text is used in some Korean American churches to single out and socially marginalize Korean immigrant wives of American soldiers who are caught by a number of complicated economic and emotional reasons in a "cycle of marriage and divorce. . . . In their desperation, these women sometimes go to church to be consoled." In church, the immorality of the Samaritan woman's story is preached to them, and they find themselves "forced to identify themselves with her." Compounded with this is the burden they bear because within their native Korean culture interracial marriage is often shameful.[37]

Other feminists, however, might ask why it is necessary to present the Samaritan woman as sexually virtuous. Marcella Althaus-Reid sees the attempt to sanitize women's sexuality as a general tendency in the Latin American liberation theologies she has studied. "Stories of sexual desire amongst the poor are a no-go area. Gutiérrez has said that poor Latin American women only care for food for their children, but I can tell him that we must care a lot about our orgasms too. If not, how is it that poor women end up having so many promiscuous relations in their lives? Is promiscuity an imposition or is it sometimes the flow of desire, a search for intimacy usually unfulfilled under the present conditions of sexual injustice?" An "indecent" approach to John 4 would not try to mask, excuse or condemn the Samaritan woman's past, which might well include a search for sexual satisfaction via multiple partners. If Jesus is depicted as taking a moralizing tone toward her sexual history, with no mention of the conditions of injustice (economic, religious, etc.) under which she no doubt lived, then what is literally indecent is not the woman's supposed promiscuity but Jesus' apparent judgmental attitude toward her (and the attitude of those exegetes who self-righteously concur). This reflects the Jesus described by Althaus-Reid when she says that "Jesus was constructed [in the biblical text and church dogma] in a way such that he was born to speak and to be silent at the same time."[38] In his interactions with the Samaritan woman in John 4, Jesus speaks explicitly about bodily needs ("Give me a drink," v. 7) and spiritual needs ("The water that I will give will become...eternal life," v. 14). He does not avoid speaking about relations that presume sex; yet his meaning is obscure ("you have had five husbands, and the one you have now is not your husband," v. 18). Is he implying that she is thereby a sinner of some sort (as Jesus called the sick man he healed on the Sabbath in John 5:14)? Jesus says both too much and too little, leaving the reader, and perhaps the Samaritan women herself, at a loss.

Many feminists are critical of the way the exegetical tradition has situated the Samaritan woman's interaction with Jesus evangelistically, with "Jesus as the messianic bridegroom at Cana (2:1–12)."[39] This characterization of Jesus as bridegroom is also linked to a narrative interpretation based on betrothal type-scenes from Hebrew scripture where a bridegroom (or his representative) finds a bride at a well, such as Abraham's servant meeting Rebekah (Gen. 24) or Jacob meeting Rachel (Gen. 29). Many exegetes argue that the author of John was making the allegorical move from courting to evangelism, in order to cast the Samaritan woman in the role of convert. The effect of seeing the Samaritan woman in the context of male-initiated betrothal rites is that she becomes the mostly passive recipient of Jesus' spiritual "wooing." The sexist, patronizing implications of this type-scene approach emerge when these exegetes point out how the Samaritan woman's meeting at the well differs from those in the Hebrew scriptures. Unlike the compliant brides-to-be in Hebrew scripture, the Samaritan woman misunderstands and resists Jesus' advances. She rather stupidly takes him literally, assuming that he wants a drink and possibly a bride, like Isaac and Jacob before him; whereas Jesus is offering living water and a spiritual marriage with himself as the bridegroom. These mostly male exegetes point out what is obvious to them: not only is Jesus not looking for a literal wife (he gives no betrothal gift to the woman) but, even if he were, the Samaritan woman is an unsuitable type-scene bride because she is evidently not a virgin, is not given in marriage by her father, and has no praiseworthy feminine features (like Rebecca who eagerly gives water to Abraham's servant, or Rachel whose beauty is noted).[40] Hence, Jesus' posture toward her is strictly missionary.

Feminist scholars dislike the negative and sexist light in which the encounter between the Samaritan woman and Jesus is cast. Some feminists attempt to reread their interaction (and redeem her reputation) by arguing that she does come around and gladly accept Jesus' offer.[41] Hence, she in effect is like those brides in Genesis (even if she does not resemble them in virtue) because she fulfills the type-scene action of going back to her people to report about the wonderful encounter (see Gen. 24:28). Others argue that traditional type-scene interpretations of John 4 gloss over the Samaritan woman's agency in the story. Not only is she not a passive recipient of a marriage proposal but she can be seen as "pursuing a careful investigation of the identity of Jesus," questioning him "on virtually every significant tenet of Samaritan theology." In short, she proves herself to be not a muddled woman of ill repute but a "genuine theological dialogue partner gradually experiencing Jesus' self-revelation even as she reveals herself to him."[42] To put this in modern day terms: she still marries the bridegroom but doesn't change her name. We have a feminist betrothal type-scene. These feminist readings go far to expose the sexism in the traditionally male type-scene approach to John 4, but some leave intact the problematic unspoken theological assumption that the woman is worthy if she eventually assumes the type-scene role of Jesus' bride by repudiating her Samaritan views in favor of his christological self-revelation.

In sum, from a feminist perspective, the Samaritan woman represents otherness in many forms. As a fairly unique female accorded missionary status, she is other within an androcentric church. She is religiously other from a first-century Jewish standpoint. She can also be seen as an oppressed immigrant Korean divorcee, a woman who dared to take on leadership in a patriarchal context, an "indecent" sexually active woman. All the above mentioned feminist readings give interpretive results that support a serious critical and appreciative engagement with the New Testament text, though not without some problematic assumptions about why the Samaritan woman is worthy of feminist attention. In what follows, I will conduct a reading of the text that reflects a feminist concern with women's otherness and agency but does not depend on finding a gyno-friendly core message in the text. Rather, I will expose the many disciplinary layers of John 4 in order to illustrate how it may be appropriated hermeneutically as a technology of care.

Deconstructive Negotiations with John 4

Methodologically, I will use a deconstructive interpretive method that seeks the gaps and fissures in the text that result from the pressure of bringing to bear various critical (feminist, postcolonial, and "indecent") questions upon it.

White deconstructive biblical exegete Gary Phillips approaches this story from a Derridean perspective, arguing for the power of its Johannine textuality to communicate "undecidability," "proliferating" meaning and, thereby "overlooked signs of Otherness."[43] Some literary and biblical critics might claim that this hermeneutic is just frivolous textual play. Phillips argues that a deconstructive reading is methodologically an ethical reading because textual indecisiveness and openness requires the reader to attend to the otherness in that text (and, by extension, all texts). I bring feminist, postcolonial, and "indecent" perspectives into play in order to give a specifically female, "brown," and sexual embodiment to the more amorphous "Other" of which deconstructive method speaks.[44]

I will demonstrate how this deconstructive approach can negotiate with the dominant biblical christology of the Johannine text in ways that open up new arenas for religious and theological performativity. The believer's performativity is widened by encountering and embracing a non-christocentric otherness that stands over against the dominant interpretation of John's text as an account of how the Samaritan woman is converted to faith in Jesus as the Christ. I am not claiming that a deconstructive reading does away with the patriarchal christocentrism in John 4. In some sense, my deconstructive reading requires the centripetal pull of the text back to the exclusive male christological missionary positioning of John's story. The scholar's pleasure of seeing the text's meanings disseminate in other directions is contingent on knowing whence it came and knowing that some canonical, regulatively traditional telling of the story will continue after the intertextual threads have dispersed into the fabric of other religious and nonreligious discourses. Another way of saying this is that deconstruction of a despised text, a text whose dominant "literal" or "plain" sense holds no allure, is not really (Derridean) deconstruction, it is simply demolition.[45]

My hermeneutical approach attempts to be deconstructive not demolishing, because it aims to empower feminist readers of the biblical text to appropriate it as a technology of care, in light of the policing of its misogynist, imperialist, and patriarchal themes. Given the disciplinary strength of traditional readings of John 4, women need a hermeneutical method that is not limited to a feminist canon-within-the-canon of liberationist narratives but rather engages problematic (sexist, heteronormative, etc.) parts of the text. My reading of the Samaritan woman story is meant to model a hermeneutical approach that shows how that story can generate desire for more reading of the New Testament text, even though the reader may be someone whose body has been docilely normalized by disciplinary discourses of sin (with misogynist overtones), atonement (with surrogacy and violent overtones), and a male savior (with patriarchal overtones). That very reader needs a textual encounter with the New Testament that will be richly open with multiplying significations that pique her desire, instill new knowledges, and disrupt her normalized Christian subjectification. She needs to experience "thirst" for more kinds of redemptive performativity in relation to the Jesus of the New Testament. My hope is that the Bible's policing phallocentrism might be deconstructively opened up to release new unruly and possibly "gift-like" meanings that can become technologies for care of the self for feminist theological readers who desire to draw from the well of the Christian tradition.[46]

First, I would suggest decentering the gender and sexual roles in the story. One way to do this is by reading the Samaritan woman story intertextually with both the bride-at-the-well and the "harlot as heroine" stories such as Tamar (Gen. 38).[47] I noted above how feminist scholars object to the way some male exegetes depict the Samaritan woman as a seductress. However, when we read her encounter with Jesus intertextually with a story like Tamar's, we can give the male exegete's titillating hypothesis about seduction an indecent twist. Seduction for Tamar was a crafty business transaction that secured her future and righted a wrong done against her as a marginalized woman in a patriarchal family system. It was, to put it bluntly, strategically orchestrated political and economic sex. (That sexual encounter, orchestrated though it was, should not thereby be automatically seen as excluding pleasure; the tendency is to say that illicit sex for women is justified only if she had no other choice and no pleasure.) We can say something analogous for the Samaritan woman. Perhaps she *is* propositioning Jesus. She is wooing him theologically, trying to make a case for her (Samaritan) messianic viewpoint over against his. Switching the gender roles of the betrothal type-scene, *she* performs the role of bridegroom and Jesus is the reluctant bride. Schneiders entertains the notion that the Samaritan woman is Jesus' theological opponent but not that she was trying to woo Jesus theologically (and certainly not sexually). Again, given the Samaritan woman's history, we cannot on principle exclude the indecent possibility that she may have been (for any number of economic or sexual reasons) trying to woo him literally. There is little reason to exclude a possible erotic subtext to a narrative that may have discretely only recounted their theologically oriented foreplay. Otherwise the text becomes only a policing discourse implying that any woman who is not sexually passive is somehow morally suspect and that Jesus would have been offended to be thusly approached.[48]

We have other possibilities for sexual- and gender-complicating interpretations, which allow us also to deconstruct the text's christocentrism postcolonially. One recent postcolonial reading steps out of the binary heteronormativity and/or neocolonialism of some exegesis of this text. Batswana exegete Musa

Dube imagines the story retold with the Jesus role played by a female figure—a woman prophet—who interacts with a woman she meets at a well. They share the water from the woman's well, which affirms in a noncolonizing way the "living water from her own well on her own land." Although Dube does not go in this direction, there is a rich queering potential to this approach when combined with the type-scene bridegroom interpretation. One can imagine a woman-to-woman wooing that resists the patriarchal and imperialist tone of a story about a man (from a more powerful ethnic and religious community) saving a woman (from a less powerful ethnic and religious community) by seducing her with his superior truth.[49]

Pursuing this postcolonial and gender-reversing idea further, we could cast the Samaritan woman in the role of the male go-between, like the servant Abraham sent to find a bride for Isaac. After meeting Rebekah at the well and concluding certain transactions with her kin, the servant takes her home with him. We have a similar sequencing in John 4, although the outcome is different. Perhaps, after their discussions, the Samaritan woman (as go-between) invited Jesus (the bride) to accompany her back home to meet the townspeople (the collective groom). There is some kind of interchange with the Samaritan woman and Jesus' kin (the disciples). But unlike Rebekah's family who, after some reluctance, let her go with Abraham's servant, Jesus' disciples do not release Jesus into the Samaritan woman's custody. Jesus does not seem particularly pleased with the disciples and subsequently chides them for impeding him: "My food is to do the will of him who sent me and to complete his work" (v. 34). Jesus, like the eager Rebekah, may have been willing to go, despite protestations from his kin (the disciples)—protestations that Jesus thinks goes against his timing for the "harvest" (v. 35). If we add a postcolonial layer to this reading, one might say that John 4 is the story of how Jesus met resistance from his disciples in his intentions of "going native."[50] This type-scene postcolonial interpretation suggests that Jesus' sojourn among the Samaritans need not be seen in an imperialist missionizing way. It could be seen in terms of the metaphor of an egalitarian "marriage" of religious views (orchestrated by the Samaritan woman as go-between). This imaginative (and I would add utopian) decolonizing, deconstructive reading is not that textually farfetched, given John 8:48: "The Jews answered him [Jesus], "Are we not right in saying that you are a Samaritan and have a demon?" Perhaps Jesus did go native (religiously and otherwise) while in Samaria in a way that earned him the pejorative (according to some Jews of that day) label of "Samaritan."

No one to my knowledge has entertained the nonimperialistic imaginative interpretive possibilities of reading Jesus as open to other messianic claims and desires.[51] On the contrary, most exegetes (including many feminists) assume that the Samaritan woman accepts Jesus' exclusivist claims to truth. When she leaves and goes back to the townspeople, saying "Come and see a man who told me everything I have ever done!" (v. 3), this is taken as proof of her star-struck awe of Jesus' powers of prophecy about her life that sparks her conversion. However if the revelation of her intimate past was what won her over to Jesus, why didn't she return to town at this point in the conversation? Nothing in the text indicates that she ever rushed back to town in a religious fervor at all. In fact, the woman and Jesus continue to converse at some length concerning meaty theological issues about which they disagree— in particular, their views of the messiah. Moreover, the text is silent on her response to Jesus' messianic self-annunciation in verse 26 ("I am he"). Why assume she converted? We cannot know the tone of her statement to the townspeople, "Come and see." There is no definitive reason not to read her statement to the townspeople with many possible tones, including a sarcastic one. In paraphrase, one could take her as saying something like: "He thinks he's the messiah just because he told me about my past." This spin on her report to the townspeople would explain the cryptic ending to this story where the people say, "[W]e have heard for ourselves and we know this is truly the Savior of the world" (v. 42). These townsfolk do convert based on Jesus' word and apparently set their belief over against the woman's position. Hence, there is textual support for attributing to her a dubious attitude toward Jesus' messianic claims.

I would also call for a feminist theological deconstruction of deconstructionist readings of this text as well. Gary Phillips argues from a Derridean perspective that the Samaritan woman's jar left at the well is a sign, a "trace" of her absence yet presence within a text whose dominant theme is the evangelist's christological polemic: "The jar sits at the well lip of the text as a sign of a woman who is not yet completely eliminated.... as a reminder to the reader of a woman who is other to Jesus ... a face that cannot be completely effaced from the text. In spite of the substantial narrative effort to discount this Other—this is the theologocentric move par excellence—... she and the text resist and the jar marks her spot."[52] Phillips reads the woman as resisting Jesus theologically and materially: she debates with him and never draws water for him to drink. For Phillips, her jar is empty; the textual encounter is incomplete, inconclusive, and open. One could, however, draw different conclusions about the jar.

I sometimes see the jar as full. Following from my imaginative postcolonial reading above, I read the woman at the well as tempting Jesus with (Samaritan) holy water. She is tempting him to taste and see that it is good and that her Samaritan messianic vision is good. When Jesus plays his messianic card with his "I am he" (v. 26), she leaves—but, I speculate, she leaves him a *full* jar, should he wish to reconsider her offer of water. (It makes little narrative or cultural sense that she would have conversed for that long with a thirsty stranger without filling her jar to offer him a drink.) Moreover, I would argue (pace Phillips) that an empty jar is too little of a symbolic trace for a woman who argued her theological case so forcefully. Moreover, later, Jesus invokes the metaphor of sowing and reaping, suggesting that he labored by planting the seeds and that his disciples will reap. I suggest that the Samaritan woman is associated in an integral way with this agricultural metaphor: she has water, without which all the seed planting comes to naught. She, in other words, has living water (too) and her jar is sitting there to remind the reader and to provoke the reader to think about what the Samaritan women (and every other woman) has to offer.

Another interpretive possibility is that the Samaritan woman leaves an empty jar for Jesus to use to draw water from her well. This is not an anti-hospitality act. She leaves Jesus the means to dip into the well, given that he comes empty-handed: "The woman said to him, 'Sir, you have no bucket, and the well is deep'" (v. 11). Phillips makes a similar claim about the jar being left in order to draw water: "The deconstructive reader seats herself by the narrative well and makes use of that jar to dip into the text."[53] The difference between my reading here and Phillips's is that I am resisting a too precipitous interpretive move away from the narrative encounter between the two figures in the story and toward an allegory for deconstructive reading generally. I would want to dwell a bit longer on the Jesus of John 4, in all his patriarchal, colonialist and missionary fullness, who must respond to a jar either left full or left empty for him to use.

My point is not to argue for the superiority of ancient Samaritan messianic views. I take the Samaritan woman, as Phillips does, as a symbol for otherness in relation to the dominant disciplinary christological interpretations of John 4 that the church has historically privileged. I would argue that one should not look for the full meaning of redemption in a Christ who might be seen as humiliating women with their sexual/marital past or wooing them into heteronormative, theological passivity. Salvation for women (and others) depends on resisting that Christ at all costs. Nor am I suggesting that the Samaritan woman represents a model for some kind of christa/community that confronts Jesus and "shatters his views of religious exclusivity" (as Rita Nakashima Brock argues in relation to Jesus' encounter with the Syro-Phoenician woman).[54] The Samaritan women is not "the" or "a" Christ figure, nor does she tell us definitively who or what is. The Samaritan woman functions more as a harlot-as-heroine type in that there is nothing particularly exemplary about her except the fact that she is feisty, and she can be read as transgressing oppressive theological, religious, and societal conventions. When John 4 is read in the deconstructive (feminist, postcolonial, indecent) ways I have been suggesting, it opens up the text's and the interpretive tradition's disciplinary discourses of christocentrism, gender rigidity, masculinism, and so on. Can this create a hermeneutical basis for cultivating new christologically oriented desires, new technologies of care, and new spiritual performativity?

Toward a Hermeneutics of Christian Performativity

Based on traditional exegesis, John 4 is meant to illicit from women the desire to take Jesus at his word (he's the bridegroom and he knows best). The desire produced by this traditional Johannine christology could be powerful both for Christian women who find they have much in common with the Samaritan woman—if they read Jesus' response to her as compassionate—and for believers who have little in common with the Samaritan woman but who might want to project themselves into this narrative scene, imaginatively giving Jesus a drink of water, conversing with him, and so on. Would desires produced by traditional readings of this story help the docile female believer expand her spiritual performativity of the *imago dei* or only reinforce the policing of a traditional message of redemption—namely, that the heterosexual-yet-celibate, sinless, male Jesus alone saves? Redemption will mean cooperating to some extent with that disciplinary discourse but it must also mean exposing one-self to the pull of alterity that enables the reader to cultivate other power/knowledges and desires that are resistant to univocal discourses about Jesus as the messianic bridegroom. In this way, the resistant reader can convert such bridegroom discourses into christological technologies of care that promote feminist, postcolonial and other forms of agency not passivity.

The question naturally arises: why go on cooperating with this normalizing biblical christology at all? My deconstructive approach to John 4 would seem to point in a post-Christian feminist direction since the Jesus of John 4 is not a particularly salvific figure for the Samaritan woman nor perhaps for anyone who is not comfortable with colonialist, exclusivist christological claims.[55] After their intense exchange, the Samaritan woman walks away. Shouldn't we all as well? But then, there is the jar. This text reminds us that however stormy one's relationship with a disciplinary discourse, we might want to leave something behind that we can return to retrieve. People in some-times contentious long-term friendships know how to come and go in each other's lives, leaving belongings at each other's houses so that one has an excuse to break the ice and renew communication. Did the Samaritan woman desire to speak with Jesus again? Did she desire only to be just good friends, not to make him her spouse? And was Jesus content with that arrangement? Those are open questions that the feminist reader might still desire to ask of the John 4 narrative—if she has not determined in advance that only an unambiguously feminist canon-with-in-the canon text is acceptable, or conversely if she has not determined in advance that John 4 is too infiltrated by misogynist, colonialist, or heteronormative themes to have any relevance for her. Having asked some questions of the text, more questions may arise, more thirst for answers to new questions. When this text is submitted deconstructively to multi-refracted feminist, postcolonial, indecent (and other) lenses, we can see that the christological encounter is fraught with complex and multiple desires and thirsts. There may be no simple, univocal, definitive resolution— theologically, spiritually, sexually—despite our Johannine-disciplined desire that there be one answer to the question of who is the Christ.

This is not an interpretation of unfettered feminist liberation. There is no good news of erotic mutual relationality. The desires, if any, produced by my deconstructive reading are not unambiguous. I would not, however, say that it is therefore shrouded in ethical penumbra and enigmatic darkness.[56] Alongside the tradition's depiction of a woman of dubious morals, one can find Jesus' most scintillating theological interlocutor (perhaps in the New Testament). Alongside the masculinist missionary positioning of Jesus, one can find Jesus the eager bride-at-the-well. Alongside the symbol of colonialistic christocentric evangelization, one can find Jesus "going native" among the indigenous Samaritans. All these images, however nebulous and under the constraints of what Grace Jantzen might call the phallic symbolic, could be important factors for a feminist theological construction of Christian performativity, which must include some desire for the tradition beyond a feminist canon-within-the-canon approach.

As I have hopefully illustrated with John 4, there are fruitful meanings that can be "jarred loose" from the text's patriarchal, heteronormative, and colonialist moorings.[57] Those fruitful meanings, however, are seemingly at the bottom of a very deep and murky well of the Christian textual tradition. One must want to sift through the tradition in order to haul them up. I would argue that mucking through the church's texts can be an experience with pleasures of a certain kind. Consider the pleasure of reading against the grain of Augustine's very disciplinary interpretation of John 4, which he takes as an allegorical lesson against concupiscence:

What means, "Whoso shall drink of this water shall thirst again?" . . . Since the water in the well is the pleasure of the world in its dark depth: from this men draw it with the vessels of lust. Stooping for-

ward, they let down the lust to reach the pleasure fetched from the
depth of the well, and enjoy the pleasure and the preceding lust let
down to fetch it. For he who has not despatched [sic] his lust in
advance cannot get to the pleasure. Consider lust, then, as the vessel;
and pleasure as the water from the depth of the well.[58]

Let me play a bit with the rich allegorical imagery of Augustine's interpretation.

I suggest that feminist readers may need to allow themselves to entertain illicit "lusts," if they are to constitute themselves as subjects via a reading
of a murky text like John 4. This may sound like feminist heresy, but let me
be clear that I am not suggesting that women should submit with a smile to
male theological domination, that they should cower under the label of tramp,
that they should acquiesce to religious dogmas that have harmful psychological, emotional or physical effects. Nor am I merely stating the obvious: that
some conservative Christian women do take the traditional reading of John 4
(and the Bible generally) as gospel, and hence for them, their deepest religious performativity is normed pleasurably by the male Jesus' claim: "I am he."
Rather, I have in mind those many feminist scholars standing uneasily
within a tradition they are trying to reform but whose very reforming impulses
have been constructed within the pleasures and constraints of a discursive
relationship with that tradition's power/knowledge. For those women, the
pressure of feminist political correctness could turn any cooperation with that
disciplinary tradition into an illicit desire, a kind of ideologically forbidden
concupiscence. I think we have to take the risk. Feminist Christian performativity today has to risk negotiating with the most disciplinary texts, like
John 4. The scholar brings to the table a full array of tools for critical and even
deconstructive readings; however, she must also come to the table willing to
become, at the very least, pleasurably intrigued by her opponent, so to speak.

Augustine believed that "having received Christ the Lord into her heart,"
the Samaritan woman left her water-pot (that is, her lust) "and hastened to
proclaim the truth." He then instructs would-be evangelists: "Let them who
would preach the gospel … throw away their water-pot at the well."[59] A fully
consistent feminist should do something analogous to what Augustine instructs evangelists: let her who would preach feminism throw away her water-
pot (i.e., her desire for the tradition) at the well. But in fact, Augustine himself
never really threw away his water-pot, his vessel of lust—if we think of his own
self-description in, for example, *Confessions*, where he meticulously describes
all the many sensual desires that mediate his sense of spiritual love for God.[60]
Analogously (and conversely), for many feminists, the ways they have been

shaped by the patriarchally oppressive Christian tradition mediates in many ways their feminism. Many Christian feminists continue to construct their feminism alongside and via the (illicit) pleasure of cooperation with the patriarchal Christian tradition. These feminists never leave behind their lust for that tradition—nor should they have to. Vibrant feminist theology will continue to develop as we highlight the dominant discursive formations with which we cooperate and which we appropriate as technologies of care to some extent—all the while formulating new and often subversive feminist religious imagery, doctrines, practices, and desires. Either that ambiguous and risky process can be used as a technology of care, or else we have to concede that the only true feminist desire is that which wells up from a pristine and nurturing dark womb of semiotic waters that are never muddied by illicit lusts and forbidden desires.

6

Rethinking Solidarity

I began this project by reflecting on the fracturing of feminist theology because of differences among women's experiences. It is my firm belief that the more feminist theologians can deepen their understanding and appreciation of difference and interrogate continually new formations of privilege, the more enriching and enlivening our discourse and practice will become. At various points throughout this text I have analyzed problematic assumptions in feminist theological writings, especially related to issues of race and sexuality. I have also noted fruitful dialogues on these issues among feminists from very different backgrounds, representing very different theological, political, and social concerns. Conversations have taken place despite the fact that in the writings of feminist theologians of privilege (especially white feminist theologians), color-blindness and lack of self-critical awareness of ongoing white racial privilege continue adversely to affect methodological approaches and theological formulations. Moreover, with some very few exceptions, most feminist theological writing is either woefully "decent" in its lack of critical attention to the politics, economics, and racialization of sexuality or else unduly romantic about the liberatory capacities of the "erotic." One could say that the current feminist theological situation is one of coalitional fragility, notwithstanding strong interpersonal collegiality in many specific cases. In light of this situation, it is important to address explicitly the much invoked yet much maligned "s" word: *solidarity*. Can we continue (or even begin) to speak of women's solidarity—not to mention sisterhood—given the fractured state of feminism today and the dire need to explore more profoundly women's differences and expose more consistently the workings of privilege? Under what conditions could we rethink solidarity?

Some feminist theologians have effectively called for a moratorium on talk of solidarity. White feminist Mary McClintock Fulkerson proposes "a feminist theology of affinity rather than...solidarity with the other" because her postmodern sensibilities suggest that academic feminist calls for solidarity risk functioning as a hegemonic discourse.[1] Other critiques of the notion of solidarity come by way of a conspicuous nonuse of the term, coupled with analyses of what appeals to solidarity can mask. Womanist theologian Jacquelyn Grant asserts that "all too often, notions of reconciliation, covenantal relationship, unity and community mirror...the system of domestic service relationships [where] those on the topside...are the beneficiaries of the system; and those one the underside...are mere victims."[2] If one substitutes "solidarity" for Grant's terms "reconciliation" or "covenantal relationship," Grant can be read as injecting a strong note of suspicion regarding an appeal to women's solidarity.

Many feminist theologians, however, still appeal to the notion of women's solidarity, cognizant of its problematic uses in the past by white feminists especially. These feminists are trying to speak of feminist solidarity in ways that avoid the imposition of the values and agendas of women in positions of privilege. White feminist theologian Sharon Welch sees solidarity linked to difference because it requires granting the other "sufficient respect to listen to their ideas and be challenged by them."[3] Sheila Greeve Davaney (also white) affirms a call for solidarity defined as a "radical commitment to the well-being of the other," if that call is made on the pragmatic grounds that "those who have adopted it have found it transformative and liberating."[4] Womanist theologian M. Shawn Copeland believes it is possible to move beyond a "facile adoption of the [white feminist] rhetoric of solidarity" by a methodological commitment to critical social analysis of oppression, a theological-moral commitment to the irreducible individual value of human persons, and a eucharistic commitment to the broken bodies of others, because "a hurting body has been the symbol of solidarity for Christians since the institution of the Holy Communion."[5]

It may be that the current state of race relations in academe and society generally is such that white feminists should never invoke anything more than affinity. Moreover, some women of color may be wary of Copeland's attempts to forge a sacramental path toward women's solidarity. Given that the issue, however contentious, is still being raised in feminist theological writing, it merits further discussion. I find aspects of what Welch, Davaney, and Copeland say compelling; nevertheless, as a white feminist, I realize that however good my intentions, my positionality renders any overtures I might make to the notion of solidarity immediately suspect (and understandably so). Discussion about solidarity may in fact be a relatively low priority for feminists from minority communities who have understandably not wanted their energies and attention displaced from research and advocacy projects focused on the needs of those communities of which they are a part. Given my postmodern leanings, I see the value in Fulkerson's move toward the more modest notion of affinity. Nevertheless, there are also postmodern (and other) reasons not to foreclose the category of solidarity—yet. In this chapter, I approach the notion of solidarity as I would any power/knowledge discourse—aware that it affords various pleasures and constraints (white feminists have historically experienced more the former than the latter) and aware that it can become a site for the construction of agency and improvisational movements of power. Current feminist writings on solidarity demonstrate that while this is an issue rife with pitfalls, more is to be gained from continuing critically to engage this notion than in excising it from the feminist theological lexicon as an irretrievably corrupted term. I am choosing my words carefully here. I do not think I am (or feminist theology generally is) in a position at this point in time to offer more than tentative observations on what feminist solidarity should look like, but we do need to engage the notion critically if only to avoid complacency when it comes to addressing difference and working toward the betterment of real women's lives.

In what follows, I will critically analyze Welch's, Davaney's, and Copeland's views on solidarity as part of an ongoing process of rethinking feminist solidarity. Positively, each is trying to reflect on solidarity based on the recognition of differences in women's experiences; however, each ends up caught in a conceptual dichotomy that either overburdens or overinflates the notion of solidarity. In Welch, one finds a dichotomy between the project of defending validity claims argumentatively (within a framework of Jürgen Habermas's communicative action) and the project of interracial solidarity, such that solidarity is made to carry too much of a burden for correcting flaws in Habermas's views. In addition, setting solidarity and communicative action in opposition may ironically undermine both. In Davaney's writings, one finds a dichotomy between supposedly overly confessional Christian appeals to solidarity and a liberal democratic form of pragmatic solidarity, such that the value of the latter is overinflated—in part because the power dynamics in pragmatism's liberal democratic procedures are obscured. Copeland implies that anything less than a traditionally understood trinitarian and christological solidarity will be insufficient to overcome our indifference to difference—a position that over-burdens solidarity by linking it uncritically to a heavily disciplinary theological rationale, thus creating an unnecessary dichotomy between traditional and nontraditional Christian feminisms.

In my contribution to this topic, I will suggest a way of thinking that moves past these dichotomies (the metaphorical character of my term "moves" will become apparent later when I use improvisational dance as a metaphor to explore new dynamics for solidarity). As a result of my critical conversations with Welch, Davaney, and Copeland, I hope to show the value of thinking about solidarity that: (1) recognizes its fragility (hence it must not be over-burdened); (2) recognizes how power differences will need to be continually renegotiated (hence solidarity must not be overinflated); and (3) explores new metaphorical perspectives that encourage feminists in positions of privilege to continue to be challenged by difference and that envision how those in nondominant positions might self-determine their participation in discussions or relations of solidarity.

I. Defending Validity Claims or Building Solidarity

Does the demand for solidarity attentive to difference mean that feminist theologians should forego mutually critical conversation whereby one defends one's own claims and interrogates those of others? The desire to find agreement and accord while downplaying conflict can be strongly tempting. For example, one volume of feminist essays on christology tries to mute the force of differences and potentially conflicting positions of the authors by suggesting that each writer's proposal offers, to quote T. S. Eliot, "'merely hints and guesses, hints followed by guesses ... the rest is prayer, observance, discipline, thought, and action.'"[6] In other words, one cannot say that there are serious christo-logical disputes going on if feminist doctrinal proposals are only hinting at something and not making any strong validity claims.

Welch's A Feminist Ethic of Risk is a sustained effort to construct a feminist ethic that sustains "work to transform conditions of injustice." In this text, she proposes how "to exercise and create a different sort of power," especially for persons of privilege (such as herself) attempting to use their status to work for justice.[7] Welch says that she has found that the experiences and stories "constitutive of white, middle-class identity" have tended to "reinforce the defense of privilege" and cannot therefore "motivate and sustain us [i.e., white people] in our work for social transformation."[8] In response to this situation, she turns to the literature (novels, essays, poetry) by African American women writers whose depictions of black women's wisdom, struggles, and hope inspire her to generate her own feminist ethics. She insists that ethics cannot be done from the vantage point of a homogeneous "cohesive community, such as the Aristotelian polis" but must emerge from "the material interaction of different communities."[9] She critically retrieves aspects of Jürgen Habermas's communicative ethics as a model of how one could adjudicate conflicting ethical claims from different communities. Her intention is to retain the notion of communicative ethics while transmuting Habermas's ideal of rational consensus into the more social justice oriented goal of forging solidarity. As she moves deeper into the demands of solidarity in this and other writings, however, not only does the project of Habermasian communicative ethics fade into the background but solidarity itself becomes burdened beyond what the notion should bear.

Communicative action is a notion Habermas develops that explains how dialogue can proceed in the absence of "foundational 'ultimate groundings.'"[10] Some kind of structure for communicative rationality is necessary because, Habermas explains, any speech act logically (and hence unavoidably) entails "a rationally motivated position of yes or no" vis-à-vis the implicit or explicit validity claims of that speech act.[11] The rationality of the consensus is based on the "noncoercively unifying, consensus-building force" of the argumentation in which the participants take part.[12] Habermas holds that this communicative consensus approach is not a return to Enlightenment transcendental philosophy because the kinds of "strong universalistic suppositions" that he posits are not a priori structures but hypotheses developed in conjunction with "empirical theories of [communicative] competence."[13] By this he means theories drawn from the human social sciences regarding the linguistic, cognitive and moral aspects of the self. (For example, he depends on the work of Jean Piaget for a theory of cognitive development.[14]) These sciences explore what Habermas calls the "lifeworld of communicative actors," which is the "intersubjectively shared" background beliefs, commitments, and assumptions of linguistically socialized subjects.[15] The scientific reconstruction of structures of linguistic competence confirms what philosophy posits—that is, any communication between people presupposes the "transcending force" of validity claims. Hence, when one lifeworld collides with another, the communicative actors "impute to everyone involved an intersubjectively shared lifeworld...and work out their differences."[16] This rational consensus in communicative action is not meant to entail "a forced integration of the many"; rather, the more dialogical one's concept of reason becomes, "the more diverse the disagreements with which we can *nonviolently* live."[17]

Notwithstanding his white, European, elite status, Habermas provides Welch with some important tools for social analysis of political and cultural interactions in light of difference. Welch concurs with Habermas that although the lifeworlds of two people (or groups of people) are always plural and "'their coexistence may cause friction . . . this *difference* does not automatically result in their *incompatibility*'";[18] hence the possibility of dialogue across difference. Nevertheless, Welch would stress (more than Habermas has) the need for material socio-political interactions between the differing individuals and groups attempting to dialogue or work together. In this sense, she is rightly critical of Habermas's thought as being too abstract and divorced from the "concrete other," a term Welch borrows from Turkish-born feminist political philosopher Seyla Benhabib, who rejects Habermas's liberal Enlightenment focus on an idealized or "generalized other."[19] Welch argues that the strict Habermasian notion of ideal consensus does not take into account "determinative differences in both access to political power and in the definition of norms" and the material social changes and the equalizations of power that would have to take place for real dialogue to occur among, say, "Euro-American feminists, African-American womanists, African-American men, and Euro-American upper-class men" where differences of race, culture and power are so marked (*FER*, 127, 133). When those realities are brought into play, Welch pulls back from Habermas's notion of consensus based on "the force of the better argument" and instead argues for the notion of solidarity based on "the fruit of work together, . . . [because] in work we create as much as we affirm the rational principles of shared humanity" (*FER*, 135). For people from very different backgrounds, this work may even have to be limited to the most basic forms: "preparing food . . . , cleaning, building houses" (*FER*, 136). When those from positions of privilege commit themselves to the work of social justice, it requires a "new chastened perspective" about one's complicity in structures of oppression, which Welch calls an "epistemology of solidarity" (*FER*, 139, 137). Out of this mode of thinking and acting in solidarity (rather than in debate) comes a "politic in which 'consensus and sharing may not always be the goal' " (*FER*, 140).

There are three concerns that could be raised about this position on solidarity. First, this approach seems to overburden the notion of solidarity by making it the necessary precondition to any dialogical move toward consensus. Welch writes that communicative action "presupposes material transformation" in the form of "solidarity . . . as a prior step" (*FER*, 133). The empathy and compassion that ensue from material practices of solidarity allow people of privilege to "transcend the blinders of our own social location" (*FER*, 151). Welch is certainly correct to attend to the material bases for effective communicative action (and many feminists have faulted Habermas for not addressing this more). Interactions of empathy, justice making, and so on would no doubt enhance most any dialogue across difference; nevertheless, Welch may be asking too much of solidarity, which is itself as fragile and rare as communicative consensus. While solidarity may offset some problems of communicative ethics, solidarity is itself also a contested notion and a complex practice that puts us face to face with the challenge of difference.

Second, notwithstanding Welch's stated support of communicative ethics, has she effectively set it aside? Other Habermasian feminists are not so quick to discard the project (and the demands) of adjudicating validity claims. Seyla Benhabib, for example, believes that some form of communicative rationality can provide a way of defending validity claims that solicit, without coercing, a response from the participants in the dialogue. Benhabib proposes a shift from Habermas's focus on "consensus to the idea of an ongoing moral conversation" that may even emerge in modes other than argumentation (e.g., narrative modes), without however abandoning arguments altogether. Ongoing moral conversation can be directed to sustaining caring relationships with concrete others "within which reasoned agreement *as a way of life* can flourish."[20] While she amends the modalities of communicative action, Benhabib is adamant on the need for "justifying the norms of universal moral respect and egalitarian reciprocity on rational grounds, no more and no less." She believes this is necessary for a philosophically sound feminist ethic ("I do not know how we could do without it"), and it seems to imply some argumentative structure.[21]

Welch does not structure her *Feminist Ethic of Risk* in the form of a rebuttal to the views of Benhabib I have just outlined; yet in later writings especially, Welch seems to move away from not only the goal of consensus but also the process of justifying validity claims as well. In the revised edition of *A Feminist Ethic of Risk*, she states that "the goal" of the kind of communicative ethics she would want "is community and solidarity, not justification and universal consensus."[22] I am not sure this resembles communicative action anymore. Instead, Welch emphasizes here the project of listening to and learning from the literature, philosophy, and spirituality of African American women which she finds "profound," "compelling," and "life-affirming."[23] When this solidarity project is in focus, the agenda of argumentative defenses of validity claims recedes into the background. She is trying to respond (in solidarity) to Emilie Townes's call to "'peoples of color and white, male and female, young and old, to carry out a communal lament'"[24]—hence her pervasive use of African American women's writings that capture themes of sorrow, tragedy, hope, and resistance. Welch realizes how much effort it takes for a white, middle-class woman to come to a deep understanding of womanist spirituality. She takes a listening (not debating) position toward the literature of African American women in an effort to draw from those writings resources for a feminist ethic that she hopes will be instructive and transformative for white women of privilege. "As we listen to other voices, we who are white can see the respect embodied therein, and learn to practice it ourselves."[25] When discussing this process, Habermasian (or even Benhabibian) notions of communicative action are conspicuously absent.

This brings us to a third concern with Welch's position on solidarity—namely, that it could, under some circumstances, raise the specter of appropriation. Welch herself writes about being criticized for "appropriating" in relation to the title of her book.[26] Some African American (and other) scholars might read her text as representing a white feminist approach that subsumes black women's experience into a white feminist agenda.[27] When does respectful reading of and listening to the ideas of women who are different than oneself mutate into appropriation? Would a more communicative action orientation worsen or ameliorate that problem? These questions are theoretically and practically complex and go to the heart of my concern about Welch's notion of solidarity.

Feminists acknowledge that there is a "religious and spiritual need for people to appropriate myths and stories that are not their own";[28] however, it is also necessary to recognize that appropriation is "about power, about how we read and make use of each other's work in a society based on relationships of domination and subordination."[29] Native American (Cherokee) scholar Laura Donaldson defines appropriation as a kind of commodity fetishization. She describes white feminist appropriation of Native American cultures as a "rummaging through" the cultural artifacts, myths and practices of those cultures in order to "abduct objects from their original context and denude them of any social identity." Relocating an object (either physically or by decontextualizing an oral or written tradition) creates "fetishized space" where one can "construct a position of mastery over [them] . . . while seeming to value and affirm them.[30] If Welch's use of the literature of African American women leaves its contextual integrity intact, then her risk of fetishization recedes. If, however, her use of that literature invests it with some decontextualized "magical or spiritual power," then the risk of commodity fetishization looms large.[31] The issue of appropriation, I believe, arises less from her methodological use of the literature of African American women in *A Feminist Ethic of Risk* and more from her recent proposals for how white social activists can be sustained by the use of African American cultural traditions.

In a recent article, Welch pursues the theme of how white people who are working for racial justice can be sustained spiritually by finding solace in the music of black spirituals. Speaking of one such group of white activists, she asks: "What did these despairing, weary people need?... An indictment of the indulgence of their despair in light of the great suffering white supremacy causes for people of color? No.... What was needed...was comfort." Welch's suggestion here of turning to black spirituals comes dangerously close to fetishizing the "creative healing power of African-American spirituality."[32] Clearly Welch intends respectfully to use a cultural artifact from another tradition. By emphasizing the performative aspect of the communal singing of spiritual songs, Welch foregrounds their very public nature. Is it appropriation for five white social justice workers to sing "A Balm in Gilead" on their front porch in Tennessee in order to sustain themselves in their grueling and often thankless work for racial equality?[33] Given the way Christian hymns are circulated widely for the express purpose of use in public worship, it would be stretching a point to call this appropriation. However, I am worried by Welch's claim that "people experience moments of solidarity when singing [spirituals]."[34] If Welch is merely continuing her thought that white people, such as the five activists mentioned above, are spiritually uplifted by these songs and feel a sustaining camaraderie with each other, then she is simply being descriptively accurate about the impact of these songs (which have a particular historical origin but have long been in the public domain). I would not find this type of borrowing to be problematic. If, however, she meant that white activists achieve solidarity with African Americans by singing their traditional spiritual songs, that would give me some pause. That would suggest that solidarity is an experience of communion transcending difference, and Welch's other writings on difference do not support that viewpoint.

I suggest that bringing aspects of communicative action back into play could serve as an important check and balance to the risk of appropriation. I draw here from Welch's own views on how communicative action presupposes the difference and even the inevitable friction between the lifeworlds of communicative actors. Given this presupposition, communicative action (or conversation, as Benhabib suggests) has a built-in mechanism that in theory could keep difference (including complex issues of appropriation) on the forefront of any intersubjective encounter. On the other hand, to imply that empathetic listening and shared work makes for solidarity that transcends boundaries of differences is the most risky position for feminists of privilege to take. (Recall from chapter 1 Elizabeth Spelman's warning about how white feminist attempts at empathy toward women of color tend to objectify them.) I am not suggesting that communicative conversation is a foolproof or sufficient way to prevent objectification or appropriation. Moreover, it may be that power disparities and the effects of privilege are too pronounced in some cases at this time to speak further of adjudicating validity claims (ethical, political, doctrinal, etc.) among feminists of different races or social locations. In the meantime, however, I believe that it is best to avoid implying an opposition between solidarity and communicative action, since this can have the ironic effect of undermining both. Implying this opposition risks lulling white feminists into the dangerous mindset that if we are at least trying to listen empathetically, we have implemented a practice of solidarity that is superior to communicative action, with its focus on defending validity claims. If, as Habermas himself acknowledges, communicative consensus is rare and difficult to achieve, solidarity is equally if not more so. Feminists of privilege would do well to approach both practices with vigilance. Argumentative defenses of validity claims can turn hegemonic; attempts at solidarity carry equally dangerous risks (however unintended) of appropriation and the elision of difference.

II. Liberal Democratic Pragmatism or Christian-based Solidarity

How can the theologian make the case for a notion like solidarity in today's world which is marked by "the complexities, ambiguities, and even contradictions of the historical events and developments to which we are heir"?[35] Davaney argues for a historicist and pragmatic approach to defending theological claims in our pluralistic context. Her comments on solidarity are brief but very instructive. They emerge out of her appreciative and critical conversations with Latin American liberation theologian Gustavo Gutiérrez and white eco-theologian Sallie McFague, for both of whom the category is deeply embedded in their respective visions of Christian ethical responsibility to the marginalized. Davaney carefully positions herself as a pragmatic historicist in relation to their views of solidarity in an attempt to instantiate a thick historicist connection to Christian normative values without, however, losing her commitment to the processes of liberal democratic pragmatism. Despite her desire to hold these aspects together, a dichotomy emerges in her writings between Christian solidarity and a liberal democratic form of pragmatic solidarity, such that the value of the latter is overinflated.

In religious studies and philosophy in America today, there are a growing number of theorists espousing pragmatism as the best workable position to take in today's pluralistic world, one of the most widely known being Richard Rorty who proposes a pragmatic approach to adjudicating differences in order to promote democratic social reform. Public debate, Rorty insists, will be unavoidably "ethnocentric"—a revealing term Rorty has taken pains to defend, meaning a person's "contingent spatio-temporal affiliations" which identify him or her as being "a Christian, or an American, or a Marxist ... or a post-modernist bourgeois liberal" (the latter is Rorty's not so tongue-in-cheek self-description).[36] Admitting in public debate that one has an ethnocentric position merely signals that one wisely renounces claims to having indubitable sources of knowledge. Rationality or truth is defined as "what is good for *us* to believe"; consensus is what *we* are able to persuade *them* to agree with us about (and vice versa) regarding the problems affecting us all.[37] Davaney does not use Rorty's language of ethnocentrism,[38] but she does affirm that decisions about what is true are made "within social communities with particular histories." Like Rorty, Davaney's call for "fostering participation in the social conversation and the public evaluation of what should count as desirable consequences" entails liberal democratic assumptions about how we should work through our differences in the civic realm.[39] For Rorty, those assumptions are not unfounded, because when we look at the "history of reformist politics," a liberal democratic world appears to be functioning all around us. It has undergone real developments large and small (e.g., the advent of trade unions, cheap newspapers, and, I would add, "blogs" and other cyberspace modes of mass communication) that have created socio-political communities by means of which large sectors of people have been able to think of themselves "as part of a body of public opinion."[40] While Davaney is concerned about "the spec-ter of balkanized communities, ... each asserting the validity of their particu-lar claims," she seems fairly confident that communities of people of good will can avoid the imposition of the "rule of power" and instead come to deci-sions about concrete matters affecting them all based on "pragmatic norms."[41] Hence she seems to share Rorty's confidence about the possibilities of dem-ocratic public debate to persuade (not force) public consensus on pragmatic grounds.

Davaney is aware of the problem of relativism that seems to dog this pragmatic approach. The acknowledgment that all values are "power-infused" and "interest-laden," Davaney explains, "could lead to a nihilistic conclusion that all views, patriarchal and feminist alike, are commensurate," with the re-sult that the status quo (i.e., patriarchy) remains unchallenged.[42] Some femi-nist theologians combat threats of relativism by standpoint theory arguments appealing to the epistemological privilege of women as an oppressed group whose experience grants them insight and authority to judge what is oppres-sive and what is liberating. Davaney argues that the notion of the oppressed having "privileged access to 'the way things really are'" is simply a version of the correspondence view of truth that she rejects.[43] She stresses that "abandoning ... ontological and epistemological certitude need not mean that therefore all standards and norms are arbitrary commitments." A pragmatic approach to adjudicating among competing sets of beliefs about justice does not necessarily mean thoroughgoing and paralyzing relativism; rather, it merely puts the process of adjudication "on the only level that really matters—the level of concrete and practical consequences."[44] People and communities do make judgments about morality and justice and act on them based on pragmatic norms.

In probing into the content of those norms, Davaney goes beyond Rorty to ask: "What is the character of these norms that guide our decision-making? Does pragmatic historicism have any content to its norms beside the maddeningly vague and general assertion that our interpretations and practices must be tested in concrete situations?"[45] Her answer is both procedural (she proposes a method for taking a pragmatic approach) and constructive (she makes claims about the traditioned nature of human communities). To admit that one's norms are shaped by values rooted in one's inherited traditions explains them but does not justify them. We must accept our "creative responsibility" critically to shape what we will carry on from our past (PH, 152). Davaney argues for a material, historicist view of culture with inevitably overlapping spheres (e.g., "theology, science, poetry, legal argument, bureaucratic institutions" [PH, 154], etc.). Theologians, for example, cannot fall back on an appeal to a primary set of religious "internal norms disconnected from other social realities," even when the subject matter seems to fall within one of those spheres (for example, religion) (PH, 155). Hence, when adjudicating competing theological claims, one cannot use religious criteria in isolation from science, politics, economics, and other public spheres. Defending one's theological claims requires "'cross-contextual obligation'" even when it is a seemingly in-house theological issue (PH, 160; quoting Delwin Brown). Correlatively, values rooted in religious traditions should not be excluded from cross-contextual public debate but can be fruitfully a part of it. As an example of this, Davaney points to the work of Cornel West.

For Davaney, West's blend of pragmatism, Gramscian, and African American cultural critique, and liberation theology gives his approach the correct balance of pragmatic nonfoundationalism and traditioned, cultural specificity. West's Gadamerian sensibilities make him comfortable (unlike Rorty) with appealing to the moral values of a religious tradition. Davaney notes: "Importantly for West, there is not an unresolvable tension between human agency and traditionedness as there seems often to be for Rorty" (PH, 142).[46] West argues that Rorty and other "avant-garde pragmatists" espouse "'thin' historical narratives which rarely dip into the complex world of politics and culture."[47] West exemplifies Davaney's call for dialogue based on cross-contextual obligation, because he insists on the need for philosophers to engage in social analysis and cultural critique (which cannot exclude the prophetic role religion can play) and for theologians to be more philosophically rigorous and politically informed. West's Christian prophetic pragmatism exemplifies a "thick historicism" that integrates tradition-shaped human agency with the "fallible and conditioned" nature of pragmatic public consensus (PH, 143). Davaney, taking her cue from West, proposes her own thick historicist pragmatic approach, guided by the liberation theological perspective on what she describes as "inclusionary practices" toward the " 'nonperson' " which liberationists widely refer to as solidarity.[48] Here one can see an internal tension emerge between Davaney's strongly liberal democratic pragmatism (influenced by Rorty) and her Christian-based historicist pragmatism (influenced by West).

By referencing a Christian notion of solidarity with the nonperson, Davaney argues that dialogue means more than meeting the demands of cross-contextual obligation; it means recognizing that "'nonpersons' have a claim to be heard and have their experiences and interpretations as part of the data to be considered in any assessment process" (PH, 168). This commitment to solidarity with the marginalized arises out of Davaney's attentiveness to elements of liberation theology; however, her relentless pragmatism does not allow her to romanticize solidarity. Achieving the radically inclusionary solidarity, which Davaney associates with liberation theology, is an ideal. In the nitty-gritty pluralistic world, however, participants may have to settle for pragmatically achievable goals—namely, "localized, and revisable consensus...or barring such agreement, that the majority comes to use its rule to work continually with others to forge ways to enlarge the range of interests met" (PH, 164). Thus, in the end, Davaney's acknowledgment about the difficulties entailed in cross-contextual obligation and radical inclusionary practices brings her back around to a pragmatic position reminiscent of Rorty's liberal democratic vision of kinder, gentler, broader (yet still ethnocentric) majority. Rorty defends its inclusionary aspects: "What takes the curse off this ethnocentrism is...that it is the ethnocentrism of a 'we' ('we liberals') which is dedicated to enlarging itself, to creating an ever larger and more variegated ethnos."[49] Because of Davaney's commitment to pragmatism, she ends up facing a choice between what pluralistic democracy can offer (the hopefully inclusive rule of the majority) and what she ideally would like to see happen (solidarity with the marginalized) based on values she draws from the Christian tradition.

How is it that Davaney, who criticizes Rorty's thin democratic liberalism (where religious traditions are relegated to "private projects"[50]) and who espouses West's Christianly thick historicism, ends up caught in an opposition between liberal democratic pragmatism and the Christian tradition—an opposition that she resolves by having to settle for the hope that the democratic majority will act inclusively? Is it a weakness of social analysis or a thin view of the Christian moral tradition (flaws West attributes to theology and avant-garde pragmatism, respectively)?

There are some notable weaknesses in Davaney's social analysis. One weakness is her appeal to inclusionary processes.[51] It is not clear that Davaney herself sees the dangers of the inclusionary metaphor. (Recall from chapter 1 Elizabeth Spelman's critique of a politics of inclusion, where the dominant group reinforces its privilege by its offer to include the other.[52]) A more central weakness of social analysis is her too sanguine belief in the processes of contemporary liberal democracy—especially its inclusionary aspects (which Davaney sees positively). Davaney confidently mentions "radical inclusionary strategies and democratic practices" in the same breath, so to speak. Indeed, Davaney suggests that inclusion is itself a democratic "ideal," which I find overinflates the solidarity that is achievable through pragmatic democratic processes (PH, 162). Moreover, if inclusion were a democratic ideal, that fact would render arguing for a Christian version of inclusion (which is a synonym Davaney uses for solidarity) redundant—unless Davaney were to recognize (and her text is not clear on this) that specifically Christian notions of solidarity present a paradigm that is meaningfully different from liberal democratic forms of inclusion. Davaney's lack of clarity on how Christian historicism adds something novel to public debate on this issue brings us to the question of her disposition toward the tradition generally.

Regarding how to evaluate the thinness or thickness of her Christian historicism, Davaney's book poses somewhat of a problem. She admits that the book's focus is "methodological and procedural" and "only points to a particular kind of substantive theology that it does not itself deliver" (PH, 188).[53] However even taking this into account, I suggest that she still seems to harbor a liberal pragmatist's reticence toward a thick Christian historicism, especially when it comes to making Christianly normative claims publicly. This is demonstrated in her treatment of Sallie McFague's theology. Davaney agrees with McFague's call for eco-solidarity with the natural world, but she criticizes one prong of McFague's method—namely, her attempt to make the argument for eco-morality on Christian, specifically biblical, terms. Davaney summarizes McFague's position thus: because of the biblical call for "radical commitment to the outcast, the other, the oppressed," Christians are "compelled to live and act in solidarity not only with the nonperson... but nature as well" (*PH*, 178). Davaney finds this biblically based appeal to be "misguided." Davaney wants eco-solidarity but she wants an argument for it that is less dependent on what she takes to be "a new appeal to authority," which can turn hegemonic (*PH*, 179). She calls instead for a "much more pragmatically oriented rationale for... inclusionary love." Solidarity, Davaney wants to argue, is good not because it reflects Jesus' message to the outcast but because "those who have adopted it have found it transformative and liberating" (*PH*, 180–81).[54] Davaney only wants a solidarity that works. The only solidarity that is pragmatically justifiable turns out to be the solidarity envisioned by the like-minded participants of the liberal democratic process, free of anything that smacks of "confessional isolationism" (*PH*, 189). Apparently, one person's thick Christian historicism is another's private confessionalism.

I find Davaney's proposal extremely compelling in one respect because it is, well, so practical. It is very hard to disagree with what works—except, however, one has to ask, works for whom? There are interests and hegemonies enmeshed in liberal democratic pragmatism, just as there are in appeals to confessional religious traditions. The supposedly nontraditioned, pragmatic cross-contextual procedures meant to ensure public democratic debate serve some constituencies and not others. Liberal pragmatism is not the procedural opposite of the purported "confessional isolationism" of appeals to tradition-specific (religious) authority; rather, liberal pragmatism is one more tradition alongside others. Davaney at times presents liberal democratic pragmatism as a more or less neutral procedural forum where diverse historical traditions can come to submit their respective claims to cross-contextual scrutiny. This image obscures the ways in which those who promote this type of pragmatism are exercising forms of power in the name of liberal democratic processes. Hence a feminist holding to the "tenets of pragmatism" cannot ensure that solidarity construed by a liberal majority will be any less hegemonic than solidarity construed, say, as a normative implication of following Jesus (*PH*, 180).[55]

My argument that a pragmatic appeal to solidarity may not be less hegemonic than a religious-based appeal raises the question: is it possible to be strongly traditioned yet not hegemonically authoritative when calling for solidarity? Ironically, it is the author with the most thickly Christian-based argument for solidarity who leads us into some new perspectives on feminist solidarity. In critical conversation with M. Shawn Copeland's writings, I will explore a new metaphor for envisioning solidarity in Christ that remains, nevertheless, dynamically open to otherness, movement and intersubjective give and take.

III. Improvising Solidarity

M. Shawn Copeland gives a tradition-specific (Roman Catholic, womanist) construal of solidarity that significantly thickens its meaning beyond the liberal pragmatic principle of inclusion forwarded by Davaney. Copeland states unambiguously: "Solidarity is grounded in the confession of Jesus as Lord [because]...standing before the Cross of Jesus of Nazareth...[we] grasp the enormity of suffering [and] our complicity and collusion in the suffering, affliction and oppression of others." Copeland appeals to nothing less than solidarity based on the eucharistic power of the "mystical Body of Christ." Copeland's mystical and sacramental christocentric solidarity is so thick that she can even speak of how it "enables each one to apprehend the 'other,' not as an instrument or a commodity..., but as 'sister.'"[56] A secular pragmatist like Rorty might see this as trafficking in murky, private narratives; even Davaney might consider Copeland's appeals to be too traditioned for the bright light of the public sphere.

The reader of this text might be struck by Copeland's unambiguous and forthright appeal to a number of images and categories from which other feminist theologians would shy away: Jesus as (male) Lord, the cross, Christ's suffering, sisterhood. The latter receives a good deal of critical analysis by Copeland, so one can see that her invocation of sisterhood is not a throwback to the white feminist "familial ideology" that masks the "de jure and de facto inequality among the sisters of the family" (TS, 12). However, her claim for christologically based oneness is asserted without provisos: "We are called to follow Jesus to those who are broken, abused, dispossessed, and marginalized....And when we stand and live in solidarity with them, we realize ourselves as the community of the Resurrected Lord....[I]n this is our salvation" (TS, 31). Copeland's definition of solidarity is a powerful and evocative example of what could be described as a thoroughly policed christological vision of unity, to use the language of Foucault (my use, not Copeland's). This type of solidarity is a function of intense disciplinary mechanisms of sin and confession, personally and corporately. The policing of these discourses provides "the grace of interruption" whereby moral conversion can take place in relation to the other (TS, 29). The pleasurable, identity-producing aspect of those policing mechanisms comes into play. Through a eucharistically inspired solidarity, one finds one's place in "communion with the whole Christ: the suffering Christ, the exalted and Risen Lord, the body of believers" (TS, 30). There are, conversely, downsides to this traditional Christian-based solidarity. Grounding feminist solidarity so unequivocally in these traditional creedal beliefs creates a dichotomy between traditional and nontraditional feminists. Moreover solidarity is overburdened with the disciplinary aspects of those creeds. The androcentrism, savior hierarchy, and cross-focused christocentrism in Copeland's discussion are untempered by her concerns voiced elsewhere about "marginalized . . . gendered . . . embodiment," the "crusted misogyny" of the church, and "cultural imperialism" (*TS*, 5, 8, 24). Must Christian feminist solidarity be bought at such an unrelenting and burdensome disciplinary price? Is the fracturing of Christian feminism such that we have an either/or situation: either return to feminism's "clichéd rhetoric" of solidarity that obscures differences of race, class, and so on; or submit to the unifying, equalizing and potentially hegemonic discourse of "the Incarnation of the Second Person of the Trinity" (*TS*, 27)? Is this perhaps a reason to accept Davaney's admonition to steer clear of confessional Christian appeals and instead rely on pragmatic norms alone? Are there other possibilities for rethinking solidarity theologically?

My response to Copeland's appeal to traditionally creedal and disciplinary forms of Christian belief is twofold. I reiterate what I have argued in previous chapters about how feminist theologians can continue to work within the Christian tradition by negotiating with it regulatively and hermeneutically. I will not rehash those arguments here, except to say that although Copeland does not cast her engagement with creedal formulas like the trinity poststructurally, she arguably is negotiating with their disciplinary aspects in various ways, such that a womanist power/knowledge of solidarity is (pleasurably) produced. Moreover, she can also be seen as envisioning how institutional mechanisms of the tradition (e.g., the eucharist) can be appropriated as a technology of care that the Christian feminist can impose on her body to effect a spiritual and ethical self-transformation. That said, I would like to explore here another idea that Copeland hints at elsewhere in her writings that helps address the dichotomy between traditional and revisionary feminists that Copeland's comments could precipitate.

In an appreciative review of Cornel West's scholarship, Copeland praises the "improvisational" nature of West's use of "the '*organic* intellectual traditions'" of preaching and musical performance in the African American community. For West and Copeland, good African American theology today requires something like jazz improvisation that taps into the "jazz cadence in American culture . . . [arising] from massive Black human suffering." Using very Foucault-sounding terms, Copeland writes: "The [jazz] musician is steeped in a discipline, a desire, and an excellence. . . . disciplined, yet transgressing boundaries."[57] There is a discipline yet also desire; there is structure yet also transgression. The result is " 'dialogue or conversation or even argument...with peers, with...the world at large.'"[58] Tradition-specific discipline with the interruption of improvisational otherness—this sounds like a basis for solidarity where policing christocentric discourses of, for example, Christ's lordship can be broken open with dissonant riffs from other "texts" that resist that discourse. In light of Copeland's and West's comments on jazz improvisation in relation to womanist and black theology, I would like to pursue an analogous line of thinking about improvisation in relation to feminist theology.[59] My focus is a medium with which I am more familiar: improvisational dance.

Improvisational dance can serve as a helpful metaphor,[60] alongside others, for thinking anew about solidarity in ways that do not imply the kinds of oppositional either/ors I have discussed in Welch's, Davaney's, and Copeland's writings.[61] Improvisation is an integral part of many new trends in dance today. A white feminist colleague of mine and professor of dance at Oberlin College observes that "improvisation is a misunderstood phenomenon.... Figured as the opposite of choreography, improvisation is often seen as free, spontaneous, nontechnical, wild, or childlike, as if one can simply erase years of physical and aesthetic training to become a blank slate into which one's imagination can project anything."[62] A dancer's body is unavoidably disciplined in various ways, and she experiences certain kinesthetic and aesthetic pleasure in conformity to those disciplines and forms. Improvisation is not freedom from all form, since it has its own technical vocabulary that one must learn. When exposed to the technique of improvisation, the dancer experiences new mental images and modes of movement that become a new body of knowledge with new forms of pleasure and constraint. "Improvisation can lead us out of our habitual responses by opening up alternative experiences—new physical sensations and movement appetites, encouraging dancers to explore new positionings and desires,"[63] including the desire to be willing to move "in a state of disorientation" where one is open to otherness.[64]

I would argue that one important precondition for reopening discussions of solidarity among feminist theologians, where racial and other differences are factors, would be a mentality analogous to that of improvisational dance. Academically disciplined, religiously normalized theologians of privilege need to discipline themselves in new ways to set aside their habitual responses to what is "other" (e.g., alternative theological and religious discourses and marginalized cultural perspectives and practices). Theologians from marginalized communities deserve a stage where roles of dominance and subordination are not already choreographed.

How could this improvisation orientation speak to the concerns I have raised above about solidarity? I argued that Welch sets up a dichotomy between solidarity and adjudicating validity claims—a dichotomy that overburdens the category of solidarity. How does the dance improvisation metaphor help us avoid this opposition? It might seem that some forms of improvisation reinforce this opposition. Take, for example, "contact" improvisation,[65] where dancers engage in movement involving confrontational physics (weight thrown against weight, unexpectedly intersecting moving bodies) as well as "moments of calm, moments of great elation."[66] Kinesthetically speaking, there seems to be an opposition between throwing one's weight around in improvisational contact with other bodies (a putative metaphor for communicative action) and finding equilibrium and connection (a putative metaphor for solidarity). I think this is a false opposition because it does not represent contact improvisation accurately and, when applied metaphorically to illustrate solidarity, distorts the power dynamics that are always present in material practices of solidarity.

Contact improvisation is not based on an opposition between dynamic confrontation and calm connection. Even in moments of calm, there are always confrontational physical dynamics at work. Living bodies are always moving, shifting weight, giving and taking. We "debate" when we dance, even in moments of stillness. This is analogous to the dynamics of feminist solidarity, especially regarding interracial relations. When a white feminist leaves the roundtable discussion in the academic conference hall and joins the Habitat of Humanity work group, she has not left behind the debate with its argumentative dynamics of communicative action. Intersubjective speech acts happen everywhere, and hence the risks entailed in Habermasian communicative ethics are present whenever people of privilege come into contact with others—even and maybe especially in modes of empathetic solidarity. In other words, we white people are socially and psychically conditioned to defend our validity claims (and our privilege) in many overt and subtle forms wherever we are—including our projects of solidarity. I argued above that we can unburden the category of solidarity by admitting that it is a fragile reality and not the panacea for the risks of communicative action. Here I suggest that thinking about solidarity in terms of contact improvisation can help feminists of privilege remember the inevitable power dynamics that are at work even in apparent moments of harmonious connection.

The improvisational dance metaphor also speaks to the dichotomy in Davaney's liberal pragmatic historicism—namely, that one may have to choose the supposedly neutral procedures of pragmatism and reject supposedly overly confessional religious appeals. Improvisational dance can help us to see how to uphold both pragmatism and tradition, without this dichotomy—in part because it calls into question those assumptions about them. Improvisation is very pragmatic in its orientation; one has to go with what works physically for the bodies and the space involved. On the other hand, improvisational dance does not pretend that bodies are blank slates; each dancer brings to the improvisational encounter a certain tradition of technical expertise, as well as various injuries, physical limitations, and so on. Ballet-trained dancers tend to contact others balletically. Over time, a contact improvisational dance troupe can build its own common language or tradition of what works, but the whole process starts over again when new dancers join the group or as bodies age and change. What works for any contact improvisation is a process of constantly recreating a shared movement language by continually drawing from each dancer's own deeply embedded tradition. The individual dancers' backgrounds as well as the pragmatics of their collective dancing are deeply historicized. Dance improvisation materially demonstrates that tradition and "what works" are both historicized and are always mutually conditioning each other.

Just as there is traditioning in pragmatism (liberal or any other kind), so also is there improvisation in tradition. We can see this in the world of dance. Improvisation is used integrally in many traditional and highly structured dance forms (e.g., flamenco and classical South Indian dance).[67] A dance tradition can be the cradle for the powerful pragmatics of improvisational performances. Classical dance forms and improvisation should not be seen as oppositional. Analogously religiously traditioned authority should not be seen automatically as necessarily competing with pragmatism. As I have argued above, religious claims are in principle no more and no less disposed to be rigidly authoritative when invoked in the public sphere than liberal democratically normed principles of, say, inclusion. Indeed, it is possible that an appeal to inclusion by a well-intentioned privileged academic elite could function more hegemonically than Christianly based appeals by grassroots believers to follow Jesus and befriend the outcast. Improvisational dance imagery is helpful for reminding us that those with privileged access to liberal (white, upper-class) democratic modes of social organization cannot continue to choreograph the modes of social change. Even white feminist theologians who enter the pragmatic process with the best of intentions (like a commitment to the Christian preferential option for the nonperson) must at some point relinquish their choreographic control of the process so that other (nondominant) modes of thought/movement can emerge on their own terms—and not be relegated to the receiving end of a pragmatic application by those in power of a principle of inclusion.

Improvisational dance addresses the dichotomy found in Copeland's discussion of solidarity where her (justified) critique of a liberal white feminist rhetoric of sisterhood seems to lead her to a cul-de-sac of heavily disciplinary

Christian doctrine as the basis for solidarity, which many revisionary feminists would find hard to accept. For Copeland, the ills of white feminist racism are so deeply rooted that nothing less than an appeal to the mystical body of the second person of the Trinity could begin to dislodge it. While it may be true (pastorally speaking) that appeals to the crucified and suffering body of Christ can precipitate the kind of moral conversion needed on the part of many traditional white feminist Christians, there are other ways to engage christological discourses that can acknowledge and channel some of its repressive policing entailments. Dance improvisation training provides an analogy that helps us think more fluidly and performatively about moral conversion.

Dancers come to contact improvisation with dance training history and prior movement vocabularies, some of which can get in the way of moving together improvisationally. Past dance training can never be erased, but retraining at the most rudimentary levels must occur so that dancers can cultivate a new orientation to movement, the dance space, and other bodies. Dancers must develop new strengths and modes of perception in order to move together improvisationally.[68] Thus, just as dancers do not lose their prior dance movement identities when they submit to contact improvisational retraining, so feminists inevitably will (and should) maintain their feminist (and other) commitments and critical perspectives if and when they respond to a call to solidarity as an outgrowth of their religious formation. Feminists (white feminists, womanists, Asian American and Latina feminists, etc.) could decide to take the risk of moving improvisationally within a disciplinary, even penitential, discourse of solidarity in Christ—a discourse where privilege is burned away by the cross, difference is celebrated as "the unmistakable stamp of the Creator's image and likeness," and the other becomes "'sister,' 'brother,' 'neighbor'" by virtue of Christ's mystical body (TS, 32). For white feminists in particular, seeing moral conversion as analogous to improvisational dance retraining gets at the "penitential" dynamic required on the part of white feminists, if one thinks of penitential practices in some of their classic forms of actual practices upon the body meant to effect spiritual change (TS, 3).[69] This analogy helps us keep a critical feminist perspective about the disciplinary aspects of solidarity in Christ. Appealing, for example, to Christ's lordship could be an effective improvisational *moment* that even a very liberal feminist might wish to pass through in a mode of improvisational solidarity with others, but it cannot be made the sole, sufficient or even extended basis for the kind of broad Christian feminist solidarity attentive to difference for which I believe Copeland hopes.

Hence, I return to the theme with which I began: difference. If difference is made methodologically and theoretically central to the way feminists with various forms of privilege do theology, then it may be possible to move beyond affinity and begin to speak of feminist solidarity—or, as Copeland boldly suggests, even sisterhood (though I would invoke this term much more tentatively). But if we do, we must attend seriously and rigorously to the genealogy of these terms, with their dominating and pleasurable forms of discipline, and to the ways they have been used to screen white, heterosexual, upper-class, and other privileges. Solidarity, like the notion of women's experience, must be used strategically and improvisationally, if at all. If what I have argued in previous chapters has been convincing, the fact of the past disciplinary force of a discursive symbol need not alone be a reason to excise that symbol from one's lexicon. Indeed, as I have argued repeatedly, resistant power/knowledges emerge not apart from but in discursive relationality with policing disciplines. "Solidarity" and "sisterhood" have rendered many women's bodies docile just as the terms "lordship of Christ" and "blood of the cross" have done. The questions Christian feminists are left with are these: Is our analysis of selfhood, power, and agency full enough to be able to reconsider how normalizing terms such as these (and many others besides) might be reworked? Can these contested terms be negotiated, even appropriated, as feminist technologies of care that could foster a spiritual performativity celebratory of difference, self-critical of privilege, and open to unexpected desires?

Notes

CHAPTER 1

1. First-wave feminism, as defined in secular women's studies, refers to women's thought and activism from the late eighteenth to mid-twentieth centuries. In religious studies circles, first-wave feminism refers to women's religious thought and activism in the late 1960s and early 1970s.

2. I am using the term "theologian" to refer not just to those with training in systematic and historical theology but to any feminist thinker working in relation to the Christian tradition who reflects on theological issues, the meaning of sacred texts, women's spirituality, or other such topics. In the 1970s some scholars in religion (mostly working with goddess traditions) began using the term "*thea*logian" (attributed to Naomi Goldenberg) as a way of decentering the masculine *theos* of Christian theology and, thus, may not wish to associate with feminist theology as an umbrella category. See Carol P. Christ, "Why Women Need the Goddess: Phenomenological, Psychological, and Political Reflections," in *Womanspirit Rising: A Feminist Reader in Religion*, ed. Carol P. Christ and Judith Plaskow (1979; repr., San Francisco, Calif.: Harper & Row, 1992), 278. Some feminist scholars working in other religious traditions also use the term theologian. While not all the topics in this book will intersect with their (or thealogians') interests, I believe that many of the issues I discuss will be relevant to them.

3. Rosemary Radford Ruether, *Sexism and God-Talk: Toward a Feminist Theology*, with new introduction (1983; repr., Boston, Mass.: Beacon, 1993), 12.

4. Mary Daly, *Gyn/Ecology: The Metaethics of Radical Feminism* (Boston, Mass.: Beacon, 1978), 39.

5. Mary Daly, *Beyond God the Father: Toward a Philosophy of Women's Liberation*, with new introduction (1973; repr., Boston, Mass.: Beacon, 1985), 1; emphasis added.

6. Rosemary Radford Ruether, "Feminist Interpretation: A Method of Correlation," in *Feminist Interpretation of the Bible*, ed. Letty M. Russell (Philadelphia, Pa.: Westminster, 1985), 114, 115.

7. Delores S. Williams, "The Color of Feminism: Or Speaking the Black Woman's Tongue," in *Feminist Theological Ethics*, ed. Lois K. Daly (Louisville, Ky.: Westminster John Knox, 1994), 49, 50; Williams's essay was originally published in 1986. I will return to the issue of demonarchy in chapter 4.

8. Elizabeth A. Johnson, *She Who Is: The Mystery of God in Feminist Theological Discourse* (New York: Crossroad, 1995), 11, 222; quoting Anne Carr.

9. Susan Brooks Thistlethwaite, *Sex, Race, and God: Christian Feminism in Black and White* (New York: Crossroad, 1989), 90.

10. See Sheila Greeve Davaney, "Problems with Feminist Theory: Historicity and the Search for Sure Foundations," in *Embodied Love: Sensuality and Relationships as Feminist Values*, ed. Paula M. Cooey et al. (San Francisco, Calif.: Harper & Row, 1987); Davaney, "The Limits of the Appeal to Women's Experience," in *Shaping New Vision: Gender and Values in American Culture*, ed. Clarissa W. Atkinson, Constance H. Buchanan, and Margaret R. Miles (Ann Arbor, Mich.: UMI Research Press, 1987); and Mary McClintock Fulkerson, *Changing the Subject: Women's Discourses and Feminist Theology* (Minneapolis, Minn.: Fortress, 1994).

11. See Serene Jones, "'Women's Experience' Between a Rock and a Hard Place: Feminist, Womanist, and *Mujerista* Theologies in North America," *Religious Studies Review* 21 (1995): 178.

12. Ruether, *Sexism and God-Talk*, xv.

13. Rebecca S. Chopp, *Saving Work: Feminist Practices of Theological Education* (Louisville, Ky.: Westminster John Knox, 1995), 3–4. For two other perspectives on the emergence of feminist theology, see Janet Martin Soskice, "General Introduction," in *Oxford Readings in Feminism and Theology*, ed. Janet Martin Soskice and Diana Lipton (New York: Oxford University Press, 2003); and Rita M. Gross, *Feminism and Religion: An Introduction* (Boston, Mass.: Beacon, 1996), 40–49.

14. See Chopp, *Saving Work*, 21, 73; and Sallie McFague, *Metaphorical Theology: Models of God in Religious Language* (Philadelphia, Pa.: Fortress, 1982). The latter text also stands as one of the early constructive feminist theological monographs, though not as doctrinally oriented as Ruether's *Sexism and God-Talk*.

15. Quoted in Chopp, *Saving Work*, 72.

16. Mary Grey, *Redeeming the Dream: Feminism, Redemption, and Christian Tradition* (London: SPCK, 1989), 11, 38.

17. Ibid., 9, 28; Judith Plaskow, *Standing Again at Sinai: Judaism from a Feminist Perspective* (San Francisco, Calif.: Harper, 1990), 1; Sheila Collins, "Reflections on the Meaning of Herstory," in *Womanspirit Rising*, 68–73.

18. Delores S. Williams, *Sisters in the Wilderness: The Challenge of Womanist God-Talk* (Maryknoll, N.Y.: Orbis, 1993).

19. See Carol P. Christ, *Diving Deep and Surfacing: Women Writers on Spiritual Quest* (Boston, Mass.: Beacon, 1980); Katie G. Cannon, *Black Womanist Ethics* (Atlanta, Ga.: Scholars, 1988); Sharon D. Welch, *A Feminist Ethic of Risk* (Minneapolis, Minn.: Fortress, 1990); Williams, *Sisters in the Wilderness*; Kathleen M. Sands, *Escape from Paradise: Evil and Tragedy in Feminist Theology* (Minneapolis, Minn.: Fortress, 1994); and Ivone Gebara, trans. Ann Patrick Ware, *Out of the Depths: Women's Experience of Evil and Salvation* (Minneapolis, Minn.: Fortress, 2002).

20. Ruether, *Sexism and God-Talk*, 1–11.

21. See Thistlethwaite, *Sex, Race, and God*; and Ellen T. Armour, *Deconstruction, Feminist Theology, and the Problem of Difference: Subverting the Race/Gender Divide* (Chicago, Ill.: University of Chicago Press, 1999).

22. See Stephanie Y. Mitchem, *Introducing Womanist Theology* (Maryknoll, N.Y.: Orbis, 2002), 87–91; and Michelle A. Gonzáles, "'One Is Not Born a Latina, One Becomes One': The Construction of the Latina Feminist Theologian in Latino/a Theology," *Journal of Hispanic/Latino Theology* 10 (2003): 17–22.

23. One important early exception is Thistlethwaite, *Sex, Race, and God*.

24. Nancy Whittier, *Feminist Generations: The Persistence of the Radical Women's Movement* (Philadelphia, Pa.: Temple University Press, 1995), 306.

25. Gloria Anzaldúa, "Bridge, Drawbridge, Sandbar, or Island: Lesbians-of-Color *Hacienda Alianzas*," in *Bridges of Power: Women's Multicultural Alliances*, ed. Lisa Albrecht and Rose M. Brewer (Philadelphia, Pa.: New Society, 1990), 222.

26. Susan Stanford Friedman, "Beyond White and Other: Relationality and Narratives of Race in Feminist Discourse," *Signs: Journal of Women in Culture and Society* 21, no. 1 (1995): 9, 11.

27. Some now-classic texts include Cherrie Moraga and Gloria Anzaldúa, eds., *This Bridge Called My Back: Writings by Radical Women of Color* (New York: Kitchen Table, 1983); Angela Y. Davis, *Women Race and Class* (New York: Vintage, 1983); bell hooks, *Ain't I a Woman: Black Women and Feminism* (Boston, Mass.: South End, 1981); Audre Lorde, *Sister/Outsider: Essays and Speeches* (Freedom, Calif.: Crossing, 1984); and Alice Walker, *In Search of Our Mothers' Gardens: Womanist Prose* (San Diego, Calif.: Harcourt Brace Jovanovich, 1984).

28. Elizabeth V. Spelman, *Inessential Woman: Problems of Exclusion in Feminist Thought* (Boston, Mass.: Beacon, 1988), 162, 163.

29. Ibid., 181.

30. Ibid., 178.

31. Nancie Caraway, *Segregated Sisterhood: Racism and the Politics of American Feminism* (Knoxville: University of Tennessee Press, 1991), 173; quoting Elizabeth Spelman.

32. Ibid., 114.

33. Ibid., 16, 19. For example, she speaks of her past as a white working-class southern girl who "envied 'the popular [white?] girls'...whose parents where able to participate in PTA meetings and school activities, who were picked up in cars after school to be taken to dance class and private swim clubs" (ibid., 18).

34. Ibid., 195.

35. Ibid., 17.

36. Ruth Frankenberg, *White Women, Race Matters: The Social Construction of Whiteness* (Minneapolis: University of Minnesota Press, 1993), 198.

37. Ibid., 243.

38. See ibid., 229. None of Frankenberg's subjects were currently severely disadvantaged (economically, educationally, etc.).

39. Some Jews do not consider themselves white, although all the Jewish women Frankenberg interviewed called themselves white and Jewish. Regarding the relationship between these experiences of marginalization and race, Frankenberg concludes: "These interviews did *not*...suggest that one experience of marginality—Jewishness, lesbianism—led white women automatically toward empathy with other oppressed communities" (*White Women, Race Matters*, 20).

40. Frankenberg notes how the rhetoric of right-wing "white pride" groups creates "a discursive bind" for the project of naming whiteness as a cultural identity. Her point is that an intentionally self-critical naming of the content and function of whiteness in its diverse manifestations will head off any attempts "[t]o call Americans of European descent 'white' in any celebratory fashion [which] is almost inevitably...a white supremacist act" (ibid., 232).

41. Katie G. Cannon et al., *God's Fierce Whimsy: Christian Feminism and Theological Education* (New York: Pilgrim, 1985).

42. I will be using Katie G. Cannon and Carter Heyward, "Can We Be Different but Not Alienated? An Exchange of Letters," in *Feminist Theological Ethics: A Reader*, ed. Lois K. Daly (Louisville, Ky.: Westminster John Knox, 1994), 59–76. Cannon and Heyward have continued their dialogue in the form of ongoing correspondence and appearances together at conferences. See Cannon and Heyward, "Alienation and Anger: A Black and a White Woman's Struggle for Mutuality in an Unjust World," *Stone Center Publication*, no. 54 (1992): 1–13.

43. Robyn Wiegman discusses this reading strategy in relation to Harriet Beecher Stowe's *Uncle Tom's Cabin* where Uncle Tom's suffering is used to evoke, via a regime of sentiment, a "political alliance between slaves and [the] white women" who made up a large segment of Stowe's original readership. See Wiegman, *American Anatomies: Theorizing Race and Gender* (Durham, N.C.: Duke University Press, 1995), 195.

44. "I find at times—much to my chagrin, actually—my image of black men is of people I cannot trust" (Cannon and Heyward, "Can We Be Different?" 69).

45. Ibid., 73, 74.

46. Black literary critic Valerie Smith's discussion of race and rape is pertinent to the submerged racial subtext in the Cannon-Heyward correspondence. See Smith, "Split Affinities: The Case of Interracial Rape," in *Conflicts in Feminism*, ed. Marianne Hirsch and Evelyn Fox Keller (New York: Routledge, 1990).

47. Susan L. Secker, "Women's Experience in Feminist Theology: The 'Problem' or the 'Truth' of Difference," *Journal of Hispanic/Latino Theology* 1 (1993): 60.

48. Jeanette Rodríguez, "Experience as a Resource for Feminist Thought," *Journal of Hispanic/Latino Theology* 1 (1993): 71; quoting from Gloria Anzaldúa.

49. Secker, "Women's Experience," 63.

50. Ibid., 58.

51. Ibid., 66, 63.

52. Rodríguez, "Experience as a Resource," 75.

53. Mitchem, *Introducing Womanist Theology*, 92.

54. Stephanie Y. Mitchem, "Response: "Reading Womanists; Repatterning Ourselves," *Journal of Feminist Studies in Religion* 19, no. 2 (2003): 72, 73; quoting Barbara Christian. Mitchem's essay was solicited by the journal's editors in response to my article in the same issue, "Reading the Raced and Sexed Body in *The Color Purple*: Repatterning White Feminist and Womanist Theological Hermeneutics," 45–66.

55. Emilie M. Townes, "Appropriation and Reciprocity in Womanist/Mujerista/ Feminist Work," in *Feminist Theological Ethics: A Reader*, ed. Lois K. Daly (Louisville, Ky.: Westminster John Knox, 1994), 110, 111.

56. Judith Butler, *Gender Trouble: Feminism and the Subversion of Identity* (New York: Routledge, 1990), 6.

57. A classic exposition on these themes is Peter Brown, *The Body and Society: Men, Women, and Sexual Renunciation in Early Christianity* (New York: Columbia University Press, 1988).

58. See Dyan Elliot, *Proving Woman: Female Spirituality and Inquisitional Culture in the Later Middle Ages* (Princeton, N.J.: Princeton University Press, 2004), 205–211. See also Rosalynn Voaden, *God's Words, Women's Voices: The Discernment of Spirits in the Writings of Late-Medieval Women Visionaries* (New York: York Medieval Press, 1999).

59. In addition to the texts by Rosemary Ruether and Mary Daly cited above, see Elizabeth Clark and Herbert Richardson, ed., *Women and Religion: A Feminist Sourcebook of Christian Thought* (New York: Harper & Row, 1977); Elizabeth Clark, *Ascetic Piety and Women's Faith: Essays on Late Ancient Christianity* (Lewiston, N.Y.: Edwin Mellen, 1986); and Nel Noddings, *Women and Evil* (Berkeley: University of California Press, 1989).

60. See Lisa Isherwood and Elizabeth Stuart, *Introducing Body Theology* (Cleveland, Ohio: Pilgrim, 1998).

61. A few titles include Carter Heyward, *Touching Our Strength: The Erotic as Power and the Love of God* (San Francisco, Calif.: Harper, 1989); Gary David Comstock, *Gay Theology without Apology* (Cleveland, Ohio: Pilgrim, 1993); Robert E. Goss, *Queering Christ: Beyond Jesus Acted Up* (Cleveland, Ohio: Pilgrim, 2002); and Vanessa Sheridan, *Crossing Over: Liberating the Transgendered Christian* (Cleveland, Ohio: Pilgrim, 2001).

62. Catherine Mowry LaCugna, *God, the Trinity, and Christian Life* (San Francisco, Calif.: Harper, 1991), 407.

63. Kelly Brown Douglas, *Sexuality and the Black Church: A Womanist Perspective* (Maryknoll, N.Y.: Orbis, 1999). See also Emilie M. Townes, *In a Blaze of Glory: Womanist Spirituality as Social Witness* (Nashville, Tenn.: Abingdon, 1995), chap. 4.

64. Douglas, *Sexuality and the Black Church*, 1, 5. Holism is an allusion to the holistic definition of black feminist in Alice Walker's definition of "womanist." See *In Search of Our Mothers' Gardens* (San Diego, Calif.: Harcourt Brace, 1983), xi–xii. The

sexual component of Walker's definition has made the term controversial, and some African American women theologians do not accept it. See Cheryl J. Sanders et al., "Roundtable Discussion: Christian Ethics and Theology in Womanist Perspective," *Journal of Feminist Studies in Religion* 5 (1989): 81–112, and the response by Kelly Brown Douglas in *The Black Christ* (Maryknoll, N.Y.: Orbis, 1994), 101.

65. Carter Heyward, Mary Hunt, et al., "Roundtable Discussion: Lesbianism and Feminist Theology," *Journal of Feminist Studies in Religion* 2, no. 2 (1986): 97, 98, 99.

66. Ibid., 103, 104.

67. Renée Leslie Hill, "Disrupted/Disruptive Movements: Black Theology and Black Power," in *Black Faith and Public Talk: Critical Essays on James H. Cone's "Black Theology and Black Power,"* ed. Dwight N. Hopkins (Maryknoll, N.Y.: Orbis, 1999), 138. For other perspectives of people of faith with marginalized ethnicities, races, and sexualities, see Gary David Comstock and Susan E. Henking, *Que(e)rying Religion: A Critical Anthology* (New York: Continuum, 1997).

68. *Feminist Theology* 11, no. 2 (2003); Althaus-Reid, *Indecent Theology: Theological Perversions in Sex, Gender, and Politics* (London: Routledge, 2000).

69. A notable difference in the 2003 forum is a male voice, that of gay theologian Robert E. Goss, which shows that feminist dialogue is now at a place where it does not feel the need to exclude males. See Goss, "Marcella Althaus-Reid's 'Obscenity no. 1: Bi/Christ': Expanding Christ's Wardrobe of Dresses," *Feminist Theology* 11, no. 2 (2003).

70. Kwok Pui-lan, "Theology as a Sexual Act," *Feminist Theology* 11, no. 2 (2003): 152.

71. Emilie M. Townes, "Panel Response to Marcella Althaus-Reid's *Indecent Theology,*" *Feminist Theology* 11, no. 2 (2003): 170.

72. Marcella Althaus-Reid, "On Non-Docility and Indecent Theologians: A Response to the Panel for *Indecent Theology,*" *Feminist Theology* 11, no. 2 (2003): 186, 187.

73. A Porteña woman is "from the port of Buenos Aires" (ibid., 186).

74. Ibid., 183.

75. All in-text biblical references in this book are to The New Revised Standard Version.

CHAPTER 2

1. Carol P. Christ, *Diving Deep and Surfacing: Women Writers on Spiritual Quest* (Boston, Mass.: Beacon, 1980); Katie G. Cannon, *Black Womanist Ethics* (Atlanta, Ga.: Scholars, 1988).

2. In addition to the texts I discuss in this chapter, some other recent feminist theological texts that mention this novel are Pamela A. Smith, "Green Lap, Brown Embrace, Blue Body: The Ecospirituality of Alice Walker," *Cross Currents* 48, 4 (1998); Karen Baker-Fletcher and Garth Kasimu Baker-Fletcher, *My Sister, My Brother: Womanist and Xodus God-Talk* (Maryknoll, N.Y.: Orbis, 1997), 37–39; Toinette Eugene, "'If You Get There Before I Do!' A Womanist Ethical Response to Sexual Violence and Abuse," in *Perspectives on Womanist Theology*, ed. Jacquelyn Grant (Atlanta, Ga.:

ITC, 1997), 106–7, 110–11; Diana L. Hayes, *Hagar's Daughters: Womanist Ways of Being in the World* (New York: Paulist, 1995), 35; M. Shawn Copeland, "'Wading through Many Sorrows': Toward a Theology of Suffering in Womanist Perspective," in *A Troubling in My Soul: Womanist Perspectives on Evil and Suffering*, ed. Emilie M. Townes (Maryknoll, N.Y.: Orbis, 1993), 123; and Mary Patricia Beckman and Mara E. Donaldson, "The Theological Significance of *The Color Purple*: A Liberation Theology?" *Saint Luke's Journal of Theology* 33 (1990).

3. Let me say a word here about white feminist critique of womanist theology. Some white feminist scholars believe that they "should not presume to be addressing black women at all," that "middle-class, white women must learn to listen and educate [them]selves." Katy Taylor, "From Lavender to Purple: A Feminist Reading of Hagar and Celie in Light of Womanism," *Theology* 97 (1994): 361. Motivating this observation is the legitimate concern about the effects of the history of white liberal entitlement, so trenchantly critiqued since the advent of the black power movement and still affecting academe today. Interrogating whiteness and its hegemony remains an extraordinarily difficult but necessary task. To bring a critique to bear on womanist theological reading practices should not be seen as an excuse by white feminists such as me to be less vigilant in interrogating racism in our own reading practices. However, I do not believe that white feminist theologians should undertake that self-critical project while recusing ourselves from multicultural critical dialogue. Indeed, the opposite is the case. To refuse to engage critically the views of feminist scholars from minority communities is to patronize them, which insidiously reinforces white privilege.

4. As Robyn Wiegman writes, "Too often...white women situate themselves as the moral guardians of 'race,' policing other white women for evidence of racist transgressions, as if [this]...demonstrates our own willful noncomplicity." Wiegman, *American Anatomies: Theorizing Race and Gender* (Durham, N.C.: Duke University Press, 1995), 189. The temptation to moral superiority can be averted, hopefully, by refusing any claim to an unimpeachable, "policing" authority on discussions of race, sexuality, and other sites of identity construction.

5. Judith Butler, *Gender Trouble: Feminism and the Subversion of Identity* (New York: Routledge, 1990), 23.

6. This theme sparked heated debates among Walker's African American readership. See Pia Thielmann, "Alice Walker and the 'Man Question,'" in *Critical Essays on Alice Walker*, ed. Ikenna Dieke (Westport, Conn.: Greenwood, 1999).

7. Alice Walker, *The Color Purple* (New York: Pocket, 1982), 1; Walker's emphasis (in this chapter, hereafter cited in text as *CP*).

8. This scene has been highlighted as an example of the "'sass' and impertinence" of the "outraged mother figure" depicted in African American women's novels. See Joanne M. Braxton, "Ancestral Presence: The Outraged Mother Figure in Contemporary Afra-American Writing," in *Wild Women in the Whirlwind: Afra-American Culture and the Contemporary Literary Renaissance*, ed. Joanne M. Braxton and Andrée Nicola McLaughlin (New Brunswick, N.J.: Rutgers University Press, 1990), 309.

9. Susan Brooks Thistlethwaite, *Sex, Race, and God: Christian Feminism in Black and White* (New York: Crossroad, 1989), 4. She is not suggesting that it is illegitimate for anyone outside the African American community to interpret or use its literature, but appropriation in feminist theological writings is an issue that must be addressed. I will discuss this in chapter 6.

10. Ibid., 115–16. A recent example of this white feminist practice can be found in Carol P. Christ, *Rebirth of the Goddess: Finding Meaning in Feminist Spirituality* (New York: Routledge, 1997), 107–8. Christ quotes this passage from *The Color Purple* without a discussion of Shug's rejection of God's whiteness.

11. Thistlethwaite, *Sex, Race, and God*, 90.

12. British feminist Daphne Hampson's book *Theology and Feminism* (Oxford: Blackwell, 1990) appeared the year following Thistlethwaite's book, so while Hampson was writing her book she most likely was not aware of the charges Thistlethwaite would level against white feminists who quote from *The Color Purple*. Hampson is virtually silent on the issue of race in her subsequently published *After Christianity* (Valley Forge, Pa.: Trinity, 1996) presented as a follow-up to *Theology and Feminism*.

13. Hampson, *Theology and Feminism*, 149–50.

14. See ibid., 166, 165.

15. See Thistlethwaite, *Sex, Race, and God*, 60–68, 112–20. We see a typical white feminist use of *The Color Purple* by Pamela Dickey Young who quotes at length from the novel and concludes that Walker gives a "powerful accounting of the interconnection of all things in terms of the satisfaction of life they derive from one another." Young, *Christ in a Post-Christian World: How Can We Believe in Jesus Christ When Those Around Us Believe Differently or Not at All?* (Minneapolis, Minn.: Fortress, 1995), 115.

16. Cheryl Townsend Gilkes, "'Mother to the Motherless, Father to the Fatherless': Power, Gender, and Community in Afrocentric Biblical Tradition," *Semeia* 47 (1989): 61. See also Thistlethwaite, *Sex, Race, and God*, 116–17.

17. Thistlethwaite argues that "the natural world is always mediated by human consciousness and its social conditions," and "no assumptions of . . . women's capacity, to relate to their 'sister,' the earth, can be made without considering the factor of race" (*Sex, Race, and God*, 58, 70). Along these lines, for an excellent introduction to how "ecowomanism" differs from white ecofeminism, see Shamara Shantu Riley, "Ecology Is a Sistah's Issue Too," in *Ecofeminism and the Sacred*, ed. Carol J. Adams (New York: Continuum, 1993), 191–204.

18. Deborah McDowell explores how the writing relationship between Celie and Nettie fosters Celie's identity development as a writer and, by extension, symbolizes the development of African American women's literary voice. See McDowell, "'The Changing Same': Generational Connections and Black Women Novelists," in *Reading Black, Reading Feminist: A Critical Anthology*, ed. Henry Louis Gates, Jr. (New York: Meridian, 1990), 101–108.

19. In this sense, one could characterize their reading as an identity politics approach, as I did in an earlier version of this material. See my "Reading the Raced

and Sexed Body in *The Color Purple*: Repatterning White Feminist and Womanist Theological Hermeneutics," *Journal of Feminist Studies in Religion* 19, no. 2 (Fall 2003): 45–66. However, the term "identity politics" may be too much of a so-called buzz word with negative connotations to be used fruitfully anymore in this context.

20. Delores S. Williams, "Black Women's Literature and the Task of Feminist Theology," in *Immaculate and Powerful: The Female in Sacred Image and Social Reality*, ed. Clarissa W. Atkinson, Constance H. Buchanan, and Margaret R. Miles (Boston, Mass.: Beacon, 1985), 88, 97.

21. Ibid., 102, 101.

22. Ibid., 102.

23. Emilie M. Townes, *In a Blaze of Glory: Womanist Spirituality as Social Witness* (Nashville, Tenn.: Abingdon, 1995), 71.

24. Ibid., 70.

25. Another reading of Walker's novel that reflects womanist ethical and political commitments is Cheryl Townsend Gilkes, "A Conscious Connection to All That Is: *The Color Purple* as Subversive and Cultural Ethnography," in *Personal Knowledge and Beyond: Reshaping the Ethnography of Religion*, ed. James V. Spikard, J. Shawn Landres, and Meredith B. McGuire (New York: New York University Press, 2002).

26. For more on the issue of the intersection of racial and gender formation, see Howard Winant, *Racial Conditions: Politics, Theory, Comparisons* (Minneapolis: University of Minnesota Press, 1994), 95–98; Karen Dugger, "Changing the Subject: Race and Gender in Feminist Discourse," in *Racism and Anti-Racism in World Perspective*, ed. Benjamin P. Bowser (Thousand Oaks, Calif.: Sage, 1995); and M. Brinton Lykes and Amelia Mallona, "Surfacing Our-Selves: ¿Gringa, White—Mestiza, Brown?" in *Off White: Readings on Race, Power, and Society*, ed. Michelle Fine et al. (New York: Routledge, 1997).

27. Some recent exceptions to this generalization include Anthony B. Pinn and Dwight N. Hopkins, eds., *Loving the Body: Black Religious Studies and the Erotic* (New York: Palgrave, 2004); Eugene F. Rogers, Jr., ed., *Theology and Sexuality: Classic and Contemporary Readings* (Oxford: Blackwell, 2002); Kelly Brown Douglas, *Sexuality and the Black Church: A Womanist Perspective* (Maryknoll, N.Y.: Orbis, 1999); Lisa Isherwood and Elizabeth Stuart, *Introducing Body Theology* (Cleveland, Ohio: Pilgrim, 1998); and Kathy Rudy, *Sex and the Church: Gender, Homosexuality, and the Transformation of Christian Ethics* (Boston, Mass.: Beacon, 1997).

28. One notable exception is womanist theologian JoAnne Marie Terrell, who explicitly highlights this passage in *Power in the Blood? The Cross in the African American Experience* (Maryknoll, N.Y.: Orbis, 1998), 129, and supports Walker's womanist principle of loving women and men "'*sexually and/or nonsexually*'" (ibid., 137). For Walker's definition of *womanist*, see *In Search of Our Mothers' Gardens: Womanist Prose* (San Diego, Calif.: Harcourt Brace, 1983), xi–xii.

29. Mary Catherine Hilkert, "Experience and Tradition—Can the Center Hold?" in *Freeing Theology: The Essentials of Theology in Feminist Perspective*, ed. Catherine Mowry LaCugna (San Francisco, Calif.: HarperSanFrancisco, 1992), 60.

30. Ibid., 78 n. 2. See Mary E. Hunt, *Fierce Tenderness: A Feminist Theology of Friendship* (New York: Crossroad, 1991).

31. Hilkert elsewhere strongly promotes attending to the particularities of marginalization and relates this point to the use of the literature from minority communities: "But attending to 'the other' does not mean borrowing their stories...without entering into real relationship with them and joining in the struggle to change unjust social and political systems. To do so, however, requires that members of dominant groups recognize their own complicity in systems of oppression." See *Naming Grace: Preaching and the Sacramental Imagination* (New York: Continuum, 1997), 176.

32. Cheryl A. Kirk-Duggan, "Gender, Violence, and Transformation in *The Color Purple*," in *Curing Violence*, ed. Mark I. Wallace and Theophus H. Smith (Sonoma, Calif.: Polebridge, 1994), 266.

33. Ibid., 273.

34. Ibid., 274.

35. Ibid., 284, 284 n. 63.

36. For Barbara Smith, the lesbian relationship in *The Color Purple* has an almost idyllic air to it. She concludes that Walker's story is not a "realistic work" vis-à-vis lesbianism; yet she writes, "I am moved by the vision of a world, unlike this one, where Black women are not forced to lose their families...because of whom they love." The complete lack of homophobia makes the story function as a moral fable—a happy vision of how things might be. See Smith's "The Truth That Never Hurts: Black Lesbians in Fiction in the 1980s," in *Wild Women in the Whirlwind*, ed. Braxton and McLaughlin, 237, 232. By contrast, bell hooks concludes that the "ideal world of true love and commitment" that Walker creates is a dangerous "fantasy of change without effort...a brand of false consciousness that keeps everyone in place and oppressive structures intact." See "Reading and Resistance: *The Color Purple*," in *Alice Walker: Critical Perspectives Past and Present*, ed. Henry Louis Gates, Jr., and K. A. Appiah (New York: Amistad, 1993), 287, 295. Townes would agree that Celie "lives an interior liberation [that] is no threat to the social order," but Townes nevertheless believes Walker's story is an important spiritual "guide" for African Americans (*In a Blaze of Glory*, 71, 72).

37. In her "Justified, Sanctified, and Redeemed: Blessed Expectation in Black Women's Blues and Gospels," Kirk-Duggan highlights the rich mix of spirituality and sexuality in the songs of blues singer Ma Rainey, a "big-hearted woman [who] was sexually involved with men and women." In Rainey's music, "[o]ne experiences hope and salvation through living life to its fullest...as a Black woman, especially sexually." In *Embracing the Spirit: Womanist Perspectives on Hope, Salvation, and Transformation*, ed. Emilie M. Townes (Maryknoll, N.Y.: Orbis, 1997), 145, 157.

38. Delores S. Williams, *Sisters in the Wilderness: The Challenge of Womanist God-Talk* (Maryknoll, N.Y.: Orbis, 1993), 53, 54. In somewhat surprising contrast is the absence of any discussion of sexuality in Gilkes's otherwise rich ethnographic study of the cultural nuances displayed in Walker's novel. Even when Gilkes quotes from a passage charged with erotic energy where Celie longs just to "'lay eyes on [Shug],'"

Gilkes avoids mention of their lesbian relationship. "A Conscious Connection to All That Is," 187; see n. 25.

39. Williams, "Black Women's Literature," 100. Irish feminist Linda Hogan gives an extensive discussion of this article by Williams, focusing on Williams's comments about Shug's role in Celie's life; however Hogan makes no mention of either character's sexuality, despite Williams's explicit reference to their sexual eroticism (ibid., 98). See Linda Hogan, *From Women's Experience to Feminist Theology* (Sheffield, U.K.: Sheffield Academic Press, 1995), 136–38. Hence, black lesbian and bisexual bodies in *The Color Purple* are rendered invisible in Hogan's text.

40. Delores S. Williams, "The Color of Feminism: Or Speaking the Black Woman's Tongue," in *Feminist Theological Ethics: A Reader*, ed. Lois K. Daly (Louisville, Ky.: Westminster John Knox, 1994), 55.

41. See Williams, "Black Women's Literature," 106. For an insightful study on black women's body image, see Cheryl Townsend Gilkes, "The 'Loves' and 'Troubles' of African American Women's Bodies and the Womanist Challenge to Cultural Humiliation and Community Ambivalence," in *A Troubling in My Soul: Womanist Perspectives on Evil and Suffering*, ed. Emilie M. Townes (Maryknoll, N.Y.: Orbis, 1993).

42. Townes, *In a Blaze of Glory*, 77.

43. Ibid., 70, 77.

44. Ibid., 87; Townes's emphasis.

45. Phyllis Trible, *Texts of Terror: Literary-Feminist Readings of Biblical Narratives* (Philadelphia, Pa.: Fortress, 1984).

46. Some important titles are Amy-Jill Levine, "Settling at Beer-lahai-roi," in *Daughters of Abraham: Feminist Thought In Judaism, Christianity, and Islam*, ed. Yvonne Yazbeck Haddad and John L. Esposito (Gainesville: University Press of Florida, 2001); Dora R. Mbuwayesando, "Childlessness and Woman-to-Woman Relationships in Genesis and African Patriarchal Society: Sarah and Hagar from a Zimbabwean Woman's Perspective (Gen. 16:1–16; 21:8–21)," *Semeia* 78 (1997); Kwok Pui-Lan, "Racism and Ethnocentrism in Feminist Biblical Interpretation," in *Searching the Scriptures*, ed. Elizabeth Schüssler Fiorenza (New York: Crossroad, 1995); Cheryl J. Sanders, "Black Women in Biblical Perspective: Resistance, Affirmation, and Empowerment," in *Living the Intersection: Womanism and Afrocentrism in Theology*, ed. Cheryl J. Sanders (Minneapolis, Minn.: Fortress, 1995), 131–38; Williams, *Sisters in the Wilderness*, esp. 15–33; Danna Nolan Fewell and David M. Gunn, "Keeping the Promise (Genesis 11–22)," in *Gender, Power, and Promise: The Subject of the Bible's First Story* (Nashville, Tenn.: Abingdon, 1993); Savina J. Teubal, *Ancient Sisterhood: The Lost Traditions of Hagar and Sarah* (Athens, Ohio: Swallow, 1990); Jo Ann Hackett, "Rehabilitating Hagar: Fragments of an Epic Pattern," in *Gender and Difference in Ancient Israel*, ed. Peggy L. Day (Minneapolis, Minn.: Fortress, 1989); J. Cheryl Exum, "'Mother in Israel': A Familiar Figure Reconsidered," in *Feminist Interpretation of the Bible*, ed. Letty M. Russell (Philadelphia, Pa.: Westminster, 1988); and Renita T. Weems, "A Mistress, a Maid, and No Mercy," in her *Just a Sister Away: A Womanist Vision of Women's Relationships in the Bible* (San Diego, Calif.: Lura Media, 1988).

47. Exum, "'Mother in Israel,'" 74.

48. By contrast, for a study of race issues related to the history of Hagar in white American women's literature, see Janet Gabler-Hover, *Dreaming Black, Writing White: The Hagar Myth in American Cultural History* (Lexington: University Press of Kentucky, 2000).

49. Many scholars argue that race is a fairly modern theoretical construction. See Cornel West, *Prophetic Fragments* (Grand Rapids, Mich.: Eerdmans, 1988), 100; Cain Hope Felder, "Race, Racism, and the Biblical Narrative," in *Stony the Road We Trod: African American Biblical Interpretation*, ed. Cain Hope Felder (Minneapolis, Minn.: Fortress, 1991), 127–45; and Alice Ogden Bellis, *Helpmates, Harlots, and Heroes: Women's Stories in the Hebrew Bible* (Louisville, Ky.: Westminster John Knox, 1994), 78.

50. Feminist interpretations of the Sarah-Hagar texts can also be mapped on another axis according to hermeneutical methodology, with canonical approaches on one end and critical approaches on the other. The possible canonical readings of Genesis are many, ranging from narrative retellings to allegorical interpretations. The critical approaches at the other pole are also diverse, encompassing historical criticism, ideology critique, literary criticism, archaeological and social sciences, and others.

51. There are a few women's scholarly readings of the Sarah-Hagar story that do not foreground women's oppression of any kind. Devora Steinmetz, who takes an extreme canonical approach, attempts to justify Sarah's (and Abraham's) oppressive actions by subsuming them under the canonical outcome of the story. See Steinmetz, *From Father to Son: Kinship, Conflict and Continuity in Genesis* (Louisville, Ky.: Westminster John Knox, 1991). Naomi Steinberg avoids any feminist critique of the sociological realities of ancient kinship practices, including those in the Sarah and Hagar story. See Steinberg, *Kinship and Marriage in Genesis: A Household Economics Perspective* (Minneapolis, Minn.: Fortress, 1993).

52. Refer to their texts cited in note 46, this chapter.

53. See Fewell/Gunn, *Gender, Power, and Promise*, 12–13.

54. Ibid., 19.

55. Ibid., 45.

56. Ibid., 46.

57. Ibid., 52, 53.

58. Perhaps one reason for the fact that both Exum and Fewell/Gunn privilege gender oppression is that they rely on Gerda Lerner's *The Creation of Patriarchy* (New York: Oxford University Press, 1986), which argues that patriarchy was at work prior to other forms of oppression such as class discrimination. See Exum, *Fragmented Women: Feminist (Sub)Versions of Biblical Narratives* (Valley Forge, Pa.: Trinity, 1993), 9, 10; and Fewell/Gunn, *Gender, Power, and Promise*, 15.

59. Exum, "'Mother in Israel,'" 76, 77.

60. Exum, *Fragmented Women*, 135, 136.

61. Ibid., 122. Esther Fuchs, in her analysis of annunciation type-scenes, makes a similar argument: biblical female characters are prevented from developing mutually

supporting allegiances. The biblical writers portray mothers-to-be (like Sarah and Hagar, Rachel and Leah) as a "*means* of reproduction" to achieve covenantal promises with fathers. The Genesis text, "[b]y perpetuating the theme of women's mutual rivalry, especially in a reproduction context...implies that sisterhood is a precarious alternative to the patriarchal system." Esther Fuchs, "The Literary Characterization of Mothers and Sexual Politics in the Hebrew Bible," in *Feminist Perspectives on Biblical Scholarship*, ed. Adela Yarbro Collins (Chico, Calif.: Scholars, 1985), 120, 132.

62. See Sanders, "Black Women in Biblical Perspective," 132. White feminist exegete Jo Ann Hackett argues to a similar conclusion: Sarah is culpable. Hackett uses historical-critical tools to analyze the story in terms of type scenes and argues that the Hagar character typifies the heroic victim, as found in comparable ancient myths, namely, the Gilgamesh epic. Hackett argues that the Sarah-Hagar relationship echoes the type scene where a hero (Gilgamesh) insults a female superior (the goddess Ishtar) who then appeals to a higher male authority (the god Anu) for revenge. With one gender change, Hackett sees a similar motif in Genesis. Sarah represents the offended goddess, Hagar represents the hero Gilgamesh, and Abraham is the higher authority to whom Sarah appeals. See Hackett, "Rehabilitating Hagar" (see note 46 above).

63. Sanders, "Black Women in Biblical Perspective," 130, 132.

64. Ibid., 133. From a perspective of interreligious and intercultural dialogue, the application of Sanders's reading is more ambiguous. Sanders recognizes the importance of Hagar for Islam and notes that "[t]he story of Hagar and Ishmael is told to account for the centuries of hostilities in the Middle East between the Ishamaelites and the Israelites" and that Ishmael's "descendants are destined to remain perpetually at war with their Hebrew cousins" (ibid., 136, 137). With no further comment on the complex relationship between ancient religious stories and the long history of often times bloody conflict (but sometimes peace) between the two religio-ethnic groups, these comments could, if misconstrued, become a dangerous wind on a tinderbox situation. For a discussion of Hagar's roles in Islamic traditions, see Reuven Firestone, *Journeys in Holy Lands: The Evolution of the Abraham-Ishmael Legends in Islamic Exegesis* (Albany: State University of New York Press, 1990), esp. chaps. 5 and 8; Barbara Freyer Stowasser, *Women in the Qur'an: Traditions and Interpretation* (New York: Oxford University Press, 1994), 43–49; Carol Delaney, *Abraham on Trial: The Social Legacy of Biblical Myth* (Princeton, N.J.: Princeton University Press, 1998), 174–75; and Hibba Abugideiri, "Hagar: A Historical Model for 'Gender Jihad,'" in *Daughters of Abraham: Feminist Thought in Judaism, Christianity, and Islam*, ed. Yvonne Yazbeck Haddad and John Esposito (Gainesville: University of Florida Press, 2001).

65. Sanders, "Black Women in Biblical Perspective," 137, 138.

66. Teubal, *Ancient Sisterhood*, xv. See also Savina Teubal, *Sarah the Priestess: The First Matriarch of Genesis* (Athens, Ohio: Swallow, 1984).

67. Teubal, *Ancient Sisterhood*, 59.

68. Teubal speculates that the loss of the birthing story of Ishmael means that a crucial piece of feminist historical evidence is missing. Had Hagar been depicted

in the symbolic posture of giving birth to Ishmael on the lap of her mistress Sarah, this would be definitive evidence supporting the matrilineal theory that Hagar's son was meant to be Sarah's (not Abraham's) heir. See ibid., 82–84.

69. Ibid., 165. Teubal is critical of womanist readings of racial antagonism between Sarah and Hagar (ibid., 186 n. 1).

70. Influential texts would include Charlotte Perkins Gilman, *Herland*, and the science fiction and fantasy texts of Ursula LeGuin.

71. See her obituary at Jewish Women's Archive, "JWA—In Memoriam—Savina Teubal," http://www.jwa.org/discover/inmemoriam/teubal/index.html (accessed June 27, 2006).

72. Sharon Pace Jeansonne, from a Jewish feminist perspective, takes a similar stance. She sees Sarah and Hagar separated by status (mistress versus servant) and by covenental privilege (Jewish insider versus non-Jewish outsider). Jeansonne tries to grapple ethically with the treatment of a subordinate and an outsider like Hagar by the dominant, covenental figure, Sarah. See Jeansonne, *The Women of Genesis: From Sarah to Potipher's Wife* (Minneapolis, Minn.: Fortress, 1990), 116.

73. Trible, *Texts of Terror*, 27, 1.

74. For example, just as Hagar "fled (*brh*)" from Sarah's abuse (Gen. 16:6b), so "Israel will flee (*brh*) from Pharaoh (Exod. 14:5a)." Just as Sarah "commands Abraham: Cast out (*grs*) this slave woman" (Gen. 21:10), so "Pharaoh cast out (*grs*) the Hebrew slaves" (Exod. 12:39) (Trible, *Texts of Terror*, 13, 20, 21). In other words, Hagar, as Sarah's slave, is viewed in a role analogous to that of the Hebrews later enslaved by Pharaoh.

75. Trible, *Texts of Terror*, 28–29.

76. Ibid., 16, 18.

77. See Phyllis Trible, "Genesis 22: The Sacrifice of Sarah," in *Not in Heaven: Coherence and Complexity in Biblical Narrative*, ed. Jason P. Rosenblatt and Joseph C. Sitterson, Jr. (Bloomington: Indiana University Press, 1991).

78. Weems, *Just a Sister Away*, 6, 7, 8.

79. Ibid., 11.

80. Williams, *Sisters in the Wilderness*, 149.

81. Weems, *Just a Sister Away*, 12.

82. Ibid., 15.

83. Ibid., 17, 18.

84. Williams, *Sisters in the Wilderness*, 35. See also Diana L. Hayes, *Hagar's Daughters: Womanist Ways of Being in the World* (Mahwah, N.J.: Paulist, 1995), 56.

85. Williams, *Sisters in the Wilderness*, 185.

86. See ibid., 120–39.

87. Weems, *Just a Sister Away*, 12.

88. Williams, *Sisters in the Wilderness*, 28.

89. Ethnography has long been part of cultural anthropological approaches to the study of religion. Ethnographies of religion with a gender focus are a growing subset of that field. See Nancy Auer Falk and Rita M. Gross, eds., *Unspoken Worlds: Women's Religious Lives* (Belmont, Calif.: Wadsworth, 2001); Susan Starr Sered,

Women as Ritual Experts: The Religious Lives of Elderly Jewish Women in Jerusalem (New York: Oxford University Press, 1992); and Karen McCarthy Brown, "Writing about 'the Other,' Revisited," in *Personal Knowledge and Beyond: Reshaping the Ethnography of Religion*, ed. James V. Spickard et al. (New York: New York University Press, 2002).

90. Linda E. Thomas, "Womanist Theology, Epistemology, and a New Anthropological Paradigm," in *Living Stones in the Household of God: The Legacy and Future of Black Theology*, ed. Linda E. Thomas (Minneapolis, Minn.: Fortress, 2004), 45, 46.

91. Gilkes, "A Conscious Connection to All that Is," 175 (see note 25 above).

92. Ibid., 276; quoting Walker.

93. Ada María Isasi-Díaz, *En la Lucha, In the Struggle: A Hispanic Woman's Liberation Theology* (Minneapolis, Minn.: Fortress, 1993), 67 (in this chapter, hereafter cited in text as *EL*).

94. Sheila Greeve Davaney, "The Limits of the Appeal to Women's Experience," in *Shaping New Vision: Gender and Values in American Culture*, ed. Clarissa W. Atkinson, Constance H. Buchanan, and Margaret R. Miles (Ann Arbor, Mich.: UMI Research Press, 1987), 42, 45, 47. In chapter 6, I will critically engage her pragmatic historicism.

95. Sheila Greeve Davaney, "Theology and the Turn to Cultural Analysis," in *Converging on Culture: Theologians in Dialogue with Cultural Analysis and Criticism*, ed. Delwin Brown, Sheila Greeve Davaney, and Kathryn Tanner (New York: Oxford University Press, 2001), 9, 13.

96. Mary McClintock Fulkerson, *Changing the Subject: Women's Discourses and Feminist Theology* (Minneapolis, Minn.: Fortress, 1994) and "'We Don't See Color Here': A Case Study in Ecclesial-Cultural Invention," in *Converging on Culture*, ed. Brown, Davaney, and Tanner.

97. See note 36 above. Townes and hooks are not explicit about whether this is a factor of the genre of fiction or of the viewpoint of the author, Alice Walker.

98. As Davaney states: "Many North American scholars of religion...foster notions of the disengaged scholar studying artifacts of other people's convictions while keeping our own at bay and steadfastly refusing to enter into serious debate about the value, meaning, truth, and function of anyone's convictions including our own" ("Theology and the Turn to Cultural Analysis," 12).

99. Isasi-Díaz notes that the term "Hispanic" originated not in Latino/Latina experience but in U.S. government agencies and the (white) media; nevertheless, she continues to use the term because it has contributed—positively and negatively—to the way Latinas see themselves (Isasi-Díaz, *En la Lucha*, 192). Since Isasi-Díaz uses the terms "Hispanic women" and "Latinas" interchangeably, I will as well. For more on this issue, see Michelle A. González, "'One is Not Born a Latina, One Becomes One': The Construction of the Latina Feminist Theologian in Latino/a Theology," *Journal of Hispanic/Latino Theology* 10, no. 3 (2003).

100. See Isasi-Díaz, *En la Lucha*, 73, 173. Although Isasi-Díaz is committed to the appeal to Latina lived-experience, she believes her approach is consistent with Davaney's critique of the appeal to experience in her article "Limits of the Appeal," cited in note 94 above. See Isasi-Díaz, *En la Lucha*, 175 n. 29.

101. Isasi-Díaz is critical about the way she sees some Latin American liberation theologians (Gustavo Gutiérrez, Leonardo and Clodovis Boff) promoting the distinctions between action and reflection or grassroots and academic theology (see *En la Lucha*, 177–78 nn. 37, 38). For an alternative interpretation of how these liberation theologians construe these distinctions, see David G. Kamitsuka, *Theology and Contemporary Culture: Liberation, Postliberal, and Revisionary Perspectives* (Cambridge: Cambridge University Press, 1999), esp. chaps. 1 and 6.

102. Marian Ronan, "Reclaiming Women's Experience: A Reading of Selected Christian Feminist Theologies," *Cross Currents* 48, no. 2 (1998): 221.

103. Ibid., 222; quoting from Isasi-Díaz, *En La Lucha*, 142 n. 16

104. Ada María Isasi-Díaz, "Creating a Liberating Culture: Latinas' Subversive Narratives," in *Converging on Culture*, ed. Brown, Davaney, and Tanner, 135.

105. Patricia Hill Collins, *Black Feminist Thought: Knowledge, Consciousness, and the Politics of Empowerment* (New York: Routledge, 1991), 82.

106. Collins, *Black Feminist Thought*, 208, 234.

107. Ibid., 30, 31.

108. Isasi-Díaz, "Creating a Liberating Culture," 123.

109. "Domestic work allowed African-American women to see white elites...from perspectives largely obscured from Black men....Accounts of Black domestic workers stress the sense of self-affirmation the women experienced at seeing white power demystified. But on another level, these Black women knew that they...were economically exploited workers and thus would remain outsiders." Collins, *Black Feminist Thought*, 11. Collins's outsider-within notion is similar but not equivalent to Isasi-Díaz's insider-outsider notion. The former has to do with the relationship between women of color and white culture. The latter has to do with scholarly women of color in relation to their own racial/ethnic community. See Isasi-Díaz, *En la Lucha*, 71–72.

110. Patricia Hill Collins, "The Social Construction of Black Feminist Thought," *Signs: Journal for Women in Culture and Society* 14, no. 4 (1989): 772, 773.

111. For more on the internal debates between *mujeristas* and Latina feminists, see González, "'One is Not Born a Latina, One Becomes One.'"

112. Isasi-Díaz does not describe the interviewees' gestures or facial expressions, but she does record numerous instances of the women disagreeing and correcting Isasi-Díaz's construals of their experience: "'No, look, I realized that...'" or "'No, I don't know, I simply said to myself...'" (*En La Lucha*, 106).

113. J. Shawn Landres, "Being (in) the Field: Defining Ethnography in Southern California and Central Slovakia," in *Personal Knowledge and Beyond: Reshaping the Ethnography of Religion*, ed. James V. Spickard et al. (New York: New York University Press, 2002), 103, 104.

114. See Ann Grodzins Gold, "Shared Blessings as Ethnographic Practice," *Method and Theory of Religion* 13 (2001): 34–49.

115. Mary Jo Neitz, "Walking between Two Worlds: Permeable Boundaries, Ambiguous Identities," in *Personal Knowledge and Beyond: Reshaping the Ethnography*

of Religion, ed. James V. Spikard, J. Shawn Landres, and Meredith B. McGuire (New York: New York University Press, 2002), 38.

116. Vicki Kirby, "Feminisms and Postmodernisms: Anthropology and the Management of Difference," *Anthropological Quarterly* 66, no. 3 (1993): 130, 131, 132. Her use of the term "imperial" is Kirby's approving nod to postcolonial critiques of first-world feminism. However Kirby criticizes some postcolonial writers of also being tied to a "Cartesian model" of subjectivity (ibid., 131).

117. Gayle Greene, quoted in Susan Stanford Friedman, "Making History: Reflections on Feminism, Narrative, and Desire," in *Feminism Beside Itself,* ed. Diane Elam and Robyn Wiegman (New York: Routledge, 1995), 27.

CHAPTER 3

1. "Marriage is itself 'honorable in all' . . . yet, whenever it comes to the actual process of generation, the very embrace which is lawful and honourable cannot be effected without the ardour of lust. . . . This is the carnal concupiscence, which, while it is no longer accounted sin in the regenerate, yet in no case happens to nature except from sin. It is the daughter of sin, as it were; and whenever it yields assent to the commission of shameful deeds, it becomes also the mother of many sins." St. Augustine, "On Marriage and Concupiscence," in *The Anti-Pelagian Writings,* vol. 5 of *A Select Library of the Nicene and Post-Nicene Fathers of the Christian Church,* ed. Philip Schaff (New York: The Christian Literature Company, 1887), bk. 1, chap. 27, 274–75.

2. It is not surprising that Augustine chooses female metaphors to speak of sexually related sins (see note 1, this chapter).

3. See Guilia Sfameni Gasparro, "Image of God and Sexual Differentiation in the Tradition of *Enkrateia,*" and Kari Elisabeth Børrensen, "God's Image. Is Woman Excluded?" in *The Image of God: Gender Models in Judaeo-Christian Tradition,* ed. Kari Elisabeth Børrensen (Minneapolis, Minn.: Fortress, 1991).

4. Anne M. Clifford, "When Becoming Human Becomes Truly Earthly: An Ecofeminist Proposal for Solidarity," in *In the Embrace of God: Feminist Approaches to Theological Anthropology,* ed. Ann O'Hara Graff (Maryknoll, N.Y.: Orbis, 1995), 183.

5. Patricia L. Hunter, "Women's Power—Women's Passion: And God Said, 'That's Good,'" in *A Troubling in My Soul: Womanist Perspectives on Evil and Suffering,"* ed. Emilie M. Townes (Maryknoll, N.Y.: Orbis, 1993), 191. For a discussion of Asian feminist views on the image of God, see Chung Hyun Kyung, *Struggle to Be the Sun Again: Introducing Asian Women's Theology* (Maryknoll, N.Y.: Orbis, 1990), 47–52.

6. M. Shawn Copeland, "Body, Representation, and Black Religious Discourse," in *Postcolonialism, Feminism and Religious Discourse,* ed. Laura E. Donaldson and Kwok Pui-lan (New York: Routledge, 2002), 191.

7. Elizabeth A. Johnson, *She Who Is: The Mystery of God in Feminist Theological Discourse* (New York: Crossroad, 1995), 71.

8. Hunter, "Women's Power—Women's Passion," 189–90. Traditionally, the image of God in relation to humanity has been spoken of in various ways, two

prominent ones being the image of God as a divine substantial endowment (e.g., within the faculties of the soul or mind), or as the capacity conferred by God for relationality with God. Many theologians today seem oriented to speaking of the image of God relationally, emphasizing how humanity as "being-in-relation" reflects a trinitarian, perichoretic God. Mary Catherine Hilkert, "Cry Beloved Image: Rethinking the Image of God," in *In the Embrace of God: Feminist Approaches to Theological Anthropology*, ed. Ann O'Hara Graff (Maryknoll, N.Y.: Orbis, 1995), 200.

9. Johnson, *She Who Is*, 70.

10. Mary McClintock Fulkerson, "Contesting the Gendered Subject: A Feminist Account of the *Imago Dei*," in *Horizons in Feminist Theology: Identity, Tradition and Norms*, ed. Rebecca S. Chopp and Sheila Greeve Davaney (Minneapolis, Minn.: Fortress, 1997), 109.

11. Mary Aquin O'Neill, "The Mystery of Being Human Together—Anthropology," in *Freeing Theology: The Essentials of Theology in Feminist Perspective*, ed. Catherine Mowry LaCugna (San Francisco, Calif.: Harper, 1993), 141, 151.

12. Catherine Mowry LaCugna, *God for Us: The Trinity and Christian Life* (San Francisco, Calif.: Harper, 1991), 407.

13. Johnson, *She Who Is*, 70–71.

14. Rebecca Alpert, *Like Bread on the Seder Plate: Jewish Lesbians and the Transformation of Tradition* (New York: Columbia University Press, 1997), 21, 22.

15. For more on how sin can be situated in the context of various doctrinal loci (i.e., creation, theological anthropology, and soteriology), see David H. Kelsey, "Whatever Happened to the Doctrine of Sin?" *Theology Today* 50 (1993): 169–78.

16. David H. Kelsey, "Human Being," in *Christian Theology: An Introduction to Its Traditions and Tasks*, ed. Peter C. Hodgson and Robert H. King (Philadelphia, Pa.: Fortress, 1982), 141.

17. See Reinhold Niebuhr, *The Nature and Destiny of Man, Vol. 1: Human Nature* (New York: Charles Scribner's Sons, 1941), esp. chs. VII and VIII.

18. Valerie Saiving Goldstein, "The Human Situation: A Feminine View," *Journal of Religion* 40 (1960): 100–112.

19. Judith Plaskow, *Sex, Sin, and Grace: Women's Experience and the Theologies of Reinhold Niebuhr and Paul Tillich* (Washington, D.C.: University Press of America, 1980). See also Susan Nelson Dunfee, "The Sin of Hiding: A Feminist Critique of Reinhold Niebuhr's Account of the Sin of Pride," *Soundings* 65 (1982): 316–27; Judith Vaughan, *Sociality, Ethics, and Social Change: A Critical Appraisal of Reinhold Niebuhr's Ethics in Light of Rosemary Radford Ruether's Works* (Lanham, Md.: University Press of America, 1983); and Daphne Hampson, "Reinhold Niebuhr on Sin: A Critique," in *Reinhold Niebuhr and the Issues of Our Time*, ed. Richard Harries (Oxford: A. R. Mowbray, 1986), 46–60.

20. Judith Butler, *Gender Trouble: Feminism and the Subversion of Identity* (New York: Routledge, 1990), 23.

21. Søren Kierkegaard, *The Sickness Unto Death: A Psychological Exposition for Upbuilding and Awakening*, trans. and ed. Howard V. Hong and Edna H. Hong (Princeton, N.J.: Princeton University Press, 1980), 29.

22. Ibid., 52, 70; see also 49, 67.

23. Wanda Warren Berry, "Images of Sin and Salvation in Feminist Theology," *Anglican Theological Review* 60 (1978): 47.

24. Sylvia I. Walsh, "On 'Feminine' and 'Masculine' Forms of Despair," in *The International Kierkegaard Commentary: Sickness Unto Death*, ed. Robert L. Perkins (Macon, Ga.: Mercer University Press, 1987), 129. Leslie Howe questions how much balancing Kierkegaard actually supports. See Howe, "Kierkegaard and the Feminine Self," in *Feminist Interpretations of Søren Kierkegaard*, ed. Céline Léon and Sylvia Walsh (University Park: Pennsylvania State University Press, 1997), 239–41. I will return to this issue below.

25. Walsh, "On 'Feminine' and 'Masculine' Forms of Despair," 128, 133.

26. Birgit Bertung, "Yes, a Woman Can Exist," in *Feminist Interpretations of Søren Kierkegaard*, ed. Léon and Walsh, 58, 57; quoting Kierkegaard. Howe suggests that some of Kierkegaard's sexist comments should be taken as ironically feminist ("Kierkegaard and the Feminine Self," 238).

27. This is not to invalidate Kierkegaard's thought as a whole and the fruitfulness of feminist engagement with it. I agree heartily with Wanda Warren Berry's call for feminists to continue critically reading Kierkegaard. See Berry, "Kierkegaard and Feminism: Apologetic, Repetition, and Dialogue," in *Kierkegaard in Post/Modernity*, ed. Martin J. Matustík and Merold Westphal (Bloomington: Indiana University Press, 1995), 110–24.

28. Walsh, "On 'Feminine' and 'Masculine' Forms of Despair," 133.

29. Howe, "Kierkegaard and the Feminine Self," 237.

30. For some current debates on Butler's views, see Sara Salih, *Judith Butler* (London: Routledge, 2001), esp. 137–52; and Annamarie Jagose, *Queer Theory: An Introduction* (New York: New York University Press, 1996), 83–90. For an insightful application of Butler's thought to ethics, see Marilyn Gottschall, "The Ethical Implications of the Deconstruction of Gender," *Journal of the American Academy of Religion* 70, no. 2 (June 2002): 279–99. Sarah Coakley finds eschatological meanings in Butler's gender theory, when read in conjunction with Gregory of Nyssa. See Coakley, "The Eschatological Body: Gender, Transformation and God," in her *Powers and Submissions: Spirituality, Philosophy and Gender* (Oxford: Blackwell, 2002). For a critical view of feminist theological uses of Butler, see Pamela Sue Anderson, "Feminist Theology as Philosophy of Religion," in *The Cambridge Companion to Feminist Theology*, ed. Susan Frank Parsons (Cambridge: Cambridge University Press, 2002), 48–50.

31. De Beauvoir, quoted in Butler, *Gender Trouble*, 8.

32. Ibid., 7. Butler argues that de Beauvoir's views were too linked to a modernist view of a subject as "a *cogito*" (ibid., 8).

33. Judith Butler, *Bodies that Matter: On the Discursive Limits of "Sex"* (New York: Routledge, 1993), 17.

34. Butler, *Gender Trouble*, 23.

35. Judith Butler, "For a Careful Reading," in *Feminist Contentions: A Philosophical Exchange*, by Seyla Benhabib, Judith Butler, Drucilla Cornell, and Nancy Fraser (New York: Routledge, 1995), 134.

36. Butler, *Gender Trouble*, 25. Butler further discusses performativity in her chapter "Critically Queer," in *Bodies that Matter*, 223–42.

37. This distinction between performativity and play-acting was made by Gayatri Chakravorty Spivak in a public lecture at Oberlin College, March 15, 1999.

38. Butler, "For a Careful Reading," 134.

39. Ibid. 136.

40. Butler, *Gender Trouble*, 31, 137. Akin to Foucault's notion of insurrectional knowledge (see note 47 below), "parody" is Butler's term that refers to how some performativity can decenter the convention it repeats. The repetition can be subversive when it *"implicitly reveals the imitative structure"* of the so-called original fact (137).

41. Ibid., 136.

42. Alice Walker, *The Color Purple* (New York: Pocket, 1982), 276.

43. Butler, *Gender Trouble*, 22.

44. At this stage in my theorizing, I am also exploring metaphors other than narrow relationality, such as fixed or rigid relationality.

45. Michel Foucault, *Power/Knowledge: Selected Interviews and Other Writings, 1972–1977*, trans. and ed. Colin Gordon et al. (New York: Pantheon, 1972), 74. The terms "discourse" and "discursive" are technical and not always used consistently in Foucault's writings. Sometimes he makes a distinction between discursive and nondiscursive power regimes. However, many interpreters of Foucault take him as precisely breaking down the dichotomy between language and materiality. In this sense, "discourse is not a synonym for language.... Discourse is not what is said; it is that which constrains and enables what can be said. Discursive practices...are the local sociohistorical material conditions that enable and constrain...knowledge practices such as speaking, writing, thinking," and so on. Karen Barad, "Posthumanist Performativity: Toward an Understanding of How Matter Comes to Matter," *Signs: Journal for Women in Culture and Society* 28, no. 3 (2003): 819.

46. Foucault, *Power/Knowledge*, 93; see Colin Gordon, "Afterword," in ibid., 236–37.

47. Ibid., 98, 81. Sharon D. Welch sees liberation theologies as examples of insurrectional knowledge. See Welch, *Communities of Resistance and Solidarity: A Feminist Theology of Liberation* (Maryknoll, N.Y.: Orbis, 1985), 19–31, 35, 44–45.

48. Foucault, *Power/Knowledge*, 98, 142. Foucault is cognizant of extreme and violent forms of oppression: penal torture, the Gulag, etc. See Michel Foucault, *Discipline and Punish: The Birth of the Prison*, trans. Alan Sheridan (New York: Random House, 1977), esp. chap. 2; and *Power/Knowledge*, 134–39. He calls these dominations to distinguish them from subject-forming power relations. See Michel Foucault, "The Subject and Power," in *Michel Foucault: Beyond Structuralism and Hermeneutics*, ed. Hubert L. Dreyfus and Paul Rabinow (Chicago: University of Chicago Press, 1982), 226.

49. Foucault, *Power/Knowledge*, 119.

50. Other terms also help display this interactive productive aspect of power (e.g., engagement, negotiation). I use these terms as well. See also note 1, chapter 5.

51. See Monique Devaux, "Feminism and Empowerment: A Critical Reading of Foucault," in *Feminist Interpretations of Michel Foucault*, ed. Susan J. Hekman (University Park: Pennsylvania State University Press, 1996), 213–17.

52. Structural sin will be discussed in chapter 4.

53. See Melissa Raphael, *Thealogy and Embodiment: The Post-Patriarchal Reconstruction of Female Sacrality* (Sheffield, U.K.: Sheffield Academic Press, 1996), 83–96; and Cheryl Townsend Gilkes, "The 'Loves' and 'Troubles' of African-American Women's Bodies and the Womanist Challenge to Cultural Humiliation and Community Ambivalence," in *A Troubling in My Soul: Womanist Perspectives on Evil and Suffering*," ed. Emilie M. Townes (Maryknoll, N.Y.: Orbis, 1993).

54. Michel Foucault, *Technologies of the Self: A Seminar with Michel Foucault*, ed. Luther H. Martin, Huck Gutman, and Patrick H. Hutton (Amherst: University of Massachusetts Press, 1988), 21, 19. I will discuss Foucault's notion of technologies of the self in more depth in chapter 4.

55. For arguments about the psychologically detrimental aspect of patriarchal family authority structures, see Rita Nakashima Brock, *Journeys By Heart: A Christology of Erotic Power* (New York: Crossroad, 1994), esp. chaps. 1 and 2. Delores Williams analyzes some effects of the incursion of white patriarchal family models on the African American family. See Delores S. Williams, *Sisters in the Wilderness: The Challenge of Womanist God-Talk* (Maryknoll, N.Y.: Orbis, 1993), esp. chap. 2.

56. Kierkegaard, *The Sickness Unto Death*, 49n, 50n. Leslie Howe finds an inherent sexism in Kierkegaard's assumptions about gendered gradations of selfhood, which threatens to undermine the androgyny model. At the religious and the secular level, Howe argues, Kierkegaard gives "no indication that a man is supposed to display devotedness (or any other supposedly feminine quality) . . . much less that woman is to show masculine qualities" ("Kierkegaard and the Feminine Self," 241).

57. Howe, "Kierkegaard and the Feminine Self," 237.

58. A criterion is clearly needed for determining what would constitute a morally and spiritually proper Christian performativity. Let me anticipate the point I will make below by saying that the way one construes the *imago dei* would be central to this determination.

59. There are a number of feminist proposals about sin's inevitability. Marjorie Suchocki sees sin as inevitable because we are born into the human race that has evolved into a society of violence. She construes original sin as the inevitability of evil as a result of anxiety due to pervasive violence. See Marjorie Hewitt Suchocki, *The Fall to Violence: Original Sin in Relational Theology* (New York: Continuum, 1995). Serene Jones brings together Calvinist and postmodern feminist insights and attributes sin's inevitability to the "'false performative scripts' into which women are born" causing us to suffer harm and do harm. See Serene Jones, *Feminist Theory and Christian Theology: Cartographies of Grace* (Minneapolis, Minn.: Fortress, 2000), 119.

60. See Søren Kierkegaard, *The Concept of Anxiety*, in *The Kierkegaard Reader*, ed. Jane Chamberlain and Jonathan Rée (Oxford: Blackwell, 2001), esp. 201–208.

61. Michel Foucault, trans. J. D. Gauthier, SJ, "The Ethic of Care for the Self as a Practice of Freedom," in *The Final Foucault*, ed. James Bernauer and David Rasmussen (Cambridge, Mass.: MIT Press, 1988), 18.

62. LaCugna, *God for Us*, 407. I borrow LaCugna's term for my performative approach; however, she does not present her discussion of the iconic image of God via performativity theory.

63. My discussion here focuses on the image of God and humankind, but the concept can (and I believe should) be extended to the natural world as well. See Sallie McFague, *Life Abundant: Rethinking Theology and Economy for a Planet in Peril* (Minneapolis, Minn.: Fortress, 2001), 199. McFague does not employ performativity theory in relation to the *imago dei*, but if that theory were to be used in relation to how the nonhuman even inanimate world reflects God's image, its use would need to be, I conjecture, metaphorical.

64. The hermeneutical approach of queering a text emerges out of queer theory. Annamarie Jagose explains that this term early on "was, at best, slang for homosexual, at worst, a term of homophobic abuse. In recent years 'queer' has come to be used differently, sometimes as an umbrella term for a coalition of culturally marginal sexual self-identifications and at other times to describe a . . . theoretical model which has developed out of more traditional lesbian and gay studies." *Queer Theory*, 1; for full citation see note 30 above). Queering has been called "a heuristic tool devised by scholars like Eve Sedgwick and Judith Butler . . . to understand the function of the (homo)social and (homo)erotic . . . in opaque, resilient texts" and to foster "a new kind of reading for the questions of 'friendships,' passion, and sex." Francesca Sautman and Pamela Sheingorn, "Charting the Field," in *Same Sex Love and Desire Among Women in the Middle Ages*, ed. Francesca Sautman and Pamela Sheingorn (New York: Palgrave, 2001), 18.

65. Elizabeth Stuart, "Camping about the Canon: Humor as a Hermeneutical Tool in Queer Readings of Biblical Text," in *Take Back the Word: A Queer Reading of the Bible*, ed. Robert E. Goss and Mona West (Cleveland, Ohio: Pilgrim Press, 2000), 29–33; Elisabeth Schüssler Fiorenza, *Bread Not Stone: The Challenge of Feminist Biblical Interpretation* (Boston, Mass.: Beacon, 1995), 15–22.

66. Robert E. Goss and Mona West, introduction to *Take Back the Word*, 5, 4.

67. I will explore some queering hermeneutics in chapter 5.

68. See Celena M. Duncan, "The Book of Ruth: On Boundaries, Love, and Truth," in *Take Back the Word*, ed. Goss and West. For related discussions of queer approaches to the Christian tradition, see Robert E. Goss, *Queering Christ: Beyond Jesus Acted Up* (Cleveland, Ohio: Pilgrim, 2002); Mary McClintock Fulkerson, "Gender—Being It or Doing It: The Church, Homosexuality, and the Politics of Identity," in *Que(e)rying Religion: A Critical Anthology*, ed. Gary David Comstock and Susan E. Henking (New York: Continuum, 1997); and Nancy Wilson, *Our Tribe: Queer Folks, God, Jesus, and the Bible* (San Francisco, Calif.: Harper, 1995).

69. This position is quite pervasive in many theological and religious circles. A recent version of it is given by Miroslav Volf, who argues that the fixed dimorphism of sexed bodies is the lesson taught by the Genesis creation stories and contributes

toward a nonsexist notion of gender fluidity. While he may make some persuasive points to address sexism in the tradition's interpretations of gender roles, he is notably silent on the issue of heterosexism. I contend that his sex binarism model in fact undergirds a discourse of compulsory heterosexuality and hence heterosexism— which is at odds with his overall theme of promoting justice and embrace of the other. See Volf, *Exclusion and Embrace: A Theological Exploration of Identity, Otherness, and Reconciliation* (Nashville, Tenn.: Abingdon, 1996), esp. chap. 4.

70. Johnson, *She Who Is*, 65 (in this chapter, hereafter cited in text as *SWI*).

71. George Lindbeck would call a theory of religion such as Johnson's "experiential-expressive." See George A. Lindbeck, *The Nature of Doctrine: Religion and Theology in a Postliberal Age* (Philadelphia, Pa.: Westminster, 1984), 31. I will return to Lindbeck's theories of religion and doctrine in chapter 5.

72. Paula Cooey discusses this distinction in relation to the issue of how feminism defines sex and gender. I agree with Cooey that seeing "essentialism and cultural constructivism as two opposing schools of thought . . . frames virtually all discussions of the significance of gender and sexual difference. . . . [D]ebate concerning the status of difference depends as a whole on an irresolvable dualism that is itself patriarchal in its roots, namely, the nature/culture dualism." Cooey, *Religion, Imagination, and the Body: A Feminist Analysis* (New York: Oxford University Press, 1994), 20.

73. Grace M. Jantzen, *Becoming Divine: Toward a Feminist Philosophy of Religion* (Bloomington: Indiana University Press, 1999), 16 (in this chapter, hereafter cited in text as *BD*). I will discuss her term "imaginary" below. Jantzen does discuss Foucault briefly (see ibid., 54–57), but the bulk of her claims are dependent on a psychoanalytic philosophical orientation.

74. The term "phallocentric" stems from a feminist critique of Jacques Lacan's term "phallus," the psychoanalytic symbol for that which makes possible the infant's eventual individuation (i.e., apart from the mother) and development toward cognition. In breaking from the mother, the young child associates with the father and enters into linguistically structured existence; hence, the phallic symbol (see ibid., 39–43). Given the unavoidably masculinist entailments of this theory, feminists deem that positing the phallus as the realm of linguistic signification institutes a framework whereby the male marginalizes and rules oppressively over the female. The phallus is thus phallocentric and phallocratic. *Jouissance* (literally enjoyment or pleasure) is the experience of reconnection with the semiotic realm by way of transgression of the phallic symbolic order. For Julia Kristeva, this transgressive *jouissance* is "enacted in various ways: in music and art, in poetry, in childbirth" (ibid., 196). For more on the notion of *jouissance* in French feminist writings, see Jane Gallop, "Beyond the *Jouissance* Principle," *Representations* 7 (1984).

75. Imaginary is a Lacanian term Jantzen uses which echoes themes from Ludwig Feuerbach who affirmed "the imagination as a divine power" (Jantzen, *Becoming Divine*, 95). She is not suggesting that a female symbolic could emerge untouched by dominant masculinist symbolics. All feminist imaginaries will be affected by the "disorder called masculinism" (ibid., 97). Bringing to light a feminist

symbolic exposes the disorder that "opens a gap, and allows . . . a reconfiguring of the symbolic . . . which allows a feminist imaginary to grow" (ibid., 99).

76. She borrows the concept of natality from Hannah Arendt. I will not delve into whether she is reading Arendt (or any of the other authors she borrows from) fairly. Indeed, she describes herself as having read Arendt, Kristeva, and others "against the grain, appropriating from them those things which enable me to say what I want to say." Jantzen, "Feminist Philosophy of Religion: Open Discussion with Pamela Anderson," *Feminist Theology* 26 (2001): 108.

77. Since the publication of Jantzen's text, Julia Kristeva has written on natality specifically in relation to the work of Arendt and Melanie Klein. See Kristeva, *Hannah Arendt*, trans. Ross Guberman (New York: Columbia University Press, 2000), and *Melanie Klein*, trans. Ross Guberman (New York: Columbia University Press, 2001). (See note 80 below.)

78. See Jantzen, *Becoming Divine*, 144, 150, 203. Although she is critical of Kristeva's romanticization of motherhood, Jantzen succumbs to it herself at points, presenting the material process of gestation, birthing, and nurturing of infants in a glowing light: "A woman who has had a new life grow within her . . . : such a woman is most unlikely to be invested in . . . [a] 'kill or be killed'" masculinist imagery; "each infant is unique and precious. . . . It emerges from its mother's womb, and unless things are badly askew, it is welcomed by its mother and by the whole community" (ibid., 243, 147, 149).

79. Among the issues I would want to include in such discussions would be the material conditions surrounding actual natality. For example, the fact that most women around the world do not have access to adequate family planning, prenatal care (including HIV/AIDS transmission prevention), and obstetric services, birthing can be a dangerous time for mother and child. Moreover, family conditions are too often such that babies are sometimes tragically greeted with heavy hearts and anxiety by their parents who must now spread meager financial and/or emotional resources even thinner. Another crucial issue would be how an appeal to natality might play out in the context of contentious debates and even violent confrontations between so-called right-to-life and pro-choice movements.

80. One could also question Jantzen's views on natality as an event of integration from a psychoanalytic perspective, since many theorists (Kristeva included) would define natality as a dual and conflictual event of pleasure and separation—an event that carries with it the seeds or, more accurately, the impulses for violence (psychological and political). Peg Birmingham comments on how this point emerges clearly in Kristeva's recent work on Arendt and Klein: "Kristeva, following Klein, shows how both anxiety . . . and gratitude . . . are part of the event of natality." Birmingham, "The Pleasure of Your Company: Arendt, Kristeva, and an Ethics of Public Happiness," *Research in Phenomenology* 33 (2003): 69. Jantzen seems to associate the notion that infant development entails a "rupture" and a "splitting of the self" with the phallocentrism of Lacan's theories, with which she contrasts her concept of natality (*Becoming Divine*, 37). She also distances herself from this psychoanalytic tradition in

her new book. See Grace M. Jantzen, *Foundations of Violence* (New York: Routledge, 2004), 24.

81. Michel Foucault, trans. Robert Hurley, *The History of Sexuality*, vol. 1 (New York: Vintage, 1990), 82.

CHAPTER 4

1. Rosemary Radford Ruether, *Sexism and God-Talk: Toward a Feminist Theology*, with new introduction (Boston, Mass.: Beacon, 1993), 2, 3.

2. Ibid., 266.

3. Carter Heyward, *Touching Our Strength: The Erotic as Power and the Love of God* (San Francisco, Calif.: HarperSanFrancisco, 1989), 191.

4. Ruether, *Sexism and God-Talk*, 163, 164.

5. Ibid., 180, 181. Ruether apparently groups racism and classism as subsets of a more basic patriarchal oppression.

6. Ibid., 180.

7. Ibid., 183, 184. To overcome the staticness of this victim status, she relies on the notion of a feminist "breakthrough experience," especially anger (ibid., 186).

8. Delores S. Williams, "The Color of Feminism: Or Speaking the Black Woman's Tongue," in *Feminist Theological Ethics*, ed. Lois K. Daly (Louisville, Ky.: Westminster John Knox, 1994), 50, 49. This article was originally published in *Journal of Religious Thought* (Spring/Summer 1986).

9. Delores S. Williams, *Sisters in the Wilderness: The Challenge of Womanist God-Talk* (Maryknoll, N.Y.: Orbis, 1993), 185. In this text in particular, where Williams discusses the complexities of the Hagar-Sarah story, she tends to avoid a too univocal view of power.

10. See ibid., 186–87.

11. Delores S. Williams, "A Womanist Perspective on Sin," in *A Troubling in My Soul: Womanist Perspectives on Evil and Suffering*," ed. Emilie M. Townes (Maryknoll, N.Y.: Orbis, 1993), 144, 146. JoAnne Marie Terrell notes that Williams has recently "backed away from" using demonarchy. Terrell, *Power in the Blood? The Cross in the African American Experience* (Maryknoll, N.Y.: Orbis, 1998), 132.

12. Ruether, *Sexism and God-Talk*, 182; Delores S. Williams, "Straight Talk, Plain Talk: Womanist Words about Salvation in a Social Context," in *Embracing the Spirit: Womanist Perspectives on Hope, Salvation, and Transformation*, ed. Emilie M. Townes (Maryknoll, N.Y.: Orbis, 2001), 97.

13. Stephanie Mitchem, "Womanists and (Unfinished) Constructions of Salvation," *Journal of Feminist Studies in Religion* 17, no. 1 (2001), 87; see also ibid., 95, 96, 98; and Cheryl Townsend Gilkes, "The 'Loves' and 'Troubles' of African American Women's Bodies: The Womanist Challenge to Cultural Humiliation and Community Ambivalence," in *A Troubling in My Soul: Womanist Perspectives on Evil and Suffering*," ed. Emilie M. Townes (Maryknoll, N.Y.: Orbis, 1993), 236–37.

14. See Leticia A. Guardiola-Sáenz, "Reading from Ourselves: Identity and Hermeneutics among Mexican-American Feminists"; Gloria Inéz Loya, "Pathways to

a Mestiza Feminist Theology," in *A Reader in Latina Feminist Theology: Religion and Justice*, ed. María Pilar Aquino, Daisy L. Machado, Jeanette Rodríguez (Austin: University of Texas Press, 2002), 85–86, 231–37; and María Pila Aquino, Daisy L. Machado, and Jeanette Rodríguez, introduction to *A Reader in Latina Feminist Theology*, ed. Aquino, Machado, and Rodríguez, xvi–xvii.

15. See Musa W. Dube, *Postcolonial Feminist Interpretation of the Bible* (St. Louis, Mo.: Chalice, 2000); and Laura E. Donaldson and Kwok Pui-lan, eds., *Postcolonialism, Feminism, and Religious Discourse* (New York: Routledge, 2002).

16. Kelly Brown Douglas, *Sexuality and the Black Church: A Womanist Perspective* (Maryknoll, N.Y.: Orbis, 1999).

17. Michel Foucault, *Power/Knowledge: Selected Interviews and Other Writings, 1972–1977*, ed. and trans. Colin Gordon et al. (New York: Pantheon, 1972), 98.

18. Michel Foucault, "The Subject and Power," in *Michel Foucault: Beyond Structuralism and Hermeneutics*, ed. Hubert L. Dreyfus and Paul Rabinow (Chicago, Ill.: University of Chicago Press, 1982), 220. Again, power relations must be distinguished from domination: "slavery is not a power relation when man [sic] is in chains" (ibid., 221).

19. Ruether, *Sexism and God-Talk*, 75; Williams, *Sisters in the Wilderness*, 87, 88.

20. Michel Foucault, "Nietzsche, Genealogy, History," in *Language, Counter-Memory, Practice: Selected Essays and Interviews*, trans. Donald Bouchard and Sherry Simon (Ithaca, N.Y.: Cornell University Press, 1977), 146, 150. Foucault explains that genealogy's purpose "is to entertain the claims to attention of local, discontinuous, disqualified, illegitimate knowledges against the claims of a unitary body of theory which would filter, hierarchise and order them in the name of some true knowledge" (*Power/Knowledge*, 83).

21. For a discussion of microlevel and macrolevel power, see Amy Allen, "Foucault on Power: A Theory for Feminists," in *Feminist Interpretations of Michel Foucault*, ed. Susan J. Hekman (University Park: Pennsylvania State University Press, 1996).

22. An excellent example of the type of genealogical study I have in mind of women's transgressive practices can be found in Mary McClintock Fulkerson, *Changing the Subject: Women's Discourses and Feminist Theology* (Minneapolis, Minn.: Fortress, 1994). For example, Fulkerson analyzes the disciplinary and productive effects of various discursive regimes in relation to poor, white, Appalachian Pentecostal women. She demonstrates a nondualistic view of power that circulates, though not without some ambiguity since these women cannot be shown to have "resisted [their oppressions] in completely successful ways" (ibid., 293).

23. Gayatri Chakravorty Spivak, "Subaltern Studies: Deconstructing Historiography," in *The Spivak Reader*, ed. Donna Landry and Gerald MacLean (New York: Routledge, 1996), 204, 211.

24. Spivak, "Subaltern Studies," 211, 213; emphasis added.

25. Ibid., 214, 216. Postcolonial theory is much wider than Spivak's concept of the strategic essentialization of the subaltern. For other facets of postcolonialism and other applications of Spivak's views in feminist religious scholarship, see Kwok Pui-lan, "Unbinding Our Feet: Saving Brown Women and Feminist Religious Dis-

course"; Meyda Yeğenoğlu, "Sartorial Fabric-ations: Enlightenment and Western Feminism"; and Musa W. Dube, "Postcoloniality, Feminist Spaces, and Religion"; all in *Postcolonialism, Feminism, and Religious Discourse*, ed. Laura E. Donaldson and Kwok Pui-lan (New York: Routledge, 2002), 64, 67–68, 87, 105–107. See also Kwok Pui-lan, *Postcolonial Imagination and Feminist Theology* (Louisville, Ky.: Westminster John Knox, 2005), esp. 103, 108.

26. See Serene Jones's use of strategic essentialization in her discussion of how diverse women cope with the sense of fragmentation that results from various societal and interpersonal oppressions. Jones, *Feminist Theory and Christian Theology: Cartographies of Grace* (Minneapolis, Minn.: Fortress, 2000), 43–48.

27. Spivak, "Subaltern Studies," 217, 220.

28. Cheryl J. Sanders, "Black Women in Biblical Perspective: Resistance, Affirmation, and Empowerment," in *Living the Intersection: Womanism and Afrocentrism in Theology*, ed. Cheryl J. Sanders (Minneapolis, Minn.: Fortress, 1995), 132, 137.

29. As we saw in chapter 2, Renita T. Weems, though largely sympathetic to Hagar, directs a critical eye to Hagar's passivity and slave mentality. Weems, "A Mistress, a Maid, and No Mercy," in *Just a Sister Away: A Womanist Vision of Women's Relationships in the Bible* (San Diego, Calif.: Lura Media, 1988), 12.

30. Gayatri Chakravorty Spivak, "In a Word," interview with Ellen Rooney, in *The Second Wave: A Reader in Feminist Theory*, ed. Linda Nicholson (New York: Routledge, 1997), 365.

31. Joanne Carlson Brown and Rebecca Parker, "For God So Loved the World," in *Christianity, Patriarchy, and Abuse*, ed. Joanne Carlson Brown and Carole R. Bohn (Cleveland, Ohio: Pilgrim, 1989), 2, 26; Carter Heyward, *Saving Jesus from Those Who Are Right: Rethinking What It Means to Be Christian* (Minneapolis, Minn.: Fortress, 1999), 176–78; Darby Kathleen Ray, *Deceiving the Devil: Atonement, Abuse, and Ransom* (Cleveland, Ohio: Pilgrim, 1998), 131.

32. Rita Nakashima Brock, *Journeys By Heart: A Christology of Erotic Power* (New York: Crossroad, 1988).

33. See Williams, *Sisters in the Wilderness*, esp. 161–67.

34. See *Redeeming the Dream: Feminism, Redemption, and Christian Tradition* (London: SPCK, 1989), 135–37.

35. Ibid., 125.

36. JoAnne Marie Terrell, *Power in the Blood? The Cross in the African American Experience* (Maryknoll, N.Y.: Orbis, 1998), 26.

37. Ibid., 124, 125.

38. Deborah Krause, "School's in Session: The Making and Unmaking of Docile Disciple Bodies in Mark," in *Postmodern Interpretations of the Bible: A Reader*, ed. A. K. M. Adam (St. Louis, Mo.: Chalice, 2001), 185, 186.

39. Stephen Moore, *Poststructuralism and the New Testament: Derrida and Foucault at the Foot of the Cross* (Minneapolis, Minn.: Fortress, 1994), 101; quoting Foucault.

40. Ibid., 106, 108.

41. Ibid., 112, quoting Foucault.

42. Foucault, *Technologies of the Self*, 18.

43. Daniel M. Bell, Jr., *Liberation Theology After the End of History: The Refusal to Cease Suffering* (New York: Routledge, 2001).

44. Ibid., 147, 150.

45. One concern has to do with Bell's first-world status in relation to his Latin American interlocutors. Bell encourages liberation theologians to turn away from their traditional discourses of justice, human rights, and the "preferential option for the poor" and toward discourses of forgiveness of one's oppressor and taking up their cross, which amounts to a "refusal to cease suffering" (ibid., 189). I find Bell's caveat that "although I critique the liberationists, I do not really have nor do I want an argument with them" to be somewhat disingenuous. His text lacks a sufficiently complex discussion of the theological, religious and cultural differences between Latin American Christians and himself (who is white, first-world, not oppressed, etc.) to warrant his call for them to "forego the justice of asserting their rights" (ibid., 190).

46. Terrell, *Power in the Blood*, 1–2.

47. Ruether, *Sexism and God-Talk*, 116. See also Rosemary Radford Ruether, *Introducing Redemption in Christian Feminism* (Sheffield, U.K.: Sheffield Academic Press, 1998), Ch. 6 "Can a Male Savior Save Women? Liberating Christology from Patriarchy."

48. Williams, *Sisters in the Wilderness*, 164–67, 3–6.

49. Ray, *Deceiving the Devil*, 141.

50. Grey, *Redeeming the Dream*, 84–93; Heyward, *Touching Our Strength*, 22–24, 56–58, 104–105; Brock, *Journeys By Heart*, 66–70.

51. See Brock's discussion of the hemorrhaging woman in Mark 5 (*Journeys By Heart*, 81–87.).

52. Heyward, *Touching Our Strength*, 114–18; Brock, *Journeys By Heart*, 114 n. 2; Susan Brooks Thistlethwaite, *Sex, Race, and God: Christian Feminism in Black and White* (New York: Crossroad, 1989), 93.

53. Jacquelyn Grant, *White Women's Christ and Black Women's Jesus: Feminist Christology and Womanist Response* (Atlanta, Ga.: Scholars, 1989).

54. Robert E. Goss, "From Christ the Oppressor to Jesus the Liberator," in *Queering Christ: Beyond Jesus Acted Up* (Cleveland, Ohio: Pilgrim, 2002), 160; reprinted from Robert Goss, *Jesus Acted Up: A Gay and Lesbian Manifesto* (San Francisco, Calif.: HarperSanFrancisco, 1993), chap. 3. Drawing from the work of Norman Perrin, Goss states that "Jesus used the symbol of God's reign (*basileia*) to speak of liberating activity of God among people" (Goss, *Queering Christ*, 154).

55. Goss, *Queering Christ*, 144.

56. This gay christocentric spirituality is akin to the sexualized and body-oriented spirituality of female believers in medieval times especially, who used highly eroticized heterosexual language to speak of their mystical union with Christ and who used gender-bending language to speak of nursing from the pierced side of Jesus. See Caroline Walker Bynum, "The Female Body and Religious Practices," in *Fragmentation and Redemption: Essays on Gender and the Human Body in Medieval Religion*

(New York: Zone, 1992). See also Goss' discussion of medieval roots of homodevotion to Jesus, in Goss, *Queering Christ*, 125–28.

57. Goss, *Queering Christ*, 118, 135.

58. Marcella Althaus-Reid, *Indecent Theology: Theological Perversions in Sex, Gender, and Politics* (London: Routledge, 2000), 111.

59. Ibid., 118, 113.

60. Kathleen M. Sands, "A Response to Marcella Althaus-Reid's *Indecent Theology: Theological Perversions in Sex, Gender, and Politics*," *Feminist Theology* 11, no. 2 (2003): 177.

61. Marcella Althaus-Reid, "On Non-Docility and Indecent Theologians: A Response to the Panel for *Indecent Theology*," *Feminist Theology* 11, no. 2 (2003): 189.

62. Althaus-Reid, *Indecent Theology*, 7.

63. See Luce Irigaray, trans. Gillian C. Gill, "*La Mystérique*," in *Speculum of the Other Woman* (Ithaca, N.Y.: Cornell University Press, 1985); Cristina Mazzoni, "Introduction" and "Interpretive Essay: The Spirit and the Flesh in Angela of Foligno," in *Angela of Foligno's* Memorial, ed. Cristina Mazzoni, trans. John Cirignano (Suffolk, U.K.: D. S. Brewer, 1999).

64. See Björn Krondorfer, ed., *Men's Bodies, Men's Gods: Male Identities in a (Post-) Christian Culture* (New York: New York University Press, 1996).

65. Goss, *Queering Christ*, 141–44, 179–82.

66. Ibid., 181, 182.

67. Foucault, quoted in Jeremy Carrette, "Beyond Theology and Sexuality: Foucault, the Self, and the Que(e)rying of Monotheistic Truth," in *Michel Foucault and Theology: The Politics of Religious Experience*, ed. James Bernauer and Jeremy Carrette (Hampshire, U.K.: Ashgate, 2004), 227.

68. Ibid., 228. "Polymorphously perverse" is a term Carrette borrows from Howard Eilberg-Schwartz, who in turn borrowed it from Freud (ibid., 218).

69. Michel Foucault, trans. Robert Hurley, *The History of Sexuality: An Introduction*, vol. 1 (New York: Vintage, 1990; first English editon, New York: Random House, 1978), 21.

70. James W. Bernauer, "Michel Foucault's Ecstatic Thinking," in *The Final Foucault*, ed. James Bernauer and David Rasmussen (Cambridge, Mass.: MIT Press, 1988), 56.

71. Michel Foucault, "On the Genealogy of Ethics: An Overview of Work in Progress," in *Ethics: Subjectivity and Truth*, ed. Paul Rabinow, trans. Robert Hurley et al. (New York: New Press, 1997), 253. Carrette notes this remark by Foucault as well ("Beyond Theology and Sexuality," 221), but he interprets it as an invitation to abandon the "boring" discourse of sex and take up new, more fluid discourses of pleasure and desire. Like Goss, Carrette implies that, somehow, these new discourses will emerge as imaginaries (Carrette does reference Grace Jantzen explicitly) independent from the policing discourses of sex (see ibid., 225).

72. Foucault, "On the Genealogy of Ethics," 270.

73. Bernauer, "Michel Foucault's Ecstatic Thinking," 63.

74. In this discussion, I am referring to some of Foucault's writings from the 1980s. Foucault wrote about Christian confessional practices in earlier works, such as

The History of Sexuality, vol. 1 (the original French version was published in 1976), in which he does portray the confessional as a place where "truth and sex are joined" (*History of Sexuality*, 61).

75. Michel Foucault, trans. Robert Hurley, *The Use of Pleasure*, vol. 2 of *History of Sexuality* (New York: Vintage, 1986), 28.

76. Michel Foucault, trans. J.D. Gauthier, S.J., "The Ethic of Care for the Self as a Practice of Freedom," an interview with Michel Foucault on January 20, 1984, conducted by Raúl Fornet-Betancourt et al., in *The Final Foucault*, ed. James Bernauer and David Rasmussen (Cambridge, Mass.: MIT Press, 1988), 4.

77. Foucault, "On the Genealogy of Ethics," 255.

78. Ibid., 263. The life circumstances of Foucault (1926–84) have been widely discussed in scholarly and nonscholarly circles (for example, he was a so-called Left Bank, politically engaged scholar in Paris who was white and gay). Foucault's political beliefs and biography do not factor into my use of Foucauldian theory; however, I acknowledge how they could factor importantly into other scholars' work. See David M. Halperin, *Saint Foucault: Towards a Gay Hagiography* (New York: Oxford University Press, 1995).

79. Foucault, "The Ethic of Care for the Self," 4.

80. Carrette, "Beyond Theology and Sexuality," 218.

81. For another perspective on Foucault's final thoughts on these issues, see James Bernauer, "Michel Foucault's Philosophy of Religion: An Introduction to the Non-Fascist Life," in *Michel Foucault and Theology: The Politics of Religious Experience*, ed. James Bernauer and Jeremy Carrette (Hampshire, U.K.: Ashgate, 2004).

CHAPTER 5

1. In this chapter, I am privileging the term "negotiation" when speaking of the feminist theologian's engagement with the Christian tradition; whereas in chapter 3, I spoke mostly (though not exclusively) of the believer's "cooperation." This is meant to signal that even if the theologian is herself a believer, there is a difference between the believer's and the scholarly theologian's engagement with the tradition. The believer often cooperates with the tradition unselfconsciously or with inconsistent critical awareness; the trained theologian, in her capacity as scholar—especially in the academy—is expected to be rigorously and consistently self-aware and critical when engaging her materials, including the Christian tradition. The term negotiation is meant to capture this intentionality.

2. Douglas, *The Black Christ* (Maryknoll, N.Y.: Orbis, 1994), 111.

3. Ibid., 113.

4. Julie M. Hopkins, *Towards a Feminist Christology: Jesus of Nazareth, European Woman, and the Christological Crisis* (Grand Rapids, Mich.: Eerdmans, 1995), 86, 87.

5. Hampson, *Theology and Feminism* (Oxford: Blackwell, 1990), 50, 51. See also Hampson, "Sources and the Relationship to Tradition: What Daphne Hampson is Supposed to Hold (and What She in Fact Holds)," *Feminist Theology* 3 (1993): 21–37.

6. Hampson claims of Ruether's position: "[I]f she is not saying of Christ that he is unique, [it] surely cannot be said so to be [a Christian position]" (*Theology and Feminism*, 65).

7. Ruether, "Is Feminism the End of Christianity? A Critique of Daphne Hampson's *Theology and Feminism*," *Scottish Journal of Theology* 43 (1990): 395, 398.

8. Ruether, *Sexism and God-Talk: Toward a Feminist Theology*, with a new introduction (Boston, Mass.: Beacon, 1983, 1993), 13, 15–16.

9. Ibid., p. 138. Julie Hopkins defends this approach to formulating a contemporary feminist Christology against Hampson as well. "If I choose to emphasize the redemptive power of messianic prophesy without worshipping Christ as God, am I...'only a humanist,'" as Hampson contends (Hopkins, *Towards a Feminist Christology*, 76)? Hopkins insists that this is not the case.

10. George A. Lindbeck, *The Nature of Doctrine: Religion and Theology in a Postliberal Age* (Philadelphia, Pa.: Westminster, 1984). Among the debaters are feminist voices critical of Lindbeck's postliberal view of theology ruled by the Christian grammar. Sheila Greeve Davaney, for example, criticizes Lindbeck for assuming a fairly unchanging notion Christianity's core grammar. See Davaney, *Pragmatic Historicism: Theology for the Twenty-first Century* (Albany: State University of New York Press, 2000), 33–36. Be that as it may, other authors have emphasized that rule theory itself need not lead to theological convervatism. See David G. Kamitsuka, *Theology and Contemporary Culture: Liberation, Postliberal, and Revisionary Perspectives* (Cambridge: Cambridge University Press, 1999), 132–38. I do not take the Christian grammar to be a static, singular concept, since all discursive systems, genealogically speaking, have gaps, heterogeneity, and fluidity.

11. Lindbeck, *The Nature of Doctrine*, 16. Ruether arguably has propositionalist elements as well in her theory of religion because she associates Christianity with certain core "themes" (*Sexism and God-Talk*, 24) and hence she could just as well represent a "hybrid" propositionalist and experiential-expressivist approach (see Lindbeck, *The Nature of Doctrine*, 16). However I am focusing on the experiential-expressivist aspects of her methodology.

12. R. R. Reno, *Redemptive Change: Atonement and the Christian Cure of the Soul* (Harrisburg, Pa.: Trinity Press International, 2002), 243, 244. Reno derives these rules from a reading of multiple creedal and doctrinal sources, including Augustine, Athanasius, the Heidelberg Confession, and the Formula of Concord. His method is modeled on "Lindbeck's discussion of the regulative role of Nicene and Chalcedonian creedal affirmations" (ibid., 194 n. 1). I am not suggesting that these soteriological rules are the true (or complete) meaning of salvation; they are theological interpretations that I am using heuristically here.

13. Ibid., 244, 231.

14. Ibid., 221.

15. "The single formal cause [of justification] is the righteousness of God...so that, when we are endowed with it, we are 'renewed in the spirit of our mind'.... Nobody can be righteous except God communicates the merits of the passion of our

Lord Jesus Christ to him or her." Council of Trent, quoted in Alister E. McGrath, *Christian Theology: An Introduction* (Oxford: Blackwell, 2001), 461.

16. "All those whom God had predestined unto life...he is pleased...effectually to call...out of that state of sin and death...; yet so as they come most freely, being made willing by his grace. This effectual call is of God's free and special grace alone, not anything at all foreseen in man, who is altogether passive therein." Westminster Confession, quoted in Alister E. McGrath, *The Christian Theology Reader* (Oxford: Blackwell, 1995), 433–34.

17. See Lindbeck, *The Nature of Doctrine*, 33. Lindbeck draws a distinction between formal doctrinal rules (the grammar) and the changeable, first-order vocabulary that marks how the church has instantiated those rules in contextually specific ways. Thus a formal grammar of the incarnation would be that Christ must be spoken of as human and divine, whereas the christological terms found in various creeds—"'substance' (ousia), 'person' (hypostasis)" are not core rules but vocabulary terms (albeit very influential and important ones) of "the late Hellenistic milieu" (ibid., 92).

18. See Williams, *Sisters in the Wilderness: The Challenge of Womanist God-Talk* (Maryknoll, N.Y.: Orbis, 1993), 203. That is not to say that Williams is not in critical conversation with the historical theological tradition in her writings. She develops her theory of redemption in dialogue with Anselm, Calvin, and others. Arguing that classic atonement theories support notions of surrogacy for African American women especially, Williams advocates an emphasis not on the cross but on Jesus' "ministerial vision of life" (ibid., 166). When I speak of regulative negotiation, I mean something more than a critical conversation.

19. Ibid., 202.

20. Ibid., 33.

21. Williams, "Womanist Perspective on Sin," in *A Troubling in My Soul: Womanist Perspective on Evil and Suffering*, ed. Emilie M. Townes (Maryknoll, N.Y.: Orbis, 1998), 143.

22. Ruether is thus very biblically oriented because she sees in the Bible a prophetic principle that resonates with contemporary feminist consciousness. I will speak more to Ruether's biblical hermeneutic in part two.

23. Hopkins, *Towards a Feminist Christology*, 111. An experiential-expressivist model has other drawbacks as well—namely, a tendency to think of symbols from many religions as being rooted in a unified underlying human experience of the holy, which might devalue the significance of inter-religious differences at the level of symbolic expression.

24. There might be ways to use the creedal tradition, understood propositionally, as a technology of care. I do not see how this could be done in any way that would not render extremely docile bodies, but I do hold open this possibility in theory.

25. Terrell, *Power in the Blood? The Cross in the African American Experience* (Maryknoll, N.Y.: Orbis, 1998), 105.

26. "Black church folks commonly confess, 'He died that I might have a right to the tree of life'" and "the community affirms the two natures of Christ Jesus, who charges them to be wholly holy" (ibid., 112, 113).

27. Salvific *dependence* is instantiated in the fact that Terrell holds in juxtaposition a liberationist "emphasis on human agency [as] integral to the salvific event" (ibid., 112) with the maximalism of the "*once for all* nature of Christ Jesus death ... 'on our behalf'" (ibid., 124, 125). Salvific *difference* is instantiated from a womanist perspective in her juxtaposition of statements about the ongoing nature of social sin (especially the "*defilement* of the African American community") and statements about the "real presence" of the resurrected Christ who effects "redemption and release from self-alienation and social alienation" (ibid., 120, 124–125).

28. Ibid., 124, 143. For more on the distinction between grammar and vocabulary, see n. 17 above. That Terrell is able to construct productive pathways for religious performativity in her regulative reappropriation of the tradition does not mean that other resources might not also be necessary. For example, I did not address the problem of the heavily masculinist imagery that Terrell imports when she uses the vocabulary of a male savior on the cross. I will speak to this issue in part two when I discuss the New Testament text.

29. Douglas, *The Black Christ*, 113.

30. Kathryn Tanner has raised (among other things) the concern that rule theory tends to squelch difference and debate on matters of doctrine and Christian practice. One might interpret rule theory as de facto saying that "all Christians should agree with the postliberal judgment about the rules." Tanner, *Theories of Culture: A New Agenda for Theology* (Minneapolis, Minn.: Fortress, 1997), 142. However, one need not view the notion of the Christian grammar so statically (see note 10 above). Furthermore, my appeal to rule theory has in fact highlighted difference and the presence of productive debate within the tradition—in this case, debate between two womanists and between womanist theology and the dominant tradition.

31. Rowan Greer explains by reference to Irenaeus' second-century approach to scripture that "by his doctrine of Christ's headship, Irenaeus has succeeded not only in defining his Savior but also in clarifying the church's Rule of faith. ... This Rule of faith is in one sense built out of specific passages in Scripture. ... It purports to make explicit what is implicit in Scripture." James L. Kugel and Rowan A. Greer, *Early Biblical Interpretation* (Philadelphia, Pa.: Westiminster, 1986), 171.

32. Ibid., 196. "One major reason that Scripture may be interpreted for its own sake is that the Rule of faith is a negative rather than a positive principle. That is, it excludes incorrect interpretations but does not require a correct one. Of a given passage there may be many interpretations that are valid because they do not contradict the rule of faith" (ibid., 197).

33. Fiorenza, *In Memory of Her: A Feminist Theological Reconstruction of Christian Origins* (New York: Crossroad, 1985), 326; Schneiders, "A Case Study: A Feminist Interpretation of John 4: 1–42," in her *The Revelatory Text: Interpreting the New Testament as Sacred Scripture* (Collegeville, Minn.: Liturgical Press, 1999); and Day, *The Woman at the Well: Interpretation of John 4:1–42 in Retrospect and Prospect* (Boston, Mass.: Brill, 2002).

34. Trible, *Texts of Terror: Literary-Feminist Readings of Biblical Narratives* (Philadelphia, Pa.: Fortress, 1984). See, for example, Musa W. Dube, "Reading for

Deconstruction (John 4:1–42)," in *John and Postcolonialism: Travel, Space, and Power,* ed. Musa W. Dube and Jeffrey Staley (London, U.K.: Sheffield Academic Press, 2002); and Jean K. Kim, "A Korean Feminist Reading of John 4:1–42," in "Reading the Bible as Women: Perspectives from Africa, Asia, and Latin America," ed. Phyllis A. Bird, *Semeia* 78 (1997): 117.

35. Schneiders criticizes Lyle Eslinger's claim to this effect. See Schneiders, *The Revelatory Text,* 189; in reference to Eslinger, "The Wooing of the Woman at the Well: Jesus, the Reader and Reader-Response Criticism," *Journal of Literature and Theology* 1, no. 2 (1987). Jane S. Webster disagrees with Schneiders. By reading John 4 in light of the Wisdom literature (which contains the female Wisdom figure and the dishonorable "Strange Woman"), Webster argues that "the Samaritan woman has affinity with Strange Woman as an adultress." Webster, "Transcending Alternity: Strange Woman to Samaritan Woman," in *A Feminist Companion to John,* vol. 1, ed. Amy-Jill Levine with Marianne Blickenstaff (Cleveland, Ohio: Pilgrim, 2003), 135. Webster recuperates the woman by arguing that she eventually admits the truth about Jesus and shares the gospel with others.

36. Teresa Okure, *The Johannine Approach to Mission: A Contextual Study of John 4:1–42* (Tubingen: JCB Mohr, 1988), 110; Day, *The Woman at the Well,* 169–72.

37. Kim, "A Korean Feminist Reading of John 4:1–42," 117.

38. Althaus-Reid, *Indecent Theology: Theological Perversions in Sex, Gender, and Politics* (New York: Routledge, 2000), 137, 107.

39. Adeline Fehribach, *The Women in the Life of the Bridegroom: Feminist Historical-Literary Analysis of the Female Characters in the Fourth Gospel* (Collegeville, Minn.: Liturgical, 1998), 47.

40. Esther Fuchs criticizes the extremely patriarchal nature of those betrothal-at-the-well type-scenes in "Structure and Patriarchal Function in the Biblical Betrothal Type-Scene: Some Preliminary Notes," in *Women in the Hebrew Bible: A Reader,* ed. Alice Bach (New York: Routledge, 1999).

41. Okure, *The Johannine Approach to Mission,* 169–74.

42. Schneiders, *The Revelatory Text,* 189, 190, 191. Stephen D. Moore uses a deconstructive method to come to a similar feminist conclusion: "the Samaritan woman . . . has outstripped her male teacher." Moore, "Are There Impurities in the Living Water That the Johannine Jesus Dispenses?" in *A Feminist Companion to John,* vol. 1, ed. Amy-Jill Levine with Marianne Blickenstaff (Cleveland, Ohio: Pilgrim, 2003), 95.

43. Phillips, "The Ethics of Reading Deconstructively, or, Speaking Face-to-Face: The Samaritan Woman Meets Derrida at the Well," in *The New Literary Criticism and the New Testament,* ed. Edgar McKnight and Elizabeth Malbon (Valley Forge, Pa.: Trinity, 1994), 299, 300, 307.

44. Although not all subaltern women are women of color, the reference to brown skin color has come to represent the subaltern person in some postcolonial feminist writings. Kwok Pui-lan borrows this metonym (originally coined by Gayatri Chakravorty Spivak) to describe the ongoing cultural colonization by first-world feminist writings marked by the agenda of "white women saving brown women from

brown men." See Kwok, "Unbinding Our Feet: Saving Brown Women and Feminist Religious Discourse," in *Postcolonialism, Feminism and Religious Discourse,* ed. Laura Donaldson and Kwok Pui-lan (New York: Routledge, 2002).

45. For Lindbeck, the "literal meaning must be consistent with the kind of text it is taken to be by the [Christian] community," that is, a text that reflects the normative rule of faith (*The Nature of Doctrine,* 120). For more on the literal or plain sense as a nonstatic term, see Kamitsuka, *Theology and Contemporary Culture,* 120–25.

46. "Deconstructive reading is attuned to what is fundamentally and necessarily gift-like." Phillips, "The Ethics of Reading Deconstructively," 312.

47. Phyllis Bird, "The Harlot as Heroine: Narrative Art and Social Presupposition in Three Old Testament Texts," in *Women in the Hebrew Bible: A Reader,* ed. Alice Bach (New York: Routledge, 1999).

48. That I entertain the possibility of a sexual overtone in the story does not mean I endorse Eslinger's very sexist and heteronormative reading that paints the woman as a sexually aggressive adulterer in contrast to Jesus who "in total control of the conversation, now openly reveals his disinterest in her charms" (Eslinger, "The Wooing of the Woman at the Well," 176, 179.) There are other ways to interpret Jesus' apparent rebuff to the woman's advances. One could, for example, queer the text and simply construct Jesus as gay.

49. Dube, "Reading for Decolonization," 73. I combine deconstructive and postcolonial approaches because, as Kwok Pui-lan so aptly states, "the postmodern emphasis on deconstructing the subject, indeterminacy of language, and excess of meaning will not be helpful ... if it does not come to grips with the colonial impulse." "Jesus/The Native: Biblical Studies from a Postcolonial Perspective," in *Teaching the Bible: The Discourses and Politics of Biblical Pedagogy,* ed. Fernando F. Segovia and Mary Ann Tolbert (Maryknoll, N.Y.: Orbis, 1998), 83.

50. See the discussion of colonialist desire for and fear of indigeneity, spoken of under the trope of "going native" in Jace Weaver, "Indigenousness and Indigeneity," in *A Companion to Postcolonial Studies,* ed. Henry Schwartz and Sargetta Ray (Malden, Mass.: Blackwell, 2000), 232.

51. Fewell and Phillips muse that Jesus "accepts for himself her [the Samaritan woman's] label Messiah" but they do not explore this idea further from a decolonizing perspective. Danna Nolan Fewell and Gary A. Phillips, "Drawn to Excess, or Reading Beyond Betrothal," *Semeia* 77 (1997): 41.

52. Phillips, "The Ethics of Reading Deconstructively," 306.

53. Ibid., 307.

54. Brock, *Journeys By Heart: A Christology of Erotic Power* (New York: Crossroad, 1988), 84.

55. Tat-Siong Benny Liew emphasizes the thrust of John's text toward a hegemonic message of consent that he finds particularly oppressive for marginalized communities of Asian Americans. See "Ambiguous Admittance: Consent and Descent in John's Community of Upward Mobility," in *John and Postcolonialism: Travel, Space, and Power,* ed. Musa W. Dube and Jeffrey Staley (London, U.K.: Sheffield Academic Press, 2002).

56. See Frank Kermode, *The Genesis of Secrecy: On the Interpretation of Narrative* (Cambridge, Mass.: Harvard University Press, 1979).

57. See Phillips, "The Ethics of Reading Deconstructively," 301.

58. St. Augustine, *Homilies on the Gospel of John*, tractate 15, chap. 4 of *A Select Library of the Nicene and Post-Nicene Fathers of the Christian Church*, vol. 7, ed. Philip Schaff (New York: Christian Literature Publishing Company, 1888), 102–3.

59. Ibid.

60. "But what do I love when I love my God? Not material beauty or beauty of a temporal order; not the brilliance of earthly light, so welcome to our eyes; not the sweet melody of harmony and song; not the fragrance of flowers, perfumes, and spices; not manna or honey; not limbs such as the body delights to embrace. . . . And, yet, it is true that I love a light of a certain kind, a voice, a perfume, a food, an embrace." Augustine, *Confessions*, book 10.6, trans. R. S. Pine-Coffin (New York: Penguin, 1986), 211.

CHAPTER 6

1. Mary McClintock Fulkerson, *Changing the Subject: Women's Discourses and Feminist Theology* (Minneapolis, Minn.: Fortress, 1994), 384.

2. Jacquelyn Grant, "The Sin of Servanthood," in *A Troubling in My Soul: Womanist Perspectives on Evil and Suffering*, ed. Emilie M. Townes (Maryknoll, N.Y.: Orbis, 1993), 215.

3. Sharon D. Welch, *A Feminist Ethic of Risk* (Minneapolis, Minn.: Fortress, 1990), 133.

4. Sheila Greeve Davaney, *Pragmatic Historicism: A Theology for the Twenty-First Century* (Albany, N.Y.: State University of New York Press, 2000), 179, 181.

5. M. Shawn Copeland, "Toward a Critical Christian Feminist Theology of Solidarity," in *Women and Theology*, ed. Mary Ann Hinsdale and Phyllis H. Kaminski (Maryknoll, N.Y.: Orbis, 1995), p. 30.

6. Maryanne Stevens, ed., *Reconstructing the Christ Symbol: Essays in Feminist Christology* (New York: Paulist, 1993), 5; quoting T. S. Eliot.

7. Welch, *Feminist Ethic of Risk*, 123, 6.

8. Ibid., 155–56.

9. Ibid., 124.

10. Jürgen Habermas, "Questions and Counterquestions," in *Habermas and Modernity*, ed. Richard J. Bernstein (Cambridge, Mass.: MIT Press, 1985), 196.

11. Ibid., 194–95.

12. Jürgen Habermas, *The Philosophical Discourse of Modernity: Twelve Lectures*, trans. Fredrick G. Lawrence (Cambridge, Mass.: MIT Press, 1987), 315.

13. Habermas, "Questions and Counterquestions," 196.

14. See Jürgen Habermas, *The Theory of Commmunicative Action*, vol. 1, trans. Thomas McCarthy (Boston, Mass.: Beacon, 1981), 67–72

15. Ibid., 82.

16. Habermas, *Philosophical Discourse*, 321, 359.

17. Jürgen Habermas, *Postmetaphysical Thinking*, trans. William Mark Hohengarten (Cambridge, Mass.: MIT Press, 1992), 140.

18. Welch, *Feminist Ethic of Risk*, 129–30; quoting Habermas. This viewpoint departs somewhat from her earlier more Foucault-oriented views. See Welch, *Communities of Resistance and Solidarity: A Feminist Theology of Liberation* (Maryknoll, N.Y.: Orbis, 1985).

19. Welch, *Feminist Ethic of Risk*, 127 (in this chapter, hereafter cited in text as *FER*).

20. Seyla Benhabib, *Situating the Self: Gender, Community and Postmodernism in Contemporary Ethics* (New York: Routledge, 1992), 38. Jane Braaten makes a similar proposal; she criticizes Habermas's orientation to argumentative "truth seeking" and proposes a more open-ended category of "communicative thinking." Braaten, "From Communicative Rationality to Communicative Thinking: A Basis for Feminist Theory and Practice," in *Feminists Read Habermas: Gendering the Subject of Discourse*, ed. Johanna Meehan (New York: Routledge, 1995), 155.

21. Seyla Benhabib, "Subjectivity, Historiography, and Politics" in *Feminist Contentions: A Philosophical Exchange*, by Seyla Benhabib, Judith Butler, Drucilla Cornell, and Nancy Fraser (New York: Routledge, 1995), 118. Although I would want to emphasize more than Benhabib does the poststructuralist perspective on rationality as itself a power relation, I see positive applications of her humanist appeal to the ideal of universal ethics when arguing, such as for fairness in citizenship procedures in light of globalized immigration. See Benhabib, "Citizens, Residents, and Aliens in a Changing World: Political Membership in the Global Era," *Social Research* 66, no. 3 (1999).

22. Sharon D. Welch, *A Feminist Ethic of Risk*, rev. ed. (Minneapolis, Minn.: Fortress, 2000), 15.

23. Ibid., 32, 33.

24. Ibid., 36.

25. Ibid., 34.

26. Her use of the term feminist (in *A Feminist Ethic of Risk*) was apparently criticized as meaning white feminist, hence obscuring how dependent the book is on African American spiritual and ethical resources. See Welch, "Sporting Power: American Feminism, French Feminisms, and an Ethic of Conflict," in *Transfigurations: Theology and the French Feminists*, ed. C. W. Maggie Kim et al. (Minneapolis, Minn.: Augsburg Fortress, 1993), 181. See also Welch, *Feminist Ethic of Risk*, rev. ed., 15.

27. Susan Brooks Thistlethwaite and Toinette M. Eugene are appreciative of Welch's concern about difference but note that Welch (as compared to womanist writers) is on "trickier ground because she is trying to reach beyond her own personal and even communal existence." Thistlethwaite and Eugene, "A Survey of Feminist Theologies," in *Critical Review of Books in Religion* (Atlanta, Ga.: Scholars, 1991), 13. Christine E. Gudorf faults Welch for "adopting the ethics of risk from the African-American community … without explaining how dependent that ethics' assumptions about power, resistance, and struggle are on lived experiences" of African Americans.

See Gudorf, "Issues of Race in Feminist Ethics: A Review Essay," *Journal of Feminist Studies in Religion* 9 (1993): 243.

28. Kwok Pui-lan, "Speaking from the Margins," Special Section on Appropriation and Reciprocity in Womanist/Mujerista/Feminist Work, *Journal of Feminist Studies in Religion* 8 (1992): 103.

29. Judith Plaskow, "Appropriation, Reciprocity, and Issues of Power," Special Section on Appropriation and Reciprocity in Womanist/Mujerista/Feminist Work, *Journal of Feminist Studies in Religion* 8 (1992): 105. See the discussion of appropriation relevant to Western Buddhist feminism in Sara Shneiderman, "Appropriate Treasure? Reflections on Women, Buddhism and Cross-Cultural Exchange," in *Buddhist Women across Cultures: Realizations,* ed. Karma Lekshe Tsomo (Albany: State University of New York, 1999).

30. Laura Donaldson, "On Medicine Women and White Shame-ans," in *Women, Gender, and Religion: A Reader,* ed. Elizabeth Castelli (New York: Palgrave, 2000), 241, 245, 246.

31. Ibid., 244.

32. Sharon D. Welch, "Human Beings, White Supremacy, and Racial Justice," in *Reconstructing Christian Theology,* ed. Rebecca S. Chopp and Mark Lewis Taylor (Minneapolis, Minn.: Fortress, 1994), 191, 193. Welch cites James H. Cone in support of white people's use of black spirituals (see ibid., 181). I do not read Cone as advocating that white activists should find sustenance in black spirituals (he recognizes that this did occur among white civil rights workers in the 1960s). His point seems to be that even those civil rights workers ignored the theology embedded in the spirituals when they returned to their "seminary or university desks" to write theology. See Cone, *For My People: Black Theology and the Black Church* (Maryknoll, N.Y.: Orbis, 1984), 69.

33. See Welch, "Human Beings, White Supremacy, and Racial Justice," 191.

34. Ibid., 194.

35. Davaney, *Pragmatic Historicism,* 1.

36. Richard Rorty, *Objectivity, Relativism, and Truth: Philosophical Papers,* vol. 1 (Cambridge: Cambridge University Press, 1991), 208.

37. Ibid., 22.

38. She implies disapproval of Rorty's views on ethnocentrism (see Davaney, *Pragmatic Historicism,* 138), but I do not see that she differs significantly on the nonfoundationalism he is trying to establish by his use of that term.

39. Sheila Greeve Davaney, "The Limits of the Appeal to Women's Experience," in *Shaping New Vision: Gender and Values in American Culture,* ed. Clarissa W. Atkinson, Constance H. Buchanan, and Margaret R. Miles (Ann Arbor, Mich.: UMI Research Press, 1987), 47. In *Pragmatic Historicism,* Davaney summarizes Rorty's pragmatic take on liberal democracy: "Contemporary liberal democracies protect an area in which humans are responsible to one another, where all voices are included, and public debate reigns" (Davaney, *Pragmatic Historicism,* 125). In this text, I found only one passing subsequent critique of Rorty on this point (see ibid., 136). Modern liberalism, which she does criticize (e.g., for its assumptions about "objective

knowledge"), does not seem to correspond to Rorty's liberal democratic pragmatism (ibid., 158).

40. Richard Rorty, *Essays on Heidegger and Others: Philosophical Papers*, vol. 2 (Cambridge: Cambridge University Press, 1991), 171.

41. Sheila Greeve Davaney, "Mapping Theologies: An Historicist Guide to Contemporary Theology," in *Changing Conversations: Religious Reflection and Cultural Analysis*, ed. Dwight N. Hopkins and Sheila Greeve Davaney (New York: Routledge, 1996), 40, 39.

42. Davaney, "Limits of the Appeal," 46, 47.

43. Ibid., 43. I share Davaney's concern about a modernist correspondence view of truth; however, I have argued for holding space methodologically for a strategically essentialized subaltern standpoint in some political contexts (see my discussion in chapter 4, part one).

44. Ibid., 47.

45. Davaney, *Pragmatic Historicism*, 149 (in this chapter, hereafter cited in text as *PH*).

46. Rorty does not reject traditionedness per se; however, he does view the "'private projects'" (Davaney, *Pragmatic Historicism*, 126; quoting Rorty) of religion and theology with a good deal of suspicion. Davaney is critical of this aspect in Rorty's thought (see ibid., 125–29).

47. Cornel West, *Keeping Faith: Philosophy and Faith in America* (New York: Routledge, 1993), 91, 127.

48. See Davaney, *Pragmatic Historicism*, 167–68. "Nonperson" (not "inclusionary practices") is Gutiérrez's term. I will say more about Davaney's appeal to inclusion below.

49. Richard Rorty, *Contingency, Irony, and Solidarity* (Cambridge: Cambridge University Press, 1989), 198.

50. See note 46 above.

51. See See Davaney, *Pragmatic Historicism*, 162–63, 166–70.

52. Davaney does explore switching from the metaphor of including the nonperson at the "theological table" to the metaphor of have the theological tables undergo "design changes." If she were to pursue the implications of this latter metaphor, I believe she would abandon the notion of inclusion because it will not help her to achieve her stated goal of finding the bases for conversations that "are not between 'we' who have power and personhood and those who do not, but entail a continual process of renegotiating the multiple 'we's' that compose the world" (Davaney, *Pragmatic Historicism*, 170).

53. Davaney's project of Christian historicism is linked to the concept of theology done in the mode of an "ethnography of belief" (Davaney, *Pragmatic Historicism*, 115, 140).

54. I doubt that McFague would see her biblical claim and Davaney's pragmatic one as mutually exclusive.

55. Davaney entertains the possibility that pragmatism could be susceptible to a "covert importation of particular, especially western, values of democracy," but she

contends that her insistence on "fallibilism" keeps that problem at bay (Davaney, *Pragmatic Historicism*, 186). An appeal to fallibilism might turn out to be an effective check and balance, but the fact remains that pragmatism is a tradition alongside others, including religious ones.

56. M. Shawn Copeland, "Toward a Critical Christian Feminist Theology of Solidarity," in *Women and Theology*, ed. Mary Ann Hinsdale and Phyllis H. Kaminski (Maryknoll, N.Y.: Orbis, 1995), 32 (in this chapter, hereafter cited in text as *TS*).

57. M. Shawn Copeland "Cornel West's Improvisational Philosophy of Religion," in *Cornel West: A Critical Reader*, ed. George Yancy (Malden, Mass.: Blackwell, 2000), 157, 162; quoting Cornel West.

58. Ibid., 162, quoting Albert Murray.

59. Welch also explores jazz improvisation as a metaphor for people to understand aspects of "power and fluidity" in social relations. This is similar to my metaphorical use of dance improvisation. However, Welch is also talking about literally listening to jazz as an existential resource for white people to create "identities as Americans outside of racism." Welch, *Sweet Dreams in America: Making Ethics and Spirituality Work* (New York: Routledge, 1999), 19. Regarding the latter use, my previous comments above about the risk of appropriation may apply. These concerns about appropriation are also voiced by one reviewer of Welch's book. See Janet R. Jakobsen, "Review of *Sweet Dreams in America*, by Sharon Welch," *Journal of the American Academy of Religion* 70, no. 1 (2002): 232–33.

60. My use of improvisational dance as a metaphor has advantages and disadvantages. The contemporary dance improvisation movement began in largely white dancer communities; hence I have not appropriated a cultural tradition, like jazz, with historical and current-day roots in the African American community. The white roots of dance improvisation would be a significant drawback for discussions of solidarity if not for the fact that this dance form is now practiced worldwide and is recognized as a historical aspect of diverse dance traditions; hence it can be affirmed as a growing multicultural phenomenon. Be that as it may, my use of it is theoretical and is not linked to empirical evidence of how it may or may not foster multiculturalism in the improvisational dance community itself. See Curtis L. Carter, "Improvisation in Dance," *Journal of Aesthetics and Art Criticism* 58, no. 2 (2000).

61. A metaphorical perspective per se is no guarantee against the imposition of privilege, even when multiple metaphors are employed tensively. Minimally, however, I believe metaphors should be chosen that encourage feminists of privilege to continue to be self-critical and those in nondominant positions to self-determine their participation in discussions or processes of solidarity. One example will suffice. Linda A. Moody, who is exemplary in her self-naming as a white feminist, proposes seeing feminist theological dialogue across racial difference in terms of a house with many rooms that we can call home: "We white women have some work to do in making home in our own [white] room, even as we venture out into the living room and kitchen to talk to others from different rooms." Moody, *Women Encounter God: Theology across Boundaries of Difference* (Maryknoll, N.Y.: Orbis, 1996), 139. While the room metaphor does suggest self-determination for women of color, the image of

making a white feminist home is troubling. As we saw in chapter 1, Ruth Frankenberg argues that whiteness is a privilege conferring culture. Moody's image of white women making their room homey does not encourage critical interrogation of white privilege.

62. Ann Cooper Albright, "Dwelling in Possibility," in *Taken By Surprise: A Dance Improvisation Reader*, ed. Ann Cooper Albright and David Gere (Middletown, Conn.: Wesleyan University Press, 2003), 261.

63. Ibid., 260.

64. Ann Cooper Albright, "Open Bodies: (X)Changes of Identity in Capoeira and Contact Improvisation," unpublished manuscript, used with permission, 10.

65. Contact improvisation can be solo movement but more often than not involves at least "two bodies in contact. Impulses, weight, and momentum are communicated through a point of physical contact that continuously rolls across and around the bodies of the dancers." Albright, "Present Tense: Contact Improvisation at Twenty-five," in *Taken By Surprise*, ed. Albright and Gere, 206).

66. Raymond W. Gibbs, Jr., "Embodied Meanings in Performing, Interpreting, and Talking about Dance Improvisation" in *Taken By Surprise*, ed. Albright and Gere, 187.

67. Michelle Heffner Hayes, "Writing on the Wall: Reading Improvisation in Flamenco and Postmodern Dance," and Avanthi Meduri, "Multiple Pleasures: Improvisation in *Bharatanatyam*," in *Taken By Surprise*, ed. Albright and Gere, 187.

68. Albright explains that contact improvisation classes train dancers with new skills for "falling without tensing up, giving one's weight to another person. . . . a more relaxed, peripheral vision," and so on. This training also works "to build physical endurance including an emphasis on upper body strength and the ability to support one's weight on unusual body parts" ("Open Bodies," 9, 7).

69. Copeland discusses the change required principally on the part of white feminists but also on the part of women of color. See Copeland, "Toward a Critical Christian Feminist Theology of Solidarity," 25.

Select Bibliography

Abugideiri, Hibba. "Hagar: A Historical Model for 'Gender Jihad.'" In *Daughters of Abraham: Feminist Thought in Judaism, Christianity, and Islam*, edited by Yvonne Yazbeck Haddad and John Esposito. Gainesville: University of Florida Press, 2001.

Albright, Ann Cooper. "Dwelling in Possibility." In *Taken By Surprise: A Dance Improvisation Reader*, edited by Ann Cooper Albright and David Gere. Middletown, Conn.: Wesleyan University Press, 2003.

———. "Present Tense: Contact Improvisation at Twenty-five." In *Taken By Surprise: A Dance Improvisation Reader*, edited by Ann Cooper Albright and David Gere. Middletown, Conn.: Wesleyan University Press.

Allen, Amy. "Foucault on Power: A Theory for Feminists." In *Feminist Interpretations of Michel Foucault*, edited by Susan J. Hekman. University Park: Pennsylvania State University Press, 1996.

Alpert, Rebecca. *Like Bread on the Seder Plate: Jewish Lesbians and the Transformation of Tradition*. New York: Columbia University Press, 1997.

Althaus-Reid, Marcella. *Indecent Theology: Theological Perversions in Sex, Gender, and Politics*. New York: Routledge, 2000.

———. "On Non-Docility and Indecent Theologians: A Response to the Panel for *Indecent Theology*." *Feminist Theology* 11, no. 2 (2003): 182–89.

Anderson, Pamela Sue. "Feminist Theology as Philosophy of Religion." In *The Cambridge Companion to Feminist Theology*, edited by Susan Frank Parsons. Cambridge: Cambridge University Press, 2002.

———. "Correspondence with Grace Jantzen." *Feminist Theology* 25 (2000): 112–19.

Anzaldúa, Gloria. "Bridge, Drawbridge, Sandbar, or Island: Lesbians-of-Color *Hacienda Alianzas*." In *Bridges of Power: Women's Multicultural*

Alliances, edited by Lisa Albrecht and Rose M. Brewer. Philadelphia, Pa.: New Society, 1990.

Armour, Ellen T. *Deconstruction, Feminist Theology, and the Problem of Difference: Subverting the Race/Gender Divide*. Chicago, Ill.: University of Chicago Press, 1999.

Augustine. *Confessions*, translated by R. S. Pine-Coffin. New York: Penguin, 1961.

———. *Homilies on the Gospel of John*. In *A Select Library of the Nicene and Post-Nicene Fathers of the Christian Church*, vol. 7, edited by Philip Schaff. New York: Christian Literature Publishing Company, 1888.

———. "On Marriage and Concupiscence." In *The Anti-Pelagian Writings. A Select Library of the Nicene and Post-Nicene Fathers of the Christian Church*, vol. 1, edited by Philip Schaff. New York: The Christian Literature Company, 1887.

Barad, Karen. "Posthumanist Performativity: Toward an Understanding of How Matter Comes to Matter." *Signs: Journal for Women in Culture and Society* 28, no. 3 (2003): 801–31.

Bell, Daniel M., Jr. *Liberation Theology After the End of History: The Refusal to Cease Suffering*. New York: Routledge, 2001.

Bellis, Alice Ogden. *Helpmates, Harlots, and Heroes: Women's Stories in the Hebrew Bible*. Louisville, Ky.: Westminster John Knox, 1994.

Benhabib, Seyla. *Situating the Self: Gender, Community, and Postmodernism in Contemporary Ethics*. New York: Routledge, 1992.

———. "Subjectivity, Historiography, and Politics." In *Feminist Contentions: A Philosophical Exchange*, by Seyla Benhabib, Judith Butler, Drucilla Cornell, and Nancy Fraser. New York: Routledge, 1995.

Bernauer, James W. "Michel Foucault's Ecstatic Thinking." In *The Final Foucault*, edited by James Bernauer and David Rasmussen. Cambridge, Mass.: MIT Press, 1988.

Berry, Wanda Warren. "Kierkegaard and Feminism: Apologetic, Repetition, and Dialogue." In *Kierkegaard in Post/Modernity*, edited by Martin J. Matustík and Merold Westphal. Bloomington: Indiana University Press, 1995.

———. "Images of Sin and Salvation in Feminist Theology." *Anglican Theological Review* 60 (1978): 25–54.

Bertung, Birgit. "Yes, a Woman Can Exist." In *Feminist Interpretations of Søren Kierkegaard*, edited by Céline Léon and Sylvia Walsh. University Park: Pennsylvania State University Press, 1997.

Børrensen, Kari Elisabeth. "God's Image. Is Woman Excluded?" In *The Image of God: Gender Models in Judaeo-Christian Tradition*, edited by Kari Elisabeth Børrensen. Minneapolis, Minn.: Fortress, 1991.

Braaten, Jane. "From Communicative Rationality to Communicative Thinking: A Basis for Feminist Theory and Practice." In *Feminists Read Habermas: Gendering the Subject of Discourse*, edited by Johanna Meehan. New York: Routledge, 1995.

Braxton, Joanne M. "Ancestral Presence: The Outraged Mother Figure in Contemporary Afra-American Writing." In *Wild Women in the Whirlwind: Afra-American*

Culture and the Contemporary Literary Renaissance, edited by Joanne M. Braxton and Andrée Nicola McLaughlin. New Brunswick, N.J.: Rutgers University Press, 1990.

Brock, Rita Nakashima. *Journeys By Heart: A Christology of Erotic Power.* New York: Crossroad, 1988.

Brown, Joanne Carlson and Rebecca Parker. *Christianity, Patriarchy, and Abuse*, edited by Joanne Carlson Brown and Carol R. Bohn. New York: Pilgrim, 1989.

Brown, Karen McCarthy. "Writing about 'the Other,' Revisited." In *Personal Knowledge and Beyond: Reshaping the Ethnography of Religion*, edited by James V. Spickard et al. New York: New York University Press, 2002.

Butler, Judith. *Bodies That Matter: On the Discursive Limits of "Sex."* New York: Routledge, 1993.

———. "Contingent Foundations." In *Feminist Contentions: A Philosophical Exchange*, by Seyla Benhabib, Judith Butler, Drucilla Cornell, and Nancy Fraser. New York: Routledge, 1995.

———. "For a Careful Reading." In *Feminist Contentions: A Philosophical Exchange*, by Seyla Benhabib, Judith Butler, Drucilla Cornell, and Nancy Fraser. New York: Routledge, 1995.

———. *Gender Trouble: Feminism and the Subversion of Identity.* New York: Routledge, 1990.

Butler, Judith, and Joan W. Scott, eds. *Feminists Theorize the Political.* New York: Routledge, 1992.

Cannon, Katie G. *Black Womanist Ethics.* Atlanta: Scholars, 1988.

Cannon, Katie G., and Carter Heyward. "Can We Be Different But Not Alienated?" In *Feminist Theological Ethics: A Reader*, edited by Lois K. Daly. Louisville, Ky.: Westminster John Knox, 1994.

———. "Alienation and Anger: A Black and a White Woman's Struggle for Mutuality in an Unjust World." *Stone Center Publication* 54 (1992).

Cannon, Katie G., et al., eds. *God's Fierce Whimsy: Christian Feminism and Theological Education.* New York: Pilgrim, 1985.

Caraway, Nancie. *Segregated Sisterhood: Racism and the Politics of American Feminism.* Knoxville: University of Tennessee Press, 1991.

Carrette, Jeremy. "Beyond Theology and Sexuality: Foucault, the Self, and the Que(e)rying of Monotheistic Truth." In *Michel Foucault and Theology: The Politics of Religious Experience*, edited by James Bernauer and Jeremy Carrette. Hampshire, U.K.: Ashgate, 2004.

Chopp, Rebecca S. *Saving Work: Feminist Practices of Theological Education.* Louisville, Ky.: Westminster John Knox, 1995.

Chopp, Rebecca S., and Sheila Greeve Davaney, eds. *Horizons in Feminist Theology: Identity, Tradition, and Norms.* Minneapolis, Minn.: Fortress, 1997.

Christ, Carol P. *Diving Deep and Surfacing: Women Writers on Spiritual Quest.* Boston, Mass.: Beacon, 1980.

———. *Rebirth of the Goddess: Finding Meaning in Feminist Spirituality.* New York: Routledge, 1997.

———. "Why Women Need the Goddess: Phenomenological, Psychological, and Political Reflections." In *Womanspirit Rising: A Feminist Reader in Religion*, edited by Carol P. Christ and Judith Plaskow. San Francisco, Calif.: Harper & Row, 1979.

Christ, Carol P., and Judith Plaskow, eds. *Womanspirit Rising: A Feminist Reader in Religion*. San Francisco, Calif.: Harper & Row, 1979.

Christian, Barbara. "The Race for Theory." In *Gender and Theory: Dialogues in Feminist Criticism*, edited by Linda Kaufman. New York: Blackwell, 1989.

Clifford, Anne M. "When Becoming Human Becomes Truly Earthly: An Ecofeminist Proposal for Solidarity." In *In the Embrace of God: Feminist Approaches to Theological Anthropology*, edited by Ann O'Hara Graff. Maryknoll, N.Y.: Orbis, 1995.

Coakley, Sarah. "The Eschatological Body: Gender, Transformation, and God." In *Powers and Submissions: Spirituality, Philosophy, and Gender*, by Sarah Coakley. Oxford: Blackwell, 2002.

Collins, Patricia Hill. *Black Feminist Thought: Knowledge, Consciousness, and the Politics of Empowerment*. New York: Routledge, 1991.

Comstock, Gary David, and Susan E. Henking, eds. *Que(e)rying Religion: A Critical Anthology*. New York: Continuum, 1997.

Cooey, Paula M. *Religion, Imagination, and the Body: A Feminist Analysis*. New York: Oxford University Press, 1994.

Copeland, M. Shawn. "Body, Representation, and Black Religious Discourse." In *Postcolonialism, Feminism, and Religious Discourse*, edited by Laura E. Donaldson and Kwok Pui-lan. New York: Routledge, 2002.

———. "Cornel West's Improvisational Philosophy of Religion." In *Cornel West: A Critical Reader*, edited by George Yancy. Malden, Mass.: Blackwell, 2000.

———. "Toward a Critical Christian Feminist Theology of Solidarity." In *Women and Theology*, edited by Mary Ann Hinsdale and Phyllis H. Kaminski. Maryknoll, N.Y.: Orbis, 1995.

Daly, Mary. *Beyond God the Father: Toward a Philosophy of Women's Liberation*. With new introduction. Boston, Mass.: Beacon, 1985.

———. *Gyn/Ecology: The Metaethics of Radical Feminism*. Boston, Mass.: Beacon, 1978.

———. *Pure Lust: Elemental Feminist Philosophy*. San Francisco, Calif.: HarperSanFrancisco, 1984.

Davaney, Sheila Greeve. "Judging Theologies: Truth in an Historicist Perspective." In *Pragmatism, Neo-pragmatism and Religion: Conversations with Richard Rorty*, edited by Charley D. Hardwick and Donald A. Crosby. New York: Peter Lang, 1997.

———. "The Limits of the Appeal to Women's Experience." In *Shaping New Vision: Gender and Values in American Culture*, edited by Clarissa W. Atkinson, Constance H. Buchanan, and Margaret R. Miles. Ann Arbor, Mich.: UMI Research, 1987.

———. "Mapping Theologies: An Historicist Guide to Contemporary Theology." In *Changing Conversations: Religious Reflection and Cultural Analysis*, edited by Dwight N. Hopkins and Sheila Greeve Davaney. New York: Routledge, 1996.

————. *Pragmatic Historicism: A Theology for the Twenty-first Century*. Albany: State University of New York Press, 2000.

————. "Problems with Feminist Theory: Historicity and the Search for Sure Foundations." In *Embodied Love: Sensuality and Relationships as Feminist Values*, edited by Paula M. Cooey et al. San Francisco, Calif.: Harper & Row, 1987.

————. "Theology and the Turn to Cultural Analysis." In *Converging on Culture: Theologians in Dialogue with Cultural Analysis and Criticism*, edited by Delwin Brown, Sheila Greeve Davaney, and Kathryn Tanner. New York: Oxford University Press, 2001.

Day, Janeth Norfleete. *The Woman at the Well: Interpretation of John 4:1–42 in Retrospect and Prospect*. Boston, Mass.: Brill, 2002.

Devaux, Monique. "Feminism and Empowerment: A Critical Reading of Foucault." In *Feminist Interpretations of Michel Foucault*, edited by Susan J. Hekman. University Park: Pennsylvania State University Press, 1996.

Donaldson, Laura. "On Medicine Women and White Shame-ans." In *Women, Gender, and Religion: A Reader*, edited by Elizabeth Castelli. New York: Palgrave, 2000.

Douglas, Kelly Brown. *The Black Christ*. Maryknoll, N.Y.: Orbis, 1994.

————. "Daring to Speak: Womanist Theology and Black Sexuality." In *Embracing the Spirit: Womanist Perspectives on Hope, Salvation, and Transformation*, edited by Emilie M. Townes. Maryknoll, N.Y.: Orbis, 1997.

————. *Sexuality and the Black Church: A Womanist Perspective*. Maryknoll, N.Y.: Orbis, 1999.

Dreyfus. Hubert L., and Paul Rabinow, eds. *Michel Foucault: Beyond Structuralism and Hermeneutics*. Chicago, Ill.: University of Chicago Press, 1982.

Dube, Musa W. "Reading for Deconstruction (John 4:1–42)." In *John and Postcolonialism: Travel, Space, and Power*, edited by Musa W. Dube and Jeffrey Staley. London, U.K.: Sheffield Academic Press, 2002.

Dugger, Karen. "Changing the Subject: Race and Gender in Feminist Discourse." In *Racism and Anti-Racism in World Perspective*, edited by Benjamin P. Bowser. Thousand Oaks, Calif.: Sage, 1995.

Duncan, Celena M. "The Book of Ruth: On Boundaries, Love, and Truth." In *Take Back the Word: A Queer Reading of the Bible*, edited by Robert E. Goss and Mona West. Cleveland, Ohio: Pilgrim, 2000.

Eslinger, Lyle. "The Wooing of the Woman at the Well: Jesus, the Reader, and Reader-Response Criticism," *Journal of Literature and Theology* 1, no. 2 (1987): 167–83.

Exum, J. Cheryl. *Fragmented Women: Feminist (Sub)Versions of Biblical Narratives*. Valley Forge, Pa.: Trinity, 1993.

————. " 'Mother in Israel': A Familiar Figure Reconsider." In *Feminist Interpretation of the Bible*, edited by Letty M. Russell. Philadephia, Pa.: Westminster, 1985.

Falk, Nancy Auer, and Rita M. Gross, eds. *Unspoken Worlds: Women's Religious Lives*. Belmont, Calif.: Wadsworth, 2001.

Fehribach, Adeline. *The Women in the Life of the Bridegroom: Feminist Historical-Literary Analysis of the Female Characters in the Fourth Gospel.* Collegeville, Minn.: Liturgical, 1998.

Felder, Cain Hope. "Race, Racism, and the Biblical Narrative." In *Stony the Road We Trod: African American Biblical Interpretation*, edited by Cain Hope Felder. Minneapolis, Minn.: Fortress, 1991.

Fewell, Danna Nolan, and David M. Gunn. "Keeping the Promise (Genesis 11–22)." In *Gender, Power, and Promise: The Subject of the Bible's First Story*, by Danna Nolan Fewell and David M. Gunn. Nashville, Tenn.: Abingdon, 1993.

Fewell, Danna Nolan, and Gary A. Phillips. "Drawn to Excess; or, Reading Beyond Betrothal." *Semeia* 77 (1997): 23–58.

Fiorenza, Elisabeth Schüssler. *Bread Not Stone: The Challenge of Feminist Biblical Interpretation.* Boston, Mass.: Beacon, 1995.

———. *In Memory of Her: A Feminist Theological Reconstruction of Christian Origins.* New York: Crossroad, 1985.

Firestone, Reuven. *Journeys in Holy Lands: The Evolution of the Abraham-Ishmael Legends in Islamic Exegesis.* Albany: State University of New York Press, 1990.

Foucault, Michel. *The Archaeology of Knowledge and the Discourse on Language*, translated by A. M. Sheridan Smith. San Francisco, Calif.: Harper & Row, 1972.

———. *Discipline and Punish: The Birth of the Prison*, translated by Alan Sheridan. New York: Random House, 1977.

———. "The Ethic of Care for the Self as a Practice of Freedom," translated by J. D. Gauthier, SJ. An interview with Michel Foucault on January 20, 1984, conducted by Raúl Fornet-Betancourt et al. In *The Final Foucault*, edited by James Bernauer and David Rasmussen. Cambridge, Mass.: MIT Press, 1988.

———. *The History of Sexuality: An Introduction*, vol. 1, translated by Robert Hurley. New York: Vintage, 1990; New York: Random House, 1978.

———. "Nietzsche, Genealogy, History." In *Language, Counter-Memory, Practice: Selected Essays and Interviews*, translated by Donald Bouchard and Sherry Simon. Ithaca, N.Y.: Cornell University Press, 1977.

———. "On the Genealogy of Ethics: An Overview of Work in Progress." In *Ethics: Subjectivity and Truth*, edited by Paul Rabinow, translated by Robert Hurley et al. New York: New Press, 1997.

———. *Power/Knowledge: Selected Interviews and Other Writings, 1972–1977*, edited and translated by Colin Gordon et al. New York: Pantheon, 1972.

———. "The Subject and Power." In *Michel Foucault: Beyond Structuralism and Hermeneutics*, edited by Hubert L. Dreyfus and Paul Rabinow. Chicago, Ill.: University of Chicago Press, 1982.

———. *Technologies of the Self: A Seminar with Michel Foucault*, edited Luther H. Martin, Huck Gutman, and Patrick H. Hutton. Amherst: University of Massachusetts Press, 1988.

———. *The Use of Pleasure*, translated by Robert Hurley. New York: Vintage, 1986.

Frankenberg, Ruth. *White Women, Race Matters: The Social Construction of Whiteness.* Minneapolis: University of Minnesota Press, 1993.

Friedman, Susan Stanford. "Beyond White and Other: Relationality and Narratives of Race in Feminist Discourse." *Signs* 21 (1995): 1–45.

———. "Making History: Reflections on Feminism, Narrative, and Desire." In *Feminism beside Itself*, edited by Diane Elam and Robyn Wiegman. New York: Routledge, 1995.

Fuchs, Esther. "The Literary Characterization of Mothers and Sexual Politics in the Hebrew Bible." In *Feminist Perspectives on Biblical Scholarship*, edited by Adela Yarbro Collins. Chico, Calif.: Scholars, 1985.

———. "Structure and Patriarchal Function in the Biblical Betrothal Type-Scene: Some Preliminary Notes." In *Women in the Hebrew Bible: A Reader*, edited by Alice Bach. New York: Routledge, 1999.

Fulkerson, Mary McClintock. *Changing the Subject: Women's Discourses and Feminist Theology*. Minneapolis, Minn.: Fortress, 1994.

———. "Contesting the Gendered Subject: A Feminist Account of the *Imago Dei*." In *Horizons in Feminist Theology: Identity, Tradition, and Norms*, edited by Rebecca S. Chopp and Sheila Greeve Davaney. Minneapolis, Minn.: Fortress, 1997.

———. "Gender—Being It or Doing It: The Church, Homosexuality, and the Politics of Identity." In *Que(e)rying Religion: A Critical Anthology*, edited by Gary David Comstock and Susan E. Henking. New York: Continuum, 1997.

———. " 'We Don't See Color Here': A Case Study in Ecclesial-Cultural Invention." In *Converging on Culture: Theologians in Dialogue with Cultural Analysis and Criticism*, edited by Delwin Brown, Sheila Greeve Davaney, and Kathryn Tanner. New York: Oxford University Press, 2001.

Gasparro, Guilia Sfameni. "Image of God and Sexual Differentiation in the Tradition of *Enkrateia*." In *The Image of God: Gender Models in Judaeo-Christian Tradition*, edited by Kari Elisabeth Børrensen. Minneapolis, Minn.: Fortress, 1991.

Gebara, Ivone. *Out of the Depths: Women's Experience of Evil and Salvation*, translated by Ann Patrick Ware. Minneapolis, Minn.: Fortress, 2002.

Gilkes, Cheryl Townsend. "A Conscious Connection to All That Is: *The Color Purple* as Subversive and Cultural Ethnography." In *Converging on Culture: Theologians in Dialogue with Cultural Analysis and Criticism*, edited by Delwin Brown, Sheila Greeve Davaney, and Kathryn Tanner. New York: Oxford University Press, 2001.

———. "The 'Loves' and 'Troubles' of African American Women's Bodies and the Womanist Challenge to Cultural Humiliation and Community Ambivalence." In *A Troubling in My Soul: Womanist Perspectives on Evil and Suffering*, edited by Emilie M. Townes. Maryknoll, N.Y.: Orbis, 1993.

———. " 'Mother to the Motherless, Father to the Fatherless': Power, Gender, and Community in Afrocentric Biblical Tradition." *Semeia* 47 (1989): 57–85.

Gonzáles, Michelle A. " 'One is Not Born a Latina, One Becomes One': The Construction of the Latina Feminist Theologian in Latino/a Theology." *Journal of Hispanic/Latino Theology* 10 (2003): 5–30.

Goss, Robert E. *Queering Christ: Beyond Jesus Acted Up*. Cleveland, Ohio: Pilgrim Press, 2002.

Gottschall, Marilyn. "The Ethical Implications of the Deconstruction of Gender." *Journal of the American Academy of Religion* 70, no. 2 (2002): 279–99.

Grant, Jacquelyn. "The Sin of Servanthood." In *A Troubling in My Soul: Womanist Perpsectives on Evil and Suffering*, edited by Emilie M. Townes. Maryknoll, N.Y.: Orbis, 1993.

———. *White Women's Christ and Black Women's Jesus: Feminist Christology and Womanist Response*. Atlanta, Ga.: Scholars, 1989.

Grey, Mary. *Redeeming the Dream: Feminism, Redemption, and Christian Tradition*. London: SPCK, 1989.

Gross, Rita M. *Feminism and Religion: An Introduction*. Boston, Mass.: Beacon, 1996.

Guardiola-Sáenz, Leticia A. "Reading from Ourselves: Identity and Hermeneutics among Mexican-American Feminists." In *A Reader in Latina Feminist Theology: Religion and Justice*, edited by María Pila Aquino, Daisy L. Machado, and Jeanette Rodríguez. Austin: University of Texas Press, 2002.

Gudorf, Christine E. "Issues of Race in Feminist Ethics: A Review Essay." *Journal of Feminist Studies in Religion* 9 (1993): 239–45.

Habermas, Jürgen. *The Philosophical Discourse of Modernity*, translated by Frederick Lawrence. Cambridge, Mass.: MIT Press, 1987.

———. *Postmetaphysical Thinking: Philosophical Essays*, translated by William Mark Hohengarten. Cambridge, Mass.: MIT Press, 1992.

———. "Questions and Counterquestions." In *Habermas and Modernity*, edited by Richard J. Bernstein. Cambridge, Mass.: MIT Press, 1985.

———. *The Theory of Communicative Action*, vol. 1, translated by Thomas McCarthy. Boston, Mass.: Beacon, 1981.

Hackett, Jo Ann. "Rehabilitating Hagar: Fragments of an Epic Pattern." In *Gender and Difference in Ancient Israel*, edited by Peggy L. Day. Minneapolis, Minn.: Fortress, 1989.

Hampson, Daphne. *After Christianity*. Valley Forge, Pa.: Trinity, 1996.

———. "Reinhold Niebuhr on Sin: A Critique." In *Reinhold Niebuhr and the Issues of Our Time*, edited by Richard Harries. Oxford: A. R. Mowbray, 1986.

———. "Sources and the Relationship to Tradition: What Daphne Hampson Is Supposed to Hold (and What She in Fact Holds)." *Feminist Theology* 3 (1993): 23–37.

———. *Theology and Feminism*. Oxford: Basil Blackwell, 1990.

Harstock, Nancy. "Foucault on Power: A Theory for Women?" In *Feminism/ Postmodernism*, edited by Linda J. Nicholson. New York: Routledge, 1990.

Hayes, Diana L. *Hagar's Daughters: Womanist Ways of Being in the World*. Mahwah, N.J.: Paulist, 1995.

Heyward, Carter. *Saving Jesus from Those Who Are Right: Rethinking What It Means to Be Christian*. Minneapolis, Minn.: Fortress, 1999.

———. *Touching Our Strength: The Erotic as Power and the Love of God*. San Francisco, Calif.: HarperSanFrancisco, 1989.

Heyward, Carter, and Mary Hunt. "Roundtable Discussion: Lesbianism and Feminist Theology." *Journal of Feminist Studies in Religion* 2, no. 2 (1986): 95–106.

Hilkert, Mary Catherine. "Cry Beloved Image: Rethinking the Image of God." In *In the Embrace of God: Feminist Approaches to Theological Anthropology*, edited by Ann O'Hara Graff. Maryknoll, N.Y.: Orbis, 1995.

———. "Experience and Tradition—Can the Center Hold?" In *Freeing Theology: The Essentials of Theology in Feminist Perspective*, edited by Catherine Mowry LaCugna. San Francisco, Calif.: HarperSanFranciso, 1993.

———. *Naming Grace: Preaching and the Sacramental Imagination.* New York: Continuum, 1997.

Hill, Renée Leslie. "Disrupted/Disruptive Movements: Black Theology and Black Power." In *Black Faith and Public Talk: Critical Essays on James H. Cone's "Black Theology and Black Power,"* edited by Dwight N. Hopkins. Maryknoll, N.Y.: Orbis, 1999.

Hogan, Linda. *From Women's Experience to Feminist Theology.* Sheffield, U.K.: Sheffield Academic Press, 1995.

hooks, bell. "Reading and Resistance: *The Color Purple.*" In *Alice Walker: Critical Perspectives Past and Present*, edited by Henry Louis Gates, Jr., and K. A. Appiah. New York: Amistad, 1993.

———. *Yearning: Race, Gender, and Cultural Politics.* Boston, Mass.: South End, 1990.

Hopkins, Julie M. *Towards a Feminist Christology: Jesus of Nazareth, European Woman, and the Christological Crisis.* Grand Rapids, Mich.: Eerdmans, 1995.

Howe, Leslie A. "Kierkegaard and the Feminine Self." In *Feminist Interpretations of Søren Kierkegaard*, edited by Céline Léon and Sylvia Walsh. University Park: Pennsylvania State University Press, 1997.

Hunter, Patricia L. "Women's Power—Women's Passion: And God Said, 'That's Good.'" In *A Troubling in My Soul: Womanist Perspectives on Evil and Suffering*, edited by Emilie M. Townes. Maryknoll, N.Y.: Orbis, 1993.

Irigaray, Luce. "*La Mystérique.*" In *Speculum of the Other Woman*, translated by Gillian C. Gill. Ithaca, N.Y.: Cornell University Press, 1985.

Isasi-Díaz, Ada María. "Creating a Liberating Culture: Latinas' Subversive Narratives." In *Converging on Culture: Theologians in Dialogue with Cultural Analysis and Criticism*, edited by Delwin Brown, Sheila Greeve Davaney, and Kathryn Tanner. New York: Oxford University Press, 2001.

———. *En la Lucha, In the Struggle: A Hispanic Women's Liberation Theology.* Minneapolis, Minn.: Fortress, 1993.

Isherwood, Lisa, and Elizabeth Stuart. *Introducing Body Theology.* Cleveland, Ohio: Pilgrim, 1998.

Jakobsen, Janet R. "Review of *Sweet Dreams in America*, by Sharon Welch." *Journal of the American Academy of Religion* 70, no. 1 (2002): 230–34.

Jagose, Annamarie. *Queer Theory: An Introduction.* New York: New York University Press, 1996.

Jantzen, Grace M. *Becoming Divine: Toward a Feminist Philosophy of Religion.* Bloomington: Indiana University Press, 1999.

———. "Feminist Philosophy of Religion: Open Discussion with Pamela Anderson." *Feminist Theology* 26 (2001): 102–9.

———. *Foundations of Violence*. New York: Routledge, 2004.

Jeansonne, Sharon Pace. *The Women of Genesis: From Sarah to Potipher's Wife*. Minneapolis, Minn.: Fortress, 1990.

Johnson, Elizabeth A. *She Who Is: The Mystery of God in Feminist Theological Discourse*. New York: Crossroad, 1992.

Jones, Serene. *Feminist Theory and Christian Theology: Cartographies of Grace*. Minneapolis, Minn.: Fortress, 2000.

———. " 'Women's Experience' Between a Rock and a Hard Place: Feminist, Womanist, and *Mujerista* Theologies in North America." *Religious Studies Review* 21 (1995): 171–78.

Kamitsuka, David G. *Theology and Contemporary Culture: Liberation, Postliberal, and Revisionary Perspectives*. Cambridge: Cambridge University Press, 1999.

Kamitsuka, Margaret D. "Reading the Raced and Sexed Body in *The Color Purple*: Repatterning White Feminist and Womanist Theological Hermeneutics." *Journal of Feminist Studies in Religion* 19, no. 2 (2003): 45–66.

Kelsey, David H. "Human Being." In *Christian Theology: An Introduction to Its Traditions and Tasks*, edited by Peter C. Hodgson and Robert H. King. Philadephia, Pa.: Fortress, 1982.

———. "Whatever Happened to the Doctrine of Sin?" *Theology Today* 50 (1993): 169–78.

Kierkegaard, Søren. *The Concept of Anxiety*. In *The Kierkegaard Reader*, edited by Jane Chamberlain and Jonathan Rée. Oxford: Blackwell, 2001.

———. *The Sickness Unto Death: A Psychological Exposition for Upbuilding and Awakening*, translated and edited by Howard V. Hong and Edna H. Hong. Princeton, N.J.: Princeton University Press, 1980.

Kim, Jean K. "A Korean Feminist Reading of John 4:1–42." In *Reading the Bible as Women: Perspectives from Africa, Asia and Latin America*, edited by Phyllis A. Bird. *Semeia* 78 (1997): 109–119.

Kirby, Vicki. "Feminisms and Postmodernisms: Anthropology and the Management of Difference." *Anthropological Quarterly* 66, no. 3 (1993): 127–33.

Kirk-Duggan, Cheryl A. "Gender, Violence, and Transformation in *The Color Purple*." In *Curing Violence*, edited by Mark I. Wallace and Theophus H. Smith. Sonoma, Calif.: Polebridge, 1994.

———. "Justified, Sanctified, and Redeemed: Blessed Expectation in Black Women's Blues and Gospels." In *Embracing the Spirit: Womanist Perspectives on Hope, Salvation, and Transformation*, edited by Emilie M. Townes. Maryknoll, N.Y.: Orbis, 1997.

Krause, Deborah. "School's in Session: The Making and Unmaking of Docile Disciple Bodies in Mark." In *Postmodern Interpretations of the Bible: A Reader*, edited by A. K. M. Adam. St Louis, Mo.: Chalice, 2001.

Kwok Pui-lan. "Jesus/The Native: Biblical Studies from a Postcolonial Perspective." In *Teaching the Bible: The Discourses and Politics of Biblical Pedagogy*, edited by Fernando F. Segovia and Mary Ann Tolbert. Maryknoll, N.Y.: Orbis, 1998.

———. *Postcolonial Imagination and Feminist Theology*. Louisville, Ky.: Westminster John Knox, 2005.

———. "Racism and Ethnocentrism in Feminist Biblical Interpretation." In *Searching the Scriptures*, edited by Elizabeth Schüssler Fiorenza. New York: Crossroad, 1995.

———. "Speaking from the Margins." In Special Section on Appropriation and Reciprocity in Womanist/Mujerista/Feminist Work. *Journal of Feminist Studies in Religion* 8 (1992): 102–5.

———. "Theology as a Sexual Act." *Feminist Theology* 11, no. 2 (2003): 149–56.

———. "Unbinding Our Feet: Saving Brown Women and Feminist Religious Discourse." In *Postcolonialism, Feminism, and Religious Discourse*, edited by Laura Donaldson and Kwok Pui-lan. New York: Routledge, 2002.

LaCugna, Catherine Mowry. *God for Us: The Trinity and Christian Life*. San Francisco, Calif.: HarperSanFrancisco, 1991.

LaCugna, Catherine Mowry, ed. *Freeing Theology: The Essentials of Theology in Feminist Perspective*. San Francisco, Calif.: HarperSanFranciso, 1992.

Levine, Amy-Jill. "Settling at Beer-lahai-ro." In *Daughters of Abraham: Feminist Thought in Judaism, Christianity, and Islam*, edited by Yvonne Yazbeck Haddad and John L. Esposito. Gainesville: University Press of Florida, 2001.

Liew, Tat-Siong Benny. "Ambiguous Admittance: Consent and Descent in John's Community of Upward Mobility." In *John and Postcolonialism: Travel, Space, and Power*, edited by Musa W. Dube and Jeffrey Staley. London: Sheffield Academic Press, 2002.

Lindbeck, George A. *The Nature of Doctrine: Religion and Theology in a Postliberal Age*. Philadelphia, Pa.: Westminster, 1984.

Lorde, Audre. *Sister Outsider*. Freedom, Calif.: Crossing, 1984.

Loya, Gloria Inéz. "Pathways to a Mestiza Feminist Theology." In *A Reader in Latina, Feminist Theology: Religion and Justice*, edited by María Pila Aquino, Daisy L. Machado, and Jeanette Rodríguez. Austin: University of Texas Press, 2002.

Lykes, M. Brinton, and Amelia Mallona. "Surfacing Our-Selves: ¿Gringa, White— Mestiza, Brown?" In *Off White: Readings on Society, Race, and Culture*, edited by Michelle Fine et al. New York: Routledge, 1997.

Mbuwayesando, Dora R. "Childlessness and Woman-to-Woman Relationships in Genesis and African Patriarchal Society: Sarah and Hagar from a Zimbabwean Woman's Perspective (Gen. 16:1–16; 21:8–21)." *Semeia* 78 (1997): 27–36.

McDowell, Deborah. " 'The Changing Same': Generational Connections and Black Women Novelists." In *Reading Black, Reading Feminist: A Critical Anthology*, edited by Henry Louis Gates, Jr. New York: Meridian, 1990.

McFague, Sallie. *The Body of God: An Ecological Theology*. Minneapolis, Minn.: Fortress, 1993.

———. *Metaphorical Theology: Models of God in Religious Language*. Philadelphia, Pa.: Fortress, 1982.

Mitchem, Stephanie Y. *Introducing Womanist Theology*. Maryknoll, N.Y.: Orbis, 2002.

———. "Response: Reading Womanists; Repatterning Ourselves." *Journal of Feminist Studies in Religion* 19, no. 2 (2003): 67–73.

———. "Womanists and (Unfinished) Constructions of Salvation." *Journal of Feminist Studies in Religion* 17, no. 1 (2001): 85–100.

Moody, Linda. *Women Encounter God: Theology across Boundaries of Difference.* Maryknoll, N.Y.: Orbis, 1996.

Moore, Stephen. *Poststructuralism and the New Testament: Derrida and Foucault at the Foot of the Cross.* Minneapolis, Minn.: Fortress, 1994.

Niebuhr, Reinhold. *The Nature and Destiny of Man: A Christian Interpretation*, vol. 1. New York: Scribner's Sons, 1964.

Okure, Teresa. *The Johannine Approach to Mission: A Contextual Study of John 4:1–42.* Tubingen: JCB Mohr, 1988.

O'Neill, Mary Aquin. "The Mystery of Being Human Together." In *Freeing Theology: The Essentials of Theology in Feminist Perspective*, edited by Catherine Mowry LaCugna. San Francisco, Calif.: HarperSanFranciso, 1993.

Pinn, Anthony B., and Dwight N. Hopkins, eds. *Loving the Body: Black Religious Studies and the Erotic.* New York: Palgrave, 2004.

Phillips, Gary A. "The Ethics of Reading Deconstructively, or, Speaking Face-to-Face: The Samaritan Woman Meets Derrida at the Well." In *The New Literary Criticism and the New Testament*, edited by Edgar McKnight and Elizabeth Malbon. Valley Forge, Pa.: Trinity, 1994.

Plaskow, Judith. "Appropriation, Reciprocity, and Issues of Power." In Special Section on Appropriation and Reciprocity in Womanist/Mujerista/Feminist Work. *Journal of Feminist Studies in Religion* 8 (1992): 105–9.

———. *Sex, Sin, and Grace: Women's Experience and the Theologies of Reinhold Niebuhr and Paul Tillich.* Washington, D.C.: University Press of America, 1980.

———. *Standing Again at Sinai: Judaism from a Feminist Perspective.* San Francisco, Calif.: Harper, 1990.

Ray, Darby Kathleen. *Deceiving the Devil: Atonement, Abuse, and Ransom.* Cleveland, Ohio: Pilgrim, 1998.

Reno, R. R. *Redemptive Change: Atonement and the Christian Cure of the Soul.* Harrisburg, Pa.: Trinity Press International, 2002.

Rodríguez, Jeanette. "Experience as a Resource for Feminist Thought." *Journal of Hispanic/Latino Theology* 1 (1993): 68–76.

Rogers, Eugene F., Jr., ed. *Theology and Sexuality: Classic and Contemporary Readings.* Oxford: Blackwell, 2002.

Ronan, Marian. "Reclaiming Women's Experience: A Reading of Selected Christian Feminist Theologies." *Cross Currents* 48, no. 2 (1998): 218–29.

Rorty, Richard. *Contingency, Irony, and Solidarity.* Cambridge: Cambridge University Press, 1989.

———. *Essays on Heidegger and Others: Philosophical Papers.* Vol. 2. Cambridge: Cambridge University Press, 1991.

———. *Objectivity, Relativism, and Truth: Philosophical Papers.* Vol. 1. Cambridge: Cambridge University Press, 1991.

Ruether, Rosemary Radford. "Feminist Interpretation: A Method of Correlation." In *Feminist Interpretation of the Bible*, edited by Letty M. Russell. Philadephia, Pa.: Westminster, 1985.

———. "Is Feminism the End of Christianity? A Critique of Daphne Hampson's *Theology and Feminism*." *Scottish Journal of Theology* 43 (1990): 390–400.

———. *Sexism and God-Talk: Toward a Feminist Theology*. With new introduction. Boston, Mass.: Beacon, 1993.

Saiving, Valerie. "The Human Situation: A Feminine View." In *Womanspirit Rising: A Feminist Reader in Religion*, edited by Carol P. Christ and Judith Plaskow. San Francisco, Calif.: Harper & Row, 1979.

Sands, Kathleen M. "A Response to Marcella Althaus-Reid's *Indecent Theology: Theological Perversions in Sex, Gender, and Politics*." *Feminist Theology* 11, no. 2 (2003): 175–81.

Sanders, Cheryl J. "Black Women in Biblical Perspective: Resistance, Affirmation, and Empowerment." In *Living the Intersection: Womanism and Afrocentrism in Theology*, edited by Cheryl J. Sanders. Minneapolis, Minn.: Fortress, 1995.

Sanders, Cheryl J., et al. "Roundtable Discussion: Christian Ethics and Theology in Womanist Perspective." *Journal of Feminist Studies in Religion* 5 (1989): 81–112.

Schneiders, Sandra M. "A Case Study: A Feminist Interpretation of John 4: 1–42." In *The Revelatory Text: Interpreting the New Testament as Sacred Scripture*. Collegeville, Minn.: Liturgical Press, 1999.

Secker, Susan L. "Women's Experience in Feminist Theology: The 'Problem' or the 'Truth' of Difference." *Journal of Hispanic/Latino Theology* 1 (1993): 56–67.

Sered, Susan Starr. *Women as Ritual Experts: The Religious Lives of Elderly Jewish Women in Jerusalem*. New York: Oxford University Press, 1992.

Smith, Barbara. "The Truth That Never Hurts: Black Lesbians in the Fiction in the 1980s." In *Wild Women in the Whirlwind: Afra-American Culture and the Contemporary Literary Renaissance*, edited by Joanne M. Braxton and Andrée Nicola McLaughlin. New Brunswick, N.J.: Rutgers University Press, 1990.

Smith, Valerie. "Split Affinities: The Case of Interracial Rape." In *Conflicts in Feminism*, edited by Marianne Hirsch and Evelyn Fox Keller. New York: Routledge, 1990.

Soskice, Janet Martin. "General Introduction." In *Oxford Readings in Feminism and Theology*, edited by Janet Martin Soskice and Diana Lipton. New York: Oxford University Press, 2003.

Spelman, Elizabeth V. *Inessential Woman: Problems of Exclusion in Feminist Thought*. Boston, Mass.: Beacon, 1988.

Spivak, Gayatri Chakravorty. "In a Word." Interview with Ellen Rooney. In *The Second Wave: A Reader in Feminist Theory*, edited by Linda J. Nicholson. New York: Routledge, 1997.

———. "Subaltern Studies: Deconstructing Historiography." In *The Spivak Reader*, edited by Donna Landry and Gerald MacLean. New York: Routledge, 1996.

Steinberg, Naomi. *Kinship and Marriage in Genesis: A Household Economics Perspective*. Minneapolis, Minn.: Fortress, 1993.

Steinmetz, Devora. *From Father to Son: Kinship, Conflict, and Continuity in Genesis.* Louisville, Ky.: Westminster John Knox, 1991.

Stevens, Maryanne, ed. *Reconstructing the Christ Symbol: Essays in Feminist Christology.* New York: Paulist, 1993.

Stowasser, Barbara Freyer. *Women in the Qur'an: Traditions and Interpretation.* New York: Oxford University Press, 1994.

Stuart, Elizabeth. "Camping about the Canon: Humor as a Hermeneutical Tool in Queer Readings of Biblical Text." In *Take Back the Word: A Queer Reading of the Bible,* edited by Robert E. Goss and Mona West. Cleveland, Ohio: Pilgrim Press, 2000.

Suchocki, Marjorie Hewitt. *The Fall to Violence: Original Sin in Relational Theology.* New York: Continuum, 1995.

Tanner, Kathryn. *Theories of Culture: A New Agenda for Theology.* Minneapolis, Minn.: Fortress Press, 1997.

Taylor, Katy. "From Lavender to Purple: A Feminist Reading of Hagar and Celie in Light of Womanism." *Theology* 97 (1994): 352–62.

Terrell, JoAnne Marie. *Power in the Blood? The Cross in the African American Experience.* Maryknoll, N.Y.: Orbis, 1998.

Teubal, Savina J. *Ancient Sisterhood: The Lost Traditions of Hagar and Sarah.* Athens, Ohio: Swallow. 1990.

———. *Sarah the Priestess: The First Matriarch of Genesis.* Athens, Ohio.: Swallow, 1984.

Thistlethwaite, Susan Brooks. *Sex, Race, and God: Christian Feminism in Black and White.* New York: Crossroad, 1989.

Thistlethwaite, Susan Brooks, and Toinette M. Eugene. "A Survey of Feminist Theologies." In *Critical Review of Books in Religion.* Atlanta, Ga.: Scholars, 1991.

Thomas, Linda E. "Womanist Theology, Epistemology, and a New Anthropological Paradigm." In *Living Stones in the Household of God: The Legacy and Future of Black Theology,* edited by Linda E. Thomas. Minneapolis, Minn.: Fortress, 2004.

Townes, Emilie M. *In a Blaze of Glory: Womanist Spirituality as Social Witness.* Nashville, Tenn.: Abingdon, 1995.

———. "Panel Response to Marcella Althaus-Reid's *Indecent Theology.*" *Feminist Theology* 11, no. 2 (2003): 167–73.

Townes, Emilie M., ed., *Embracing the Spirit: Womanist Perspectives on Hope, Salvation, and Transformation.* Maryknoll, N.Y.: Orbis, 1997.

———. *A Troubling in My Soul: Womanist Perspectives on Evil and Suffering.* Maryknoll, N.Y.: Orbis, 1993.

Trible, Phyllis. "Genesis 22: The Sacrifice of Sarah." In *Not in Heaven: Coherence and Complexity in Biblical Narrative,* edited by Jason P. Rosenblatt and Joseph C. Sitterson, Jr. Bloomington: Indiana University Press, 1991.

———. *Texts of Terror: Literary-Feminist Readings of Biblical Narratives.* Philadelphia, Pa.: Fortress, 1984.

Walker, Alice. *The Color Purple.* New York: Pocket, 1982.

———. *In Search of Our Mother's Gardens.* San Diego, Calif.: Harcourt Brace, 1983.

Walsh, Sylvia I. "On 'Feminine' and 'Masculine' Forms of Despair." In *The International Kierkegaard Commentary: Sickness Unto Death*, edited by Robert L. Perkins. Macon, Ga.: Mercer University Press, 1987.

Weems, Renita T. "A Mistress, a Maid, and No Mercy." In *Just a Sister Away: A Womanist Vision of Women's Relationships in the Bible*, by Renita T. Weems. San Diego, Calif.: Lura Media, 1988.

Welch, Sharon D. *Communities of Resistance and Solidarity: A Feminist Theology of Liberation*. Maryknoll, N.Y.: Orbis, 1985.

———. *A Feminist Ethic of Risk*. Minneapolis, Minn.: Fortress, 1990.

———. *A Feminist Ethic of Risk*. Revised edition. Minneapolis, Minn.: Fortress, 2000.

———. "Human Beings, White Supremacy, and Racial Justice." In *Reconstructing Christian Theology*, edited by Rebecca S. Chopp and Mark Lewis Taylor. Minneapolis, Minn.: Fortress, 1994.

———. "Sporting Power: American Feminism, French Feminisms, and an Ethic of Conflict." In *Transfigurations: Theology and the French Feminists*, edited by C. W. Maggie Kim et al. Minneapolis, Minn.: Augsburg Fortress, 1993.

———. *Sweet Dreams in America: Making Ethics and Spirituality Work*. New York: Routledge, 1999.

West, Cornel. *Keeping Faith: Philosophy and Faith in America*. New York: Routledge, 1993.

———. *Prophetic Fragments*. Grand Rapids, Mich.: Eerdmans, 1988.

Wiegman, Robyn. *American Anatomies: Theorizing Race and Gender*. Durham, N.C.: Duke University Press, 1995.

Williams, Delores S. "Black Women's Literature and the Task of Feminist Theology." In *Immaculate and Powerful: The Female in Sacred Image and Social Reality*, edited by Clarissa W. Atkinson et al. Boston, Mass.: Beacon, 1985.

———. "The Color of Feminism: Or Speaking the Black Woman's Tongue." In *Feminist Theological Ethics: A Reader*, edited by Lois K. Daly. Louisville, Ky.: Westminster John Knox, 1994.

———. *Sisters in the Wilderness: The Challenge of Womanist God-Talk*. Maryknoll, N.Y.: Orbis, 1993.

———. "A Womanist Perspective on Sin." In *A Troubling in My Soul: Womanist Perspectives on Evil and Suffering*, edited by Emilie M. Townes. Maryknoll, N.Y.: Orbis, 1993.

Winant, Howard. *Racial Conditions: Politics, Theory, Comparisons*. Minneapolis: University of Minnesota Press, 1994.

Index

Abraham, 42–48, 50, 78, 126, 130
agency, 23, 24, 26–28, 33, 37, 38,
    40–53, 55, 62, 63, 70, 73–75,
    77, 91, 94–95, 100, 102–4,
    109–10, 114, 119, 120, 122, 127,
    133, 139, 148–49, 158
    women's moral, 37, 40, 41
Albright, Ann Cooper, 154, 199n.68
Alpert, Rebecca, 67
Althaus-Reid, Marcella, 20–21,
    107–8, 125–26
androcentrism, 8, 19, 31, 38, 43, 91,
    105, 108–10, 127, 153
anthropology, 63
    theological, 67–68, 72, 78–79,
    82–83
Anzaldúa, Gloria, 11
Apostles' Creed, 116
appropriation, 144–46, 166n.10,
    198n.59
    and The Color Purple, 29
atonement, 100–101, 104, 128
    disciplinary aspects of, 102–3
    theories of, 97–99, 103, 114
Atwood, Margaret, 45
Augustine, 64, 102, 134–35, 175n.2
Austin, J.L., 70

basileia, 106, 186n.53
Beck, Evelyn Torton, 20

Bell, Daniel, 102–4, 186n.44
Benhabib, Seyla, 142–45
Bernauer, James, 112
binarism, 76, 82
    sex, 23–24, 64–69, 71–72, 76,
    79, 81, 129, 181n.69
    victim/victimizer, 23
bisexuality, 34–35, 37
body, 18, 69, 71, 85, 101, 111, 120,
    138, 157, 194n.60
    black, 29, 34–35, 37
    Christ's mystical, 152, 157
    and dance, 154, 199n.68
    as disciplined, 74, 128
    erotic, 105
    Jesus' male, 107, 109–10, 114
    lesbian and bisexual, 29, 34–35,
    169n.39
    and mind/soul dualism, 18, 66, 87
    as rendered docile, 74, 114, 128
    See also embodiment
Brock, Rita Nakashima, 98, 105, 132
Brooten, Bernadette, 20
Brown, Delwin, 148
Brown, Joanne Carlson, 98
Butler, Judith, 18, 29, 64, 115,
    177nn.30, 32, 178nn.36, 40,
    180n.64
    and theory of performativity, 23,
    68–71

Cannon, Katie, 14–15, 28
Caraway, Nancie, 11–14
Carrette, Jeremy, 111–14, 187n.70
Chalcedon, 116–20, 189n.12
Chopp, Rebecca, 8
Christ, 98, 99, 101, 107, 110, 117–21,
    132, 134, 135, 151
  as bi-, 109
  as black, 107
  as black woman, 106
  body of, 107, 152, 157
  as queer, 108
  as transvestite, 105
  See also christology; Jesus
Christ, Carol, 28, 166n.10
Christa, 106–7, 132
Christian, Barbara, 17
christocentrism, 128–29, 133–34, 153
christology, 27, 97, 99, 106–7, 116–18,
    127–28, 132–34, 140
  exclusivist, 124, 133
  high, 117, 121
  low, 117, 119, 121
  queer, 110
  See also Christ; Jesus
Chung, Hyun Kyung, 175n.5
Collins, Patricia Hill, 53, 56, 57, 92
  See also standpoint theory
colonialism, 92, 134
  See also imperialism; postcolonial
    thought
communicative action, 139, 141–46, 155
  See also Habermas, Jürgen
concupiscence, 64, 66, 112, 134–35
Copeland, M. Shawn, 25, 65, 138–40,
    151–58, 199n.69
cross, 24, 90, 97, 114, 152, 157–58
  as disciplinary, 102–3, 113, 122
  as empowering symbol, 98–100, 104
  surrogacy symbolism of, 100, 122
  violence of, 98, 103

Daly, Mary, 5, 107, 124
Davaney, Sheila Greeve, 25, 52, 138–40,
    146–55, 196nn.38, 39, 197nn.46,
    52–55
Day, Janeth, 124–25
De Beauvoir, Simone, 69
democracy, 139, 146–47, 149, 156
demonarchy, 6, 91, 95

Derrida, Jacques, 70, 94, 128, 131
desire, 21, 22, 25, 63, 73, 81, 85, 109–14,
    125, 128–30, 133–36, 153–54, 158,
    187n.70
  for the divine, 24, 79, 82–84,
    86–87, 102–3
  mimetic, 35–36
  policing of, 112
  sexual, 23–24, 36, 38, 64, 66, 70, 71,
    81, 107–9, 112–13
  for the tradition, 116, 134–35
difference, 3–4, 6–7, 22, 24–27, 91,
    95–96, 123, 137–43, 145–47, 157–58,
    181n.72, 190n.23, 191n.30
  and ethnography, 53, 61
  and the Hagar-Sarah story, 41, 45–50
  principle of maximal salvific, 119–20,
    122, 191n.27
  and race, 10–18, 63, 142, 153, 154
  and reading The Color Purple, 28, 32,
    33, 3, 37
  and sexuality, 20–22, 69, 107
  theorizing, 14–15, 26
discursivity, 23–24, 38, 52, 61–62, 64,
    68–75, 77–80, 82, 85, 87, 92, 94, 96,
    103, 105, 135–36, 178n.45, 184n.21
  See also Foucault, Michel
doctrine, 5, 7–9, 23, 25, 26, 58, 62, 65, 67,
    79, 102, 115–19, 136, 140, 157
  of atonement, 98
  of creation, 87, 176n.15
  rule theory of, 25, 116, 118–21, 123,
    189nn.10, 12, 190n.17
  of sin, 78
Donaldson, Laura, 144
Douglas, Kelly Brown, 19, 92, 116, 119
Duba, Musa, 129–30

embodiment, 19, 28, 34, 37–38, 62, 66,
    109, 153
  of Jesus, 106, 109
  sexual, 23, 29, 37, 66, 106, 128
  See also body; sexuality
Enlightenment, the, 141–42
erotic, the, 21–22, 26, 64, 81, 105–110,
    129, 134, 137, 168nn.38, 39,
    180n.64
ethnocentrism, 146–47
ethnography
  feminist, 23, 60

ethnography (*continued*)
  as means of advocacy, 51, 54
  method of, 28, 51, 54, 63
  postmodern critiques of, 60–62
evil, 19, 44, 77, 89, 90–91, 179n.59
Eugene, Toinette, 195n.27
Exum, J. Cheryl, 40–45

feminist theology
  Asian American, 3, 98, 175n.5
  and biblical exegesis, 38–40, 123–33
  as a discipline, 3–4
  eco-, 146, 150
  and ethnography, 9, 23, 28, 51–52,
    60–62
  first-wave and/or white, 5–7, 9–11, 17,
    19, 28–29, 31–35, 38, 41, 65, 90, 93,
    96, 105, 144, 156, 159n.1, 165n.3
  Kierkegaardian, 68–69, 72, 76
  Latina, 11, 92
  lesbian, 3, 19–20
  liberationist, 93, 104–107, 128
  post-Christian, 31, 33, 97, 117
  postcolonial, 129–30, 184n.24
  postmodern, 7, 138
  sources and norms for, 4–8, 27, 116–20
  and thealogy, 159n.2
  See also indecent theology; *mujerista*
    theology; womanist theology
Fewell, Danna, 40–42, 45
Foucault, Michel, 24, 70, 72–75, 88, 90,
    92–93, 97, 100–3, 110–13, 152–53,
    178nn.40, 45, 48, 179n.54, 181n.73,
    187nn.70, 73, 188n.77, 195n.18
  genealogical approach of, 93, 184n.19
  See also discursivity; poststructuralism;
    power/knowledge; technology of
    care of the self
Frankenburg, Ruth, 11, 13–14
Friedman, Susan, 11–12
Fulkerson, Mary McClintock, 52, 66,
    138–39, 184n.21

gay theology, 19, 105–7, 109, 164n.69,
    186n.55
  See also queer theology
gender, 19–20, 23–24, 34, 41, 63,
    65–71, 74, 76, 81, 87, 92, 98, 107,
    129–30, 172n.89, 181nn.61, 72
  as constituted performatively, 64, 71

  as culturally constructed, 38, 69
  and embodiment, 4, 22
  oppression, 6, 40–43, 46–47, 92,
    170n.58
  and race, 12, 14, 39, 47, 64, 98
  and sin, 64, 66, 68, 81
Genesis, 24, 41, 46, 78
  allegorical interpretations of, 44,
    47–48
  creation narratives, 66–67,
    69, 82
  See also Abraham; Hagar; Sarah
Gilkes, Cheryl Townsend, 51–52,
    168n.38, 169n.41
Goss, Robert, 106–8, 110
Grant, Jacquelyn, 106, 138
Grey, Mary, 8, 99, 106
Gudorf, Christine, 195–96n.27
Gunn, David, 40–42, 45
Gutiérrez, Gustavo, 125, 146

Habermas, Jürgen, 139, 141–46, 155
  See also communicative action
Hagar, 9, 22, 27, 38–50, 62, 65, 77–79,
    81–82, 95–96, 105, 122
  See also Sarah
Hampson, Daphne, 31–34, 117–18, 121,
    166n.12, 189nn.6, 9
heteronormativity, 19, 23–25, 109–10,
    112–13, 132
  and biblical interpretation, 124,
    193n.48
  defined, 65
  and John 4, 128–29, 134
  and Sarah-Hagar story, 81
heterosexuality, 3, 10, 21, 22, 35, 64, 71,
    81, 110–11, 133
  compulsory, 67, 81–82, 107, 181n.69
  dominant discourse of, 69–70
  naturalized, 29, 68–69, 71
  and privilege, 18–20, 22, 26, 27,
    37–38, 66–67, 81–82, 158
Heyward, Carter, 14–15, 19, 89, 98, 105
Hilkert, Mary Catherine, 35, 168n.31
Hill, Renée, 20
historicism, 37
  pragmatic, 146, 148–151, 155
Hogan, Linda, 169n.39
homophobia, 108, 124, 168n.36,
    180n.64

homosexuality, 18, 19, 108, 180n.64
hooks, bell, 52, 168n.36, 173n.97
Hopkins, Julie, 121, 189n.9
Hunt, Mary, 19, 35
Hunter, Patricia, 66
Hurston, Zora Neale, 9

image of God, 4, 23–24, 62, 64–67, 72,
    79–83, 175–76n.8, 180nn.62, 63
  in *The Color Purple*, 30, 33
  See also imago dei
imaginary, 84–85, 87, 181n.73,
    181–82n.75, 187n.70
  See also Jantzen, Grace
imago dei, 24, 64–65, 68, 72, 79–83, 133,
    179n.58, 180n.63
imperialism, 25, 26, 92, 128, 130, 153
  See also colonialism; postcolonial
    thought
improvisational dance, 25, 140, 154–57
indecent theology, 20–21, 107–8
  and biblical texts, 125, 127–29, 133–34
  See also queer theology
Irigaray, Luce, 84–85
Isasi-Díaz, Ada María, 23, 51, 53–62, 96,
    173nn99, 100, 174nn.101, 112

Jantzen, Grace, 24, 65, 79, 84–86, 110,
    134, 181nn.73, 75, 182nn.76, 77, 78,
    80, 187n.70
Jesus, 21, 58, 97–98, 104, 107–8, 116–18,
    120–23, 151–52, 156, 190nn.18, 26
  as bridegroom, 126, 129–30, 133
  cross and death of, 98–101, 104,
    191n.27
  heterosexual construction of, 110
  and homoeroticism, 109–10
  maleness of, 4, 90, 97–98, 105–110,
    114, 117, 122, 133
  and Samaritan woman, 25, 124–35,
    193nn.48, 51
  See also Christ; christology
Johnson, Elizabeth, 6, 24, 65, 79,
    82–84
Jones, Serene, 179n.59
jouissance, 65, 84–85, 110, 181n.74

Kamitsuka, David, 174n.101, 189n.10,
    193n.45
Kamitsuka, Margaret, 163n.54

Kelsey, David, 176n.15
Kierkegaard, Søren, 67–69, 72, 76, 77,
    177nn.24, 26, 27
Kim, Jean, 125
Kirby, Vicki, 61, 175n.116
Kirk-Duggan, Cheryl, 35–36, 168n.37
Krause, Deborah, 100–1
Kristeva, Julia, 84–86, 181n.74, 182nn.76,
    77, 78, 80
Kwok, Pui–lan, 21, 184n.24, 192n.44,
    193n.49

LaCugna, Catherine, 66, 180n.62
lesbianism, 6, 10, 14, 20, 46, 67,
    180n.64
  and *The Color Purple*, 29, 34–37, 71,
    168n.36, 169nn.38, 39
  and theology, 3, 19–20
liberation, 5, 8, 21, 91, 105, 108–9, 113–14,
    120, 124, 134
  and Foucault, 110, 113
  themes in *The Color Purple*, 33, 168n.36
  themes in the Sarah-Hagar story,
    49–50
liberation theology, 80, 93, 102, 108,
    148–49, 178n.47
  black, 91
  feminist, 93, 104–7, 128
  Latin American, 20, 54, 57–58, 108,
    125, 146, 174n.101, 186n.44
Lindbeck, George, 118–19, 181n.71,
    189nn.10, 12, 190n.17, 193n. 45

McFague, Sallie, 146, 150
misogyny, 19, 87, 101, 115–16, 128, 153
  and the Bible, 43, 123–24, 128, 134
Mitchem, Stephanie, 17, 163n.54
Moody, Linda, 198–99n.61
Moore, Stephen, 100, 101
Mud Flower Collective, 14–15
mujerista theology, 3, 11, 23, 51–59, 92, 96
  See also Isasi-Díaz, Ada María
mysticism, 84, 110
  and body of Christ, 152, 157

natality, 85–87, 182nn.76, 79, 80
  See also Jantzen, Grace
Nicaea, 116–19, 189n.12
Niebuhr, Reinhold, 67, 68
Nietz, Mary Jo, 60

Okure, Teresa, 125
oppression, 13, 23, 28, 49, 51, 55–57,
  90–97, 103, 111, 120, 122, 138, 142,
  152, 178n.48
  and Bible, 124–25
  and Christian symbols, 24, 97–98,
    100, 103, 106–110, 115
  class, 40, 42, 47, 49
  gender, 6, 40–43, 46, 92,
    170n.58
  heterosexist, 20, 107, 113
  racial, 6, 30, 33–35, 39–43, 46–48,
    50, 91, 105
  and resistance, 26, 41, 44, 51, 61,
    91–92, 103
  structural, 4, 24, 79, 89–91, 93–94, 96
  See also patriarchy, racism, sexism
otherness, 4, 29, 151, 154
  and the Samaritan woman, 127–28, 132

Parker, Rebecca, 98
patriarchy, 3, 5–6, 24, 27, 39–40, 50,
  65–66, 74–76, 78, 91–92, 98, 106,
  110, 115–16, 136, 147, 170n.58,
  170n.55
  and Bible, 26, 38–39, 42, 123–24
  and Hagar–Sarah story, 40, 42–48
  and John 4, 128–30, 132, 134
  and racism, 33, 37, 39
  See also oppression, gender
performativity, 23–24, 64, 68, 70–82, 84,
  95–96, 115, 121–23, 128–29, 133–35,
  157, 191n.28
  spiritual, 122–23, 133, 158
  See also Butler, Judith
phallocentrism, 24, 84–87, 97, 110, 123,
  134, 181n.74, 182n.80
  and Bible, 123, 129
Phillips, Gary, 128, 131–32
Plaskow, Judith, 68
postcolonial thought, 4, 21, 24, 24, 26, 51,
  53, 61–62, 63, 90, 9, 94–95, 125,
  127–34, 175n.116, 184–85n.24,
  192n.44, 193n.49
postmodernism, 4, 7, 52–53, 60, 62, 65,
  70, 79, 83–84, 94, 100, 138, 139,
  193n.49
  See also poststructuralism
poststructuralism, 23–24, 26, 38, 51–52,
  53, 61–62, 63–65, 68–72, 76–77,

79–82, 84, 87–90, 92–94, 97,
  100–1, 103–4, 109–10, 113, 153
  See also Butler, Judith; Foucault,
    Michel; postmodernism
power, 12, 16, 20 22, 26, 43, 44, 46,
  50, 62, 70, 73, 89, 92, 95, 100–1,
  103, 108–11, 139–40, 142, 144–45,
  147, 151, 152, 155, 158, 165n.3,
  174n.109, 178n.50, 181n.75, 184n.20,
  198n.59
  disciplinary, 72–75, 77–78, 88, 90, 92,
    98, 100–1, 103, 115
  dualistic view of, 89–92, 101, 109, 111
  erotic, 106
  good versus bad, 24, 90, 101, 109
  oppressive, 23, 24, 28, 40–41, 44, 51,
    61, 73, 89–90, 97, 104, 106,
    108–9, 111
  relations of, 24, 61, 73, 75, 77, 80, 87,
    93–94, 111, 113, 178n.48, 184n.18,
    195n.21
power/knowledge, 73–78, 92–94, 100,
  103, 111, 115, 121, 133, 135, 139, 153, 158
  See also Foucault, Michel
pragmatism, 146–49, 151–52, 156
  See also Davaney, Sheila Greeve; Rorty,
    Richard
privilege, 4, 6, 22, 25, 38, 46, 62, 91,
  137–38, 140, 142, 145, 150, 154–58
  epistemological, 52, 147
  heterosexual, 18–20, 22, 26, 27, 37–38,
    66–67, 81–82, 158
  white racial, 10–14, 16–18, 19–20, 26,
    27, 30, 37, 49, 137, 144, 165n.3

queer theology, 19–22, 64, 105, 107,
  109–10
  and the Bible, 25, 81–82, 130, 193n.48
queer theory, 26, 62, 111, 113, 180n.64

race. See difference, and race; oppression,
  racial; racism
racism, 11–12, 24, 27, 29–30, 34, 39–40,
  48, 66, 90–91, 93, 95, 97, 107,
  120, 157
  See also privilege, white racial
Rahner, Karl, 79, 82
Ray, Darby, 98, 105
redemption, 80, 98–99, 102, 104, 105–6,
  119, 121, 132–33

relativism, 78, 147–48
resistance, 1, 4, 12, 23, 26, 28, 40–41, 43–44, 46–51, 61, 63, 73–75, 85, 89, 91–96, 103–5, 109, 143, 131–32
Rodríguez, Jeanette, 16
Ronan, Marian, 53–56, 58–61
Rorty, Richard, 146–50, 152, 196n.38, 196–97n. 39, 197n.46
Ruether, Rosemary Radford, 4–5, 7, 9, 66, 89, 90–91, 93, 105, 117–18, 121
rule theory. See doctrine
Ruth, 38, 82

Saiving, Valerie, 68
salvation, 79, 85, 98, 106, 113–14, 132
Samaritan woman at the well, 25, 124–33
Sanders, Cheryl, 40–45, 95
Sands, Kathleen, 108
Sandys, Edwina, 106
Sarah, 9, 22, 27, 38–50, 62, 65, 77–79, 81–82, 95, 96
    See also Hagar
Schneiders, Sarah, 124–25, 129
Schüssler Fiorenza, Elisabeth, 124
Secker, Susan, 16–17
selfhood, 4, 50, 68, 69, 76, 80, 92, 112, 158
    androgynous, 69, 76
    Christian, 104
    embodied, 4, 26, 28, 62
    as performatively constituted, 64, 68, 71–72, 79–81
    poststructuralist approach to, 61–62, 64, 66, 89, 94
    sexed, 23, 38
sex, 10, 18–19, 22–24, 43, 47, 61, 63–72, 79, 81, 108, 181n.72
    binarism, 24, 64, 66–69, 72, 76, 79, 81–82, 180n.69
    as constituted performatively, 64, 71, 82
    and Foucault, 111–12, 187n.70, 188n.73
    naturalness of, 63, 69
sexism, 1, 5, 37, 90–93, 97, 105–6, 117
    and biblical interpretation, 125–27
    and Kierkegaard, 68, 179n.56
sexuality, 4, 10, 15, 18–22, 24, 27–30, 34–38, 63–64, 67–68, 70–71, 74, 79, 81–82, 110–12, 164n.67

and Foucault, 111–12
and Jesus, 106–10
and Samaritan woman, 125–27, 129, 193n.48
sin, 23–24, 64, 66, 72–81, 91, 112, 128, 175n.1,
    anthropological approach to, 67–68, 72–79, 176n.15
    gendered, 68
    original, 64, 179n.56
    as performatively constituted, 72–81
    poststructuralist account of, 72–79, 80–81
    social or structural, 4, 24, 79, 90–91, 93, 96, 111, 120, 191n.27
sisterhood, 11–12, 15, 78, 96, 138, 152, 156, 158
solidarity, 4, 25, 99, 106, 137–38, 154–58
    Christian notion of, 150
    and Copeland, 138–40, 151–54, 156–57
    and Davaney, 136–40, 146, 149–51, 154, 155
    disciplinary discourse of, 157
    eco-, 150–51
    and Welch, 138–45, 154
soteriology, 109, 119, 121–22, 176n.15, 189n.12
Spelman, Elizabeth, 11–14, 145, 150
spirituality, 9, 22, 35, 92, 102, 107, 109–10, 114, 121
    and The Color Purple, 29, 30–34, 168n.37
    as embodied, 34–35, 64
    performativity of, 84, 122–23, 133
    womanist, 122, 143–45
Spivak, Gayati Chakravorty, 24, 90, 94–96, 178n.37, 184n.24, 192n.44
standpoint theory, 53, 56, 60, 147
    See also Collins, Patricia Hill
strategic essentialization, 90, 94–97, 184n.24, 192n.44
    See also Spivak, Gayatri Chakravorty
subalterneity, 24, 61, 79, 94–96
    See also Spivak, Gayatri Chakravorty
subject, 70, 77–78, 80, 84–85, 93–94, 104, 113–114
    as discursively constituted, 24, 52, 61–62, 73, 84, 96, 102, 105, 109, 113, 115, 135
    female, 40, 52, 61

subject (*continued*)
  Latina, 54
  sexed, 69
  subaltern, 94
surrogacy, 99–100, 122
symbols, 48, 54, 103, 106, 109, 117–18,
    121, 134
  of the cross, 98–105, 122
  disciplinary Christian, 87, 90, 97,
    113, 114–15
  expressive religious, 83, 118, 190n.23
  and Jantzen, 84–87, 181–82n.75
  of male savior, 105–7
  masculinist and phallocentric, 84–87,
    134, 181nn.74, 75
  oppressive Christian, 24, 90, 97,
    100, 114–15
  and otherness, 132
  power of, 100
  of solidarity, 138, 158
  and women's experience, 6, 8–9

Tanner, Kathryn, 191n.30
technology of care of the self, 75, 90, 97,
    100–4, 110–15
  Bible as, 127–29, 133
  Christian tradition as, 119, 121–23, 136
Terrell, JoAnne Marie, 99–100, 104,
    114, 119, 121–22, 167n.28, 183n.11,
    191nn.27, 28
Teubal, Savina, 41, 45–47, 50,
    171–72n.68, 172nn.69, 71
thealogy, 74, 159n.2
theology, 18, 52, 59, 64, 67, 87, 90, 113
  androcentric, 10, 117
  dominant Christian, 21, 59, 110
  liberal, 5, 100
  See also feminist theology; gay
    theology; indecent theology;
    liberation theology; *mujerista*
    theology; queer theology; womanist
    theology
Thistlethwaite, Susan Brooks, 6, 31–32,
    166nn.9, 12, 17, 195n.27
Thomas, Linda, 51
Townes, Emilie, 18, 21, 33–34, 36–37, 52,
    143, 168n.36, 173n.97
tradition, Christian, 4–5, 9, 19, 56, 59, 84,
    102–3, 106, 113, 134, 150–51

anti-erotic, 108
and Bible, 126, 134
creedal, 25, 53, 113, 115–23, 190n.24
disciplinary, 25, 88, 115, 121, 123,
    133, 135
feminist desire for, 65, 116, 129, 134–35
negotiating with, 24–25, 84, 110,
    113–16, 121, 123, 153, 188n.1
patriarchal, 3, 66, 136
patristic, 63–64, 123
Trible, Phyllis, 38, 41, 47, 82, 125

Volf, Miroslav, 180–81n.69

Walker, Alice, 9, 14, 22, 27–38, 51–52, 71,
    163–64n.64, 165n.6, 166n.15,
    167nn.25, 28, 168nn.36, 38
  and *The Color Purple*, 14, 15, 22, 27–38,
    51–52, 62, 64, 71, 166nn.15, 18,
    168nn.36, 38, 169n.39
Weems, Renita, 41, 47–50, 185n.28
Welch, Sharon, 25, 138–45, 154, 195nn.18,
    26, 27, 196n.32, 198n.59
West, Cornell, 148–50, 153–54
Williams, Delores, 6, 9, 20, 33–34, 36–37,
    41, 47–50, 91, 93, 95, 98–99, 105,
    119–22, 169n.39, 179n.55, 183nn.9,
    11, 190n.18
womanist theology, 3, 6, 9, 11, 17–20, 22,
    25, 27–29, 31–35, 39, 48–49, 51–52,
    66, 91, 93, 95, 99, 104, 116–17,
    120–23, 138, 152, 154, 157
  and Alice Walker, 163–64n.64
  lesbian, 20
  and white feminist critique of,
    165n.3
women's experience, 20, 31, 52, 68, 83,
    118, 144,
  the appeal to, 4–10, 26, 63, 113, 115,
    137, 158
  and the Bible, 23, 39, 41, 43, 52, 124
  and *The Color Purple*, 22, 27–28, 31,
    33–34
  differences in, 4, 12, 16, 20, 25, 35,
    137, 139
  and ethnography, 23, 28, 51–53, 59,
    61–62
  and Jesus Christ, 98, 100, 120
  and standpoint theory, 56–57, 59, 96